14580825

CONTENTS

WISCONSIN AMERICAN INDIAN HISTORY AND CULTURE

A Survey of Selected Aspects

John Boatman
University of Wisconsin
Milwaukee

KENDALL/HUNT PUBLISHING COMPANY
4050 Westmark Drive   Dubuque, Iowa 52002

Edited by Carla Dorgay
Typeset by Angela M. Schefft
Cover design by Sharon L. Scholten

PREFACE

In the twenty years I have been teaching in the area of American Indian Studies at the university level, I have found that there are very few texts available which deal with aspects of both the history and the traditional culture of the American Indian peoples of Wisconsin. Most of the available books are written by non-natives who do not emphasize those aspects which were taught by American Indian Elders, nor do these writers have a strong appreciation of and connection with the traditions the Elders describe. In addition, many of these books contain a great deal of Eurocentric bias and are often inaccurate from the perspective of the tribal peoples themselves.

As was the case with my previous book, *My Elders Taught Me: Aspects of Western Great Lakes American Indian Philosophy*, I have written *Wisconsin American Indian History and Culture: A Survey of Selected Aspects* from my perspective as an individual who was privileged to learn from several Western Great Lakes American Indian Traditional Elders. In the 1960's and 1970's, these included the Elders Pauees and Wallace Pyawasit of the Menominee American Indian Nation, who offi-cially recognized and accepted me in a traditional Naming Ceremony in 1976 at the Zoar village on the Menominee Indian Reservation in Wisconsin.

Pauees and Wallace Pyawasit died more than ten years ago. In this book I honor their spirits, and the spirits of the other Elders I have known, for accepting me as their student and sharing their knowledge. To them I am indebted and gratefully acknowledge their patient guidance.

I wish to thank Nancy O. Lurie, the present Curator of Anthropology at the Milwaukee Public Museum, who over the years has been teacher, friend, and advisor. I am grateful to UWM Associate Dean G. Richard

Meadows, who, as was the case with my previous books, encouraged me and allowed me the time to write this book.

I dedicate this book to the Spirits of Pauees and Wallace Pyawasit and to Irene Pyawasit, who taught me a great deal, as well as to my children, my wife Patricia, and my grandson, John Michael Katchenago.

INTRODUCTION

A BRIEF HISTORY OF WISCONSIN

"Wiscooseh," as this area was called by Menominee tribal peoples, means "a good place in which to live" and has been the Menominee homeland since at least as early as 10,000 B.C., when the last remnants of the Pleistocene glaciers were retreating northward.[1] It remained an aboriginal homeland, undisturbed by the presence of non-natives, until 1634, when Jean Nicolet first arrived as a representative of the French government.

The French were the dominant Europeans in the Wisconsin area until 1761, when they were defeated by the English in what many scholars call the French and Indian War. Actually, this war was fought between England and France with American Indian tribal groups participating on both sides. English troops then occupied the French fort at La Baye (Green Bay). Several English North American colonies, including the colony of Virginia, claimed the Wisconsin area after the English victory.[2]

The area that would one day become the state of Wisconsin officially remained an English possession until 1783, when the colonies defeated the English in the American Revolution. In 1787 Wisconsin became a part of the United States Northwest Territory. By 1800, with the Northwest Territory about to be broken up by Ohio's (1802) admission into the union as a state, Wisconsin became part of the newly organized Indiana Territory. When the territory of Michigan separated from the Indiana Territory in 1805, Wisconsin remained a part of Indiana, as did the area that is now the Upper Peninsula of Michigan. In 1810 when the Illinois Territory was separated from the Indiana Territory, most of Wisconsin became part of the Illinois Territory.[3] During that time, even though the Wisconsin area was officially part of the United States, the English continued to be the dominant non-native group in the region until their second defeat by the United States in the War of 1812. Even then, United States troops did not enter Wisconsin until 1816.

When Illinois became a state in 1818, all of Wisconsin became part of the Michigan Territory. In October of the same year, three separate counties were formed in the part of the Michigan Territory located north and west of Lake Michigan. They were Michilimackinac County in the Upper Peninsula, Brown County in the eastern half of Wisconsin, and Crawford County in the western half of Wisconsin.[4]

On April 20, 1836, the separate territory of Wisconsin was formed. At that same time, the Upper Peninsula was officially annexed by the territory of Michigan. In 1837 Michigan became a state. Eleven years later, in 1848, Wisconsin became a state.[5]

A WORD ABOUT THIS BOOK

Part one of this book consists of a brief overview that examines, in chronological order, aspects of the history of those American Indian groups who made Wisconsin their home. Following this historical overview, aspects of each separate group are examined in more detail, beginning with the aboriginal ancestors of the Menominee, one of the only indigenous people of the area that became Wisconsin.[6] The second part of the book examines aspects of the traditional Algonquian tribal culture as it existed prior to and after European intrusion.[7]

It is important to note that some of the resources consulted in writing this book are based on accounts that were first recorded by Europeans shortly after early contact. These accounts were examined, interpreted, and re-recorded much later, mainly by Euro-American scholars. Other available information is based on accounts of scholars, primarily Euro-Americans, who interpreted and recorded what they saw and heard while doing field research in American Indian tribal communities. Still other information in this book is derived directly from the author's notes and recollections from his years of direct contact with tribal Elders.

All of these sources leave some room for error resulting from the individual recorder's bias in interpreting what was seen and heard. These biases may have resulted from a variety of factors, including the recorder's European or Euro-American culture and belief system. Other biases were a result of natural human memory faults or of the fact that there were several different native languages, which left scholars open to errors of interpretation. All of these errors could have been made and probably were.

In addition, the reader would do well to keep in mind that the intrusion of Europeans into native regions significantly disrupted indigenous life-styles, and the continued European presence and escalating European influence caused rapid change in many aspects of traditional tribal ways.

NOTES

1. R.E. Ritzenthaler, *Prehistoric Indians of Wisconsin*, revised by Lynne G. Goldstein (Milwaukee: Milwaukee Public Museum, 1985), 29-30.

2. D.S. Durrie, "The Public Domain," *History of Wisconsin*, compiled by C.W. Butterfield (Western Historical Company, 1880), 212.

3. Ibid., 219.

4. Ibid.

5. Ibid.

6. Principal source of information for the historical overview is John Boatman, "Historical Overview of the Wisconsin Area: From Early Years to the French, British, and American Intrusions," *An Anthology of Western Great Lakes Indian History*, ed. Donald L. Fixico, rev. ed. (Milwaukee: University of Wisconsin-Milwaukee, 1989).

7. Principal source of information about the traditional culture was acquired from various Great Lakes tribal Elders over a period of many years. Some information is also based on material from B.G. Trigger, ed., *Handbook of North American Indians, volume 15: Northeast*, (Washington, D.C.: Smithsonian Institution, 1978); and Basil Johnston, *Ojibway Heritage* (Lincoln: University of Nebraska Press, 1990).

PART ONE

SELECTED ASPECTS
OF
THE HISTORY
OF
WISCONSIN INDIANS

CHAPTER ONE
HISTORICAL OVERVIEW
OF THE WISCONSIN AREA

THE WISCONSIN AREA
BEFORE EUROPEAN-CONTACT[1]

American Indian people have been living in the Western Great Lakes area since as early as 10,000 B.C., when the last remnants of the Pleistocene glaciers were retreating northward. Some scholars call these people, who were skilled big-game hunters, the **Paleo People**. In January of 1988, the Milwaukee Public Museum reported that a recent archaeological excavation, near the edge of the Sheboygan Marsh in the Elkhart Lake area of Wisconsin's Sheboygan County, had uncovered artifacts and features that indicate the site supported American Indian populations from as early as 8,000 B.C. to the mid-1840's.[2]

As the climate became warmer around 3,000 B.C., tools were adapted to woodworking, and what is known as the **Old Copper Culture** developed in the area that became Wisconsin. The American Indian people in the area were becoming proficient metal smiths, utilizing copper mined and brought to their villages from the Lake Superior region of northern Wisconsin and from the western region of the Upper Peninsula of Michigan, both some distance away. Two major Copper Culture population centers developed in the Wisconsin area. One was located in northeastern Wisconsin in what is now eastern Oconto County. The other was in the southwestern corner of the state in what is now Grant County.

Apparently, by this time trade was occurring over a large geographical area. Archaeologists excavating burial sites have found Gulf Coast origin sea shells, in addition to the copper and pieces of iron ore from the Upper Peninsula of Michigan, among grave goods. These items have been found in present-day Manitowoc and Waukesha counties, as well as in Oconto and Grant counties.

The Copper Culture peoples, who are quite likely the ancestors of the **Menominee** people, made copper jewelry as well as copper tools, weapons, and utensils. The fact that they made jewelry is evidence that they must have had ample leisure time in their daily lives, since one must have spare time in order to devote it to making jewelry.

Approximately 2,600 years ago, during the period that scholars call the Early Woodland Period, people were carving pictures, which scholars call petroglyphs, on rocks and in caves of Wisconsin.

By 300 B.C. the climate was growing warmer, serving as a powerful impetus for cultural changes that had been building up within older societies. The period from approximately A.D. 400 to approximately A.D. 800 was generally colder again, but after that, it again became warmer, giving rise to conditions that were conducive to the further development of efficient agricultural systems.

Scholars refer to the period from 300 B.C. until A.D. 400 as the Hopewell Period, and they call the people the **Hopewell People** or Hopewellians. During that time, peoples from the southern Ohio and the lower middle Mississippi areas migrated into Wisconsin.

The Hopewell peoples brought with them into Wisconsin their previously developed trade contacts extending all the way from the Gulf of Mexico to Lake Superior, and from Wisconsin westward to Wyoming. The evidence for this extensive trade network is the presence of Gulf Coast area sea shells, obsidian (black volcanic glass), and western grizzly bear teeth found in grave goods dating from that period.

In addition, the **Hopewellians** brought into Wisconsin their material culture, including fine artistry skills. The **Hopewellians** also brought their knowledge and practice of limited sustained agriculture, which proved to be very important. Corn, pumpkins, beans, and squash were among the crops that the **Hopewellians** introduced into Wisconsin.

The relatively colder period from approximately A.D. 400 to approximately A.D. 800 witnessed somewhat of a cultural decline. Later, however, with the coming of warmer temperatures the pace of cultural development once more began to accelerate.

Recent archaeological evidence uncovered during field research in the Lake Poygan area of present-day Winnebago County in Wisconsin supports earlier evidence indicating that beginning in approximately A.D. 800, and continuing until approximately A.D. 900, another group of relatively stable and somewhat sedentary agricultural people came into Wisconsin from the area of present-day Illinois and Indiana.[3] Called the **Oneota People** by scholars, it appears that these people left their home region and came north into Wisconsin in order to escape domination by the politically and economically complex society of peoples whom scholars call the Mississippian **Cahokians**. The Cahokians, it appears, were the most dominant group in the entire middle and upper Mississippi region by that time and were becoming even more dominant.

Cahokia, the main settlement base of the Cahokians, was located in southwestern Illinois where the Missouri and Mississippi Rivers join together near present-day East St. Louis, Illinois. There is evidence that the Cahokians had contacts and influenced cultures as far north as northern Wisconsin, and even perhaps in the islands between upper and lower Michigan. By approximately A.D. 900, and until approximately 1250, Cahokia consisted of a settlement built within a three hundred acre area that was surrounded by a large fortification. Within the walls of the fortification were approximately seventeen very large and high earthen mounds, many of which contained wooden platforms. Outside of the walled area were additional mound groupings. Scholars estimate that Cahokia had a population of approximately 10,000 people at that time and that its influence extended from the Lower Mississippi Valley region to the Upper Great Lakes region.

The **Oneota** who, as previously noted, migrated north into Wisconsin to escape domination by the Cahokians, were probably the ancestors of the tribal group that later became known as the Ho-chung-gra, the present-day **Winnebago**. The Oneota established farming settlements in the area around Lake Winnebago, Butte des Morts, Winneconne, as well as at Lake Poygan.

Also beginning in approximately A.D. 800, and continuing until approximately 1300, peoples scholars call the **Effigy Mound People**, who probably developed from a mixture of Hopewell and earlier peoples, began to build earthen mounds in Wisconsin. More than five thousand of these mounds have been identified, mostly in southern and south-central Wisconsin.

Many of the mounds appear to be shaped like birds or animals.

Some mounds contain graves; however, many do not. They were probably used for special religioceremonial purposes. Some may also have served as group boundary markers.

Some of the finest mounds are located northeast of present-day West Bend, Wisconsin in Washington County's Lizard Mound Park. There are still twenty-eight mounds observable in that park. In 1883 when they were recorded on a sketch map, there were still forty-seven distinguishable mounds existing from an estimated original sixty. Most of the mounds were destroyed by early European settlers who didn't know what they were.

In approximately the year A.D. 1200, the major settlement site in southern Wisconsin known as Aztalan, near Lake Mills in present-day Jefferson County, was built. Scholars describe it as Wisconsin's largest "prehistoric" village. Various scholars theorize that Aztalan was built by Cahokians, either as a colony of Cahokia established to relieve population pressures at Cahokia, or for use by Cahokians as an outpost for planned exploitation of resources to the north. At Aztalan, over twenty acres were contained inside a walled fortification similar to the one at Cahokia. Inside there were at least three large, high mounds, one of which was double-terraced. Refuse pits have been found containing maize and squash; however, very few graves have been found--a puzzle to scholars.

For many years a widespread belief has persisted, based on sketchy and faulty evidence, that the residents of Aztalan practiced cannibalism. Some scholars have erroneously reinforced this belief; for example, as recently as 1988, Carol I. Mason, in her book *Introduction to Wisconsin Indians: Prehistory to Statehood*, wrote: "Evidence of cannibalism also exists at Aztalan. . . it is not known who was eating whom. . . ." In my review of Mason's book published in the *American Indian Culture and Research Journal*, I quoted from Lynne G. Goldstein, a highly respected archaeologist and a widely recognized expert on Aztalan. In commenting on Mason's statements about cannibalism at Aztalan, I wrote:

Goldstein (in her 1985 revision of Robert E. Ritzenthaler's, *Prehistoric Indians of Wisconsin*) states (p. 61-63) "There are. . . popular notions about Aztalan which archaeologists would like to dispel. . . [one] is the presumed cannibalism. The only evidence for cannibalism at Aztalan is that some broken human bones were found in refuse pits. . . there is a great deal of misunderstanding and oversimplification about what these bones might mean. . . many societies process the bodies of their dead. . . some parts may be curated or kept for years before burial, while other parts are discarded. . . [this is] a common practice. . .well documented for both Late Woodland and Mississippian societies. . . there is no clear evidence of cannibalism at Aztalan. . . ."[4]

The inaccurate statements about cannibalism at Aztalan are a good example of how sensationalistic writing and verbal accounts spread and persevere.

Aztalan is located near the Rock River. During the summer of 1989, investigators began exploring the depths of nearby Rock Lake, a 1,371 acre, 56 foot deep lake. Since the 1930's, reports of pyramids located at the bottom in the center of the lake have been widely circulated. Divers using sonar equipment have located structures that some believe are man-made pyramids. Whether or not these structures are actually man-made, or even pyramids, and whether they are related to Aztalan, awaits the results of additional scholarly investigation.

Another Wisconsin area mound group, containing ceramics similar to those found in the southern Wisconsin Effigy Mounds, was found as far north as the present-day Wisconsin-Michigan border along the Menominee River northwest of the present-day city of Marinette, Wisconsin. Scholars, who have dated the mounds to approximately A.D. 1300, call them the Backlund Mounds.

Still other mounds were found as early as 1890 within the boundaries of the present-day **Menominee** Reservation, along the lake shores north and northeast of Keshena. In 1890 Major Thomas Savage, the U.S. government Indian Agent there, supervised the excavation and opening of several of those mounds located about eight miles east of Keshena. Human remains were found in some, but most were barren of human remains.[5]

It appears that by 1400 most large, native, aboriginal settlements in Wisconsin had fragmented into smaller, dispersed communities during a period of cooler and wetter summers.

By the time of the arrival of the French in the region south of the

Western Great Lakes in the early to mid-1600's, Cahokia and other Mississippian culture "temple towns" were no longer occupied. Some scholars theorize that this lack of occupation may have been due to earlier disease epidemics, which quickly spread from the east following previous European contact and intrusion.

Before European intrusion, the tribally organized descendants of the aboriginal, ancient Copper Culture peoples, the **Menominee**, were the primary residents of the northeastern quarter and much of the eastern half of the area that was to become the state of Wisconsin. The Menominee are members of the language/culture group that scholars call **Algonquian**. They peacefully shared the present-day Fox River Valley, Lake Winnebago, and city of Green Bay areas with the **Winnebago**, tribally organized descendants of the earlier intrusive Oneota peoples. The **Winnebago**, who were also the primary residents of the south-central and southwestern areas of the future state of Wisconsin, had their own distinctive language and culture and were not of the Algonquian language/culture group. The tribally organized **Santee**, probably also aboriginal, were the primary residents of the northwestern quarter of the future state of Wisconsin. They also were not members of the Algonquian language/culture group, but rather were of the language/culture group that scholars call Siouan.

All of these tribal groups, the **Menominee**, **Winnebago**, and **Santee**, led a partially nomadic, hunting-fishing-gathering way of life; at the same time, they were somewhat sedentary, as they engaged in limited, but sustained, agriculture.

PRELUDE TO EUROPEAN CONTACT IN WISCONSIN

Among the most significant events in the history of the indigenous peoples in the Western Great Lakes area, including those in Wisconsin, was the European **French** contact and subsequent intrusion. The devastating and far-reaching effects of this contact forever changed the lives of the aboriginal people. In order to understand the impact that contact and intrusion had on the native peoples of Wisconsin, it is important to examine in detail the events of this period.

Beginning with the initial French contact and intrusion in the Green Bay area, the stage was set for continuing significant cultural change among indigenous peoples in Wisconsin. From this point forward, European and later American influences would replace climactic conditions and intertribal contact as the major impetus for change.

In 1608 the **French** established the growing settlement of Quebec along the St. Lawrence River in what is now Canada. The first French contact with the native peoples of the Western Great Lakes probably occurred when Samuel de Champlain, the French governor of New France, reached Lake Huron in 1615.

Champlain's reports to France noted that many of the natives he encountered, including the **northern Iroquoian** tribal group, the **Huron**, were already suffering from European diseases. These diseases had been introduced by other natives from farther east who had been in physical contact with Europeans. European diseases were also introduced through other means such as animal "carriers."

Shortly after having made contact with the Hurons, the French began hearing reports from them, as well as from **Algonquian-speaking Ottawa** traders, concerning a group of people whom they called the "strange people of the sea." The Huron and the Ottawa called these people that because their own languages and cultures were very different from the language and culture of these ''strange people.'' Both the Huron and the Ottawa cautioned the French that the "strange peoples of the sea" would be a serious hindrance to French expansion into the lands further west. The Huron and the Ottawa were referring to the **Winnebago of Wisconsin**, whose language and culture were vastly different from either of their own.

The French, as was the case with most Europeans at that time, did not realize that the new "American" continent was extremely large. Hearing about the "strange peoples of the sea," and thinking that the Pacific Ocean could not be too far away from Quebec, the French immediately decided that these reports must be about China, or at the very least, about a Chinese outpost located west of Lake Huron. At that time, the French, like the English, Spanish, and Dutch, were quite interested in finding and gaining control of a short, safe route from Europe to China.

Consequently, in 1632 de Champlain prepared a map of areas already somewhat known to the French as result of explorations or from information obtained from their native contacts. De Champlain noted on his map that a "Nation des Puants" (whom we now know to be the **Winnebago**) lived near the shores of a lake that lay some distance up river from where the river mouth meets a large bay. He used the word "puants" because both the Huron and the Ottawa referred to the "strange peoples of the sea" as being "stinking people," largely because their major villages were located near areas of shallow water where fish, after dying from summer heat, decayed, causing a distinctive odor to permeate much of the area.

Although the map de Champlain prepared contains a number of inaccuracies, it is clear that de Champlain was referring to what is now called Lake Winnebago, lying upstream of the Fox River in Wisconsin. Much later, the *Jesuit Relations*, annual reports compiled by the Jesuit Superior at Quebec from the accounts furnished to him by missionaries in the "field," refer to the Winnebago as "The People of the Sea."

THE NATIVES AND THE FRENCH
MAKE CONTACT IN WISCONSIN

In 1634 de Champlain sent his official representative, a young man by the name of Jean Nicolet, traveling by canoe and guided and escorted by a group of seven **Huron**, to make contact with "The People of the Sea."

The commonly accepted version of this event revolves around French hopes of being the first Europeans to reach China via the "Northwest Passage." Thus, while Nicolet was sent to make contact and establish a peaceful trading agreement with the peoples of the **Chinese** mainland or with a colony-outpost of Chinese, the people Nicolet encountered were, in actuality, the **Winnebago**.

In late August or early September, Nicolet and his Huron companions landed at a site below the red clay banks along the shore of Lake Michigan's largest bay, presently called the bay of Green Bay. The place, later called Red Banks, is located approximately ten miles northeast of the mouth of the Fox River in the Benderville area near the present-day city of Green Bay.

In order to impress the supposed "Chinese" with the fact that the French knew about them and possessed gunpowder (which the Chinese had originally invented), Nicolet put on a Chinese ceremonial robe as they neared the bay shore, then stood up in the canoe, and with a pistol in each hand, fired into the air.

On the shore, having been alerted by their lookouts that canoes were approaching, tribal peoples from nearby American Indian villages gathered. The peoples were from three tribal groups: the aboriginal **Menominee**, the early intrusive **Winnebago**, and some later intrusive **Potawatomi**, who also were of the Algonquian language/culture group. These tribal peoples, according to the oral traditions of the native peoples, were quite fearful of this light-skinned man, who was of questionable mental stability because he was standing in a canoe on the choppy bay waters, and who carried thunder in both hands.

Nicolet quickly realized that he had not made contact with the Chinese, but rather that he had met native tribal peoples previously unknown to the Europeans. He did, however, hold the hope that they might be tributary peoples of the Chinese. He quickly claimed all of the lands in the area for the French Crown and concluded what he thought was a peace and trade agreement with them. The Menominee, Winnebago, and Potawatomi neither spoke nor understood the French language and spoke and understood very little of the Huron language. The Huron spoke and understood a little of the Menominee, Winnebago, and Potawatomi languages, so some meaningful communication did take place at the time, although the entire agreement was not mutually understood.

According to the *Jesuit Relations* of 1643, between 4,000 and 5,000 native peoples took part in a special feast that the tribal peoples held in honor of the visit of the man who carried thunder in his hands and his companion Hurons.[6]

One of the things that Nicolet did learn from the native peoples at the feast was that there were some "Great Waters" some distance west of the Green Bay area. He assumed that these were waters of a Chinese sea. The native peoples were in fact referring to the Mississippi River.

Since it was already autumn, and the Hurons sensibly wanted to return to their home area before the big lake (Lake Michigan) became too rough for travel, Nicolet returned to Quebec without traveling to the "Western Chinese Sea."

Nicolet drowned near present-day Three Rivers, Canada, eight years after his voyage to the Wisconsin area. Apparently, his own notes about his trip were lost with him. An alleged copy of his account was very briefly reported by a second person, the Jesuit Bartelmy Vimont, nearly ten years after Nicolet's voyage took place. Fragments of data apparently obtained from Nicolet appear in the *Jesuit Relations* prior to 1643, but it is not known whether Nicolet transmitted more details of his trip to de Champlain, his official sponsor and supervisor. De Champlain died in 1635, a year after Nicolet's voyage, and Nicolet possibly did not have the opportunity to officially convey all of his information.

Other than the *Jesuit Relations*, the only other available information on this period are accounts by Pierre d'Esprit, Sieur Radisson (first copied in 1665 for presentation to King Charles II of England), Nicolas Perrot (written between 1680 and 1702), and Charles le Roy, Sieur de Bacqueville de la Potherie. Perrot's account, *Memoir of the Manners, Customs and Religion of the Savages of North America*, was not published until 1864 in Paris. Perrot, who traveled to the Green Bay area in 1667, was a French representative, agent, and interpreter among many of the Western Great Lakes tribes during the period from 1665 to 1680. La Potherie's work, *Histoire de l'Amerique Septentrionale*, was published in Paris in 1716. La Potherie, who had not actually been in the Wisconsin area, based his account on Perrot's manuscripts and makes no mention of Nicolet in connection with his account of the Winnebago.

Twenty-four years went by before the French sent anyone else to Wisconsin to follow-up on Nicolet's visit. France was experiencing very serious problems with the English in Europe and in North America as well as with tribal groups from the **Eastern Iroquois League**, who were being supplied with English weapons and who were encouraged to harass French colonial settlements. These problems kept the French from following up in the Western Great Lakes area.

Meanwhile, in the Green Bay area, the initial French contact had an almost immediate and long-lasting effect. The peoples of the area were exposed to some previously unknown European diseases through interaction with both Nicolet and the Hurons.

There were two other, more long-ranging effects of the contact by Nicolet. One involved the fact that twenty-four years later, other French people followed, and with them came aspects of the French economy, French politics, and the Christian religion, which soon had a growing influence on the native peoples' lives. The other long-range effect was that with the increasing dependence of the native peoples on the European fur trade came the subsequent increasing loss of many of their traditional cultural ways.

WAR, DISRUPTION, AND MORE CHANGES
FOR THE TRIBAL PEOPLES

East of Wisconsin, but still in the Western Great Lakes area, two tribal groups were already becoming extremely dependent on the French: the **Hurons** and the neighboring **Ottawa**. Both of these tribal groups were vying for middlemen positions in the trade between the French and other tribes further west.

The **Huron**, consisting of five, large, northern **Iroquoian** groups gathered into a confederacy, at that time called themselves the *Wen-dat*, the meaning of which is unknown. The word *Huron* is derived from *hure*, the French word for the head of a wild boar. The word began to be used to refer to the Wen-dat after French sailors reported that the Wen-dat males' hairstyle reminded them of the ridge of erect bristles on the head of the boar.

It was not long afterward that the Huron's major settlement area became known as "Huronia."

The Huron society began to disintegrate quickly with a series of devastating European disease epidemics that swept through the region between 1634 and 1640, culminating in a massive smallpox epidemic in 1639. With the death of most of their Elders, the carriers and transmitters of their traditional culture, much of the Huron culture came to an abrupt end.

Then, beginning in the late 1640's, tribes of the **Eastern Iroquois League**, supplied with English and Dutch weapons and encouraged by the English, began to raid and destroy the villages of Huronia. The English at that time were attempting to wrest control of the lucrative fur trade away from the French, and the Huron at that time were the major middlemen in the French and tribal trade. Furs were in heavy demand in Europe at that time, and in addition, the English delighted in making general trouble for their longtime European enemies, the French.

Soon, with English encouragement, the tribes of the **Eastern Iroquois League** were attacking the mostly Algonquian tribal groups in lower Michigan as well.

Between 1648 and 1650, the Eastern Iroquois League invaded the principal lands of the Hurons in the area of Georgian Bay, destroying Huronia. This was so devastating to the Huron that they never regrouped as before. Their survivors were absorbed by the neighboring **Ottawa** and by other tribal groups further west, including some as far west as the Mississippi River area of northwestern Wisconsin. Those Huron who were able to regroup later during the English period were often called the **Wyandot** by the English.

Eastern Iroquois League attacks on the tribes in lower Michigan, and the league's subsequent invasion of the region, forced the native tribal peoples, all of whom were of the **Algonquian language and culture group**, to flee the area in the 1650's. Most of those who fled at that time took refuge in Wisconsin.

Among the Michigan tribal peoples who fled from Michigan into Wisconsin were those **Potawatomi** who had not previously migrated to and settled in Wisconsin. The other Michigan tribes who fled into Wisconsin at that time were: the Mesquaki-haki (who became known as the Renards to the French, and as the **Fox** to the English), the Asa-ki-wa-ki (later commonly called the **Sauk**), the Kiikipoa (later called the **Kickapoo**), the **Mascouten**, and the **Miami**. All of the foregoing groups fled southward, out of lower Michigan, and then westward, past the ''Stinking-Place'' (Chi-ca-goa: the place of the skunk-cabbage in the marshes), into Wis-cooh-seh (the place of the wide, flower-banked rivers, where it was good to live).

In addition, some **Ottawa** (O-da-wa) who didn't join those already living on Manitoulin and other islands in northern Lake Huron also fled northward into Michigan's Upper Peninsula and westward into Wisconsin. Some of them settled for a time on the islands at the mouth of the Bay of Green Bay (present-day Washington and Rock Islands). Wanting to get as far from the Iroquois as possible, in the late 1650's, some **Ottawas**, accompanied by some remnant **Hurons**, migrated all the way to the eastern shores of the Mississippi River.

These **Ottawa**, initially with the permission of the native **Santee**, settled for a time on some of the upper Mississippi islands. Other Ottawas settled for a time in the area of the present-day Lac Courte Oreilles Chippewa reservation, where for a time the main lake was known as Ottawa Lake. By 1666 conflicts with that area's native tribal peoples, later commonly known as the **Sioux**, caused the relatively few Ottawa and Huron remnants who had not merged with other tribal groups to migrate back eastward again.

After 1670 many **Ottawa** who temporarily had been living elsewhere migrated to Manitoulin Island, where they joined other Ottawas. Some Ottawas also gradually returned to lower Michigan. By 1712 a significant number were settled in the Saginaw Bay area, and by 1742 Ottawas had settled in the Traverse and Little Traverse Bay areas of lower Michigan. Others also settled with **Ojibwe** (more commonly known as **Chippewa**) peoples on the Beaver Islands, located between upper and lower Michigan. Gradually, during the early United States period, the Ottawa lost most of their Michigan lands; however, there are still some Ottawa communities in Michigan, notably in the Charlevoix, Traverse, and Leelanau Peninsula areas.

Once they were in Wisconsin, the tribal peoples from Michigan encountered the **Winnebago**, as well as the indigenous **Santee** and **Menominee**.

During this time, the **Santee** were still settled in their apparent aboriginal homeland in the northwestern third of Wisconsin and had also settled as far southeast as the present-day Shawano County area of central Wisconsin. Some tribal Algonquian groups in Wisconsin, particularly the **Chippewa** who came into Wisconsin from the Upper Peninsula of Michigan in approximately 1679, called the Santee, who were not Algonquian, *Na-dou-es-siw*, meaning "snakes in the grass." Later the French and other Europeans, hearing the Santee referred to as the Na-dou-es-siw, mispronounced and shortened the word, calling the Santee "**Sioux**." The Santee and related tribal peoples from farther west, who later were also known as the "Sioux," did not initially call themselves by that name.

The French first made contact with the Santee in 1660 in the area of present-day Lac Courte Oreilles in Sawyer County of northwestern Wisconsin. In the late 1700's, itinerant French traders began calling the area "Courte Oreilles," (which describes the area natives' "short ears") because they noticed that the Bear Clan Chippewa who had settled there by that time did not wear the heavy earrings that stretched their ear lobes like the other Chippewas and Ottawas they had previously met.

Meanwhile, the intrusion of Michigan tribal peoples into Wisconsin during the 1650's became an increasingly disruptive force in the lives of both the Michigan peoples and the Wisconsin native peoples. In addition, it eventually resulted in a great deal of cultural exchange, and intermarriage, and other liaisons, which produced many mixed-blood children.

In 1653 the **Eastern Iroquois League**'s warriors, again encouraged by the English, attempted to follow the fleeing Michigan area natives into Wisconsin with the intent of gaining control over both them and the Wisconsin area territory and trade. The Iroquois invaders soon weakened and grew disorganized due to starvation resulting from the fleeing Michigan native groups' efforts to destroy the available food supply in their wake. The Eastern Iroquois League warriors actually faced a situation quite similar to that faced by Napoleon's troops in Russia during the 1800's, and by Hitler's troops in Russia in the 1940's.

In Wisconsin, the **Eastern Iroquois League** warriors were soon confronted by **Winnebago** and **Menominee** warriors, as well as by some **Potawatomis** and other Michigan natives. Put in the position of having to beg for food from the peoples they had come to conquer, the **Eastern Iroquois League** warriors retreated northward and southward. Those Iroquois warriors who turned north were attacked in the Upper Peninsula of Michigan by **Chippewa** warriors. Those who turned back toward the south were attacked by **Illinois** warriors. Only a few Iroquois survivors made it back to their home area east of the Appalachian and Allegheny mountains.

In 1662 another group of Eastern Iroquois League warriors began to move against a combined **Chippewa** and **Ottawa** trade center located in the Sault Ste. Marie area of Michigan's Upper Peninsula. The Iroquois were again defeated, this time in an area of the present-day Bay Mills Reservation.

THE FRENCH INCREASE
THEIR WISCONSIN AREA ACTIVITY

In 1658, twenty-four years after Nicolet's initial contact, Pierre d'Esprit, Sieur Radisson, and his brother-in-law, Medard Chouart, Sieur des Groseilliers, traveled to the Green Bay area and spent the winter of

1658-59 in a native village.

In 1667, thirty-three years after Nicolet's initial Wisconsin contact, the young Frenchman Nicolas Perrot formed a series of French and American Indian trading alliances in Wisconsin, thereby depriving the **Ottawa** of the trade monopoly they had enjoyed since becoming the only tribal middlemen in the trade at the end of the Huron era. Perrot also journeyed to and claimed the lead-rich area located within **Winnebago** territory in southwestern Wisconsin and northwestern Illinois, where he built several combined military and trading posts. He and his companions additionally "took possession" of **Santee** territory, as well as other **Siouan** territory, for the French Crown. Two years later in 1669, the French also began to exploit native copper mines located in the south shore of Lake Superior area.

By 1667 the **Potawatomi**, who had become important middlemen in the French fur trade, were heavily involved in the trade based at Green Bay. **Menominees** and **Sauk** were also present in large numbers in the Green Bay area. At that time, a large **Potawatomi** village was located near present-day Kewaunee. Many **Fox** tribal members were also in the Green Bay area, as well as along the Wolf River, drawn to the areas by the fur trade. In approximately 1677, the **Fox** moved in large numbers to the Upper Fox River area, establishing a large village near present-day Neenah. Both the **Menominee** and the **Sauk** remained in large numbers in the Green Bay area.

By 1679 a French trading post was operating on present-day Jones Island in the Milwaukee harbor.

Meanwhile, in 1669 Nicolas Perrot left the Green Bay area and another French trading expedition arrived under the leadership of Louis Jolliet. Jolliet's traders stirred up tribal animosity and quarreled with tribal leaders over payment for furs. In response, a **Potawatomi** delegation traveled to Sault Ste. Marie, complained about the activities of the French traders in the Green Bay area, and requested that a "Black Robe" visit the area to arbitrate their grievances. In response to the **Potawatomi** request, Claude Allouez, a French Jesuit Priest, returned with them to the bay of Green Bay area.

While in Wisconsin, Allouez established the first French mission, the mission of St. Francis Xavier, at Oka'to (present-day Oconto in Oconto County), the site of a long-inhabited **Menominee** village. A combined **Potawatomi** and **Sauk** village was also located there when Allouez arrived. Today, a large wood cross on Highway 41 along the Oconto River in the city of Oconto marks the site of the mission.

The following year, in 1670, Allouez and his fellow missionary priest, Claude Dablon, established a second mission near the mouth of the Fox River at the present-day city of Green Bay. There they deliberately defaced a special "spirit stone," which was thought of as being very special by both the Menominee and the Potawatomi. The missionaries defaced the stone, located in the Fox River rapids near Green Bay, in order to demonstrate to the natives living in the area the power of the Christian religion.

This act by the French priests had two major effects on the native peoples. First, when nothing negative happened to the priests as a result of their action, some natives began to doubt the efficacy of their own native religions. Second, it caused many natives to begin to hate the "Black Robes."

In 1671 the French Catholic priest Jacques Marquette founded the very important mission of St. Ignace at the eastern end of Michigan's Upper Peninsula along the western shore of the Straits of Mackinac. By that time, the French Catholic Jesuits had also established other missions at Sault Ste. Marie and at the bay called Chequamegon located in the southwestern shore area of Lake Superior.

THE CONTINUED IMPACT OF EUROPEAN CONTACT ON THE TRIBAL PEOPLES

The impact of the French contact on tribal peoples, particularly that resulting from the fur trade, was staggering. Areas with large beaver populations, rather than traditional tribal considerations, determined village locations and trade routes. This in turn led to the establishment of Catholic missions, then trading posts, and then army forts. These locations soon began to develop into French settlements. A prime example of this evolution is the settlement called Green Bay, initially called Fort St. Francis and La Baye by the French.

The establishment of French trading centers brought together tribal peoples who previously had little contact with each other. It also resulted in the development of new intertribal competition, which sometimes deteriorated into intertribal hostility.

The increasing French presence also brought European diseases that devastated entire villages and adversely affected traditional cultures. To understand what happened, it is important to know that the native peoples of much of North America, including those of Wisconsin, over a very long period of time, had developed a metaphysics that included a contractual relationship with the natural world based upon reciprocity. The humans believed that as long as they kept their part of the contractual relationship and did not abuse and overkill animals, their life experiences would be generally positive. The primary rule of this relationship was that one only took another being's life when there was a real need, as opposed to a "want." As a result, there appeared to be a ready availability of animal life, when needed.

Then alien diseases came in epidemic proportion, spreading throughout the Western Great Lakes. The medicine people were ineffective against these diseases, which were inexplicable from both a traditional medicinal and metaphysical standpoint. The religious leaders' supplications appeared to be unheeded by the Spirit-World. The tribal peoples concluded that the animals must have decided to break the contractual relationship and had sent the new, devastating diseases to signal this rupture of the reciprocal relationship. In retaliation, tribal peoples declared "war" on the animals.

This decision came at the same time that Europeans applied increasing pressure upon tribal peoples for more and more furs to be delivered to trading centers. All of this culminated in the escalation of the fur trade and resulted in the near extermination of fur-bearing animals in the Western Great Lakes area. The natives did not realize until it was too late that it was the Europeans, not the animals, who were responsible for the devastating diseases.

The increasing French presence had another devastating impact on the tribal peoples' community lives and material culture. As they became more involved in the fur trade, they became increasingly dependent upon European trade goods. This in turn escalated the slaughter of the animals, which only made tribal peoples more dependent upon the Europeans for food as their own primary food supplies, the animals, rapidly diminished. In addition, they were spending so much time in the fur trade seasonal cycle that they did not spend nearly enough time maintaining traditional subsistence cycles. As a result, they began to lose some necessary knowledge regarding traditional ways and subsistence methods, which was made more serious by their increasing dependence on the European goods made available through the trade.

The cultural losses were further and devastatingly complicated by the introduction of alcoholic beverages in the European fur trade. Previously unknown to the tribal peoples, liquor became a popular item among those who felt increasingly alienated from their previous lifestyles, traditions, and cultures. Physical addiction followed.

Meanwhile, the French Catholic missionary message was not having much of a positive effect on the tribal peoples. Most of the tribal peoples were hardly touched by the missionary message. The French missionary priest Louis Andre, for example, spent three months at a **Menominee** village at Pensaukee (located along the bay shore in present-day Oconto County), and reported having baptized only nine children and ten adults. These baptisms meant little, since the missionaries would move on quickly, providing little or no follow-up for converts. During that early period of missionary activity, there was not one historically notable convert![7]

By 1683 the number of French Catholic missionaries on the Western Great Lakes frontier had dropped drastically after an initially strong start. At the time, there were only seven priests responsible for covering the geographically immense area. Four of the seven were disabled due to age and disease. By the next year, there were no missionaries at Green Bay, and by 1711 there were only two in the entire Western Great Lakes area.

As one reads about the early efforts of the French missionaries and their apparent lack of success, one may wonder why they were among the natives in the first place, and why they persisted as long as they did.

Why did the French send missionaries among the American Indians of the Western Great Lakes? According to Louise Phelps Kellogg, the best source for the history of the early French missions is the *Jesuit Relations*. Kellogg points out that the term "mission" was used differently in the seventeenth century than it is used in the twentieth century (now usually referring to an organization involved with attempts to convert and spiritually "improve" a people). To the seventeenth century Jesuits, a mission was "the substance of things hoped for." If only one dying infant of a tribe was baptized, the first fruits of that mission were thought to have been garnered for heaven. If any members of a tribe expressed a wish to talk with the missionary, the mission for that tribe was thought of as having been established. Any contact with a native tribe was considered the beginning of a mission, whether or not there had been any acceptance of the missionary's message or any substantial plan for continued contact.[8]

Religious and secular politics also played a role in the missionary effort. In 1632 in France, a stronghold of Catholicism in the seventeenth century, the king gave the Jesuits exclusive rights to the conversion of North America's native peoples. For two successive generations, the prime ministers of France were also Roman Catholic cardinals. Members of the Jesuit order were largely recruited from the powerful families of France. One can see the inevitability of imperial plans mixing with religious fervor in outlining the goals of the Western Great Lakes missions.

There were several reasons for the severe decline in missionary activity by 1684. Interest in and enthusiasm for missionary work had suffered a sharp decline in France. The publication of the annual *Jesuit Relations*, the report of colonial missions in New France, was halted. France was also engaged in a serious struggle with Rome over the question of independence for the French Catholic Church. It also appears that some highly influential members of the French court were fearful that the Jesuits, many of whom came from the families of French nobility, had aspirations of creating a Jesuit Empire in North America.

MORE TURMOIL

In 1689 France and England were again at war, and the governor of New France requested assistance from the Wisconsin area tribes. Just as a group of warriors from these tribes was about to arrive in the Quebec area in response to the governor's request, they learned that the **Eastern Iroquois League** had inflicted heavy losses on the French. The Wisconsin warriors quickly realized that it was unlikely that the French would be able to protect the Western Great Lakes area from English inspired and armed Iroquois attacks. The western tribal groups returned to Mackinac in a sullen mood, deciding to ally themselves with the

Iroquois, attack the French, and switch their trade to the English. About that time, the French governor sent word to Mackinac that French military reinforcements had arrived from France. Approximately 150 French troops had been sent with the messenger, Jolliet. On their way to Mackinac, these French troops had the good fortune to defeat an Iroquois war group and to capture the leader. The French tied the leader to the bow of the lead canoe and forced him to sing out as they approached the Mackinac shore. The Wisconsin area warriors still at Mackinac were deeply impressed by this French military act and abandoned their plans for rebellion against the French.

In 1693 a French army officer named Pierre Le Sueur arrived at Chequamegon Bay and established the first French settlement in the area, Fort La Pointe, on the southwest corner of Madeline Island.

By 1697 many of the political, religious, and economic pressures, which had begun to exert their influence as early as twelve years before, culminated in the French king ordering all trading posts, forts, and missions in the Western Great Lakes area closed and razed.

The situation at St. Ignace under the command of Antoine de Cadillac had grown particularly chaotic. Apparently Cadillac was involved in a series of intrigues against the Jesuits of St. Ignace, who claimed that the natives were being corrupted by the French army and the traders. Liquor was everywhere, and problems involving Indian women and French men were numerous. Fur, women, and liquor appeared to have become common ingredients of the French frontier.

As early as 1685, the king, by royal edict, had banished the French Protestants from their homes in the Normandy area of France. It had been the Huguenots in particular who had utilized the North American furs, mostly the beaver, in the manufacture of hats. Their banishment almost ended the market for the fur in France.

In addition, by 1697 the warehouses of Europe were glutted with furs. That meant there was little demand anywhere in Europe for beaver or other North American furs. Intermediate merchants wanted the supply of furs drastically reduced in order to keep fur prices high in France and other parts of Europe. Montreal's warehouses were also glutted with furs.

To further complicate the situation, some pro-Jesuits had secured the ear of the king. They impressed upon him the view that the fur trade was evil, particularly because of the devastating impact of liquor upon the tribal peoples of New France. They claimed that the fur trade meant the abuse of both brandy and women. The anti-Jesuits in the court replied that the natives, if not furnished with French brandy through the trade, would certainly exchange their furs for English rum. King Louis XIV, however, decided in 1697 to withdraw official Crown permission for the fur traders to remain in the area of colonial New France.

In spite of this decision, many French traders ignored the Crown order, pursued their own interests, and became known as the "coureurs de bois," the outlawed "runners of the woods." They often lived with and had children with American Indian women, giving rise to a large population of Metis (French and Indian mixed) in Wisconsin and throughout the Western Great Lakes region. These Metis (mixed-bloods) eventually came to have a great and long-lasting influence among the tribes.

As a result of the Crown's order, military posts, including the posts at Mackinac and St. Ignace, were abandoned. Many French missions were also abandoned, including the very important mission at DePere, south of Green Bay in Wisconsin. For almost one hundred years thereafter, until about 1810, no Christian missionary visited the Wisconsin area.

Although none of the Wisconsin area tribal groups had become Christian up to the time of the closing of the missions in the Green Bay area, some memories of Christianity were preserved among some of the tribes, particularly among the **Menominee**, where there had been considerable intermarriage with French fur traders. Eventually over time, the French Catholic religion did finally permeate many of the tribal communities to a certain extent. Many tribal peoples became nominally Catholic, and even in some of the more traditional pre-Christian religious ceremonies, some of the words used in prayers are Christian-derived. For example, in the mid-1970's, the words "Jesu" and "Maria," were used in traditional Mitiwin Drum religious services on a Wisconsin Indian reservation without the Elders being aware that those words were of Christian origin![9]

Oddly enough, in 1697 the Jesuits felt that they had "won" with the closing of the French posts, even though they also had been forced to close most of their missions. Now they were determined to establish new missions along the lower Mississippi River. In mid-September of 1698, a group of Jesuits set out from Mackinac and went to Green Bay, determined to reach the Mississippi by the Fox-Wisconsin river route; however, without the presence of French troops or French government-authorized traders to control or inhibit them, the **Fox** tribal people in the area decided to oppose the missionaries' passage on the Fox-Wisconsin river route. The Jesuits detoured east, traveling down the east shore of the Door Peninsula to a **Potawatomi** village at Kewaunee, and from there they traveled south to the Chicago area.

The French military and trading post that had been established at La Pointe in 1693 was abandoned in 1700 as a result of the Crown's order. For seventeen years thereafter, there was no authorized French presence in the area. The account of French reestablishment of the post by Captain St. Pierre in 1718 provides a striking picture of the devastating effects of the fur trade on native people. St. Pierre reported that when he arrived he found starving and ragged natives, who had apparently either forgotten, or, for some reason, were not able to pursue their traditional pre-fur trade means of subsistence.

SOME MICHIGAN NATIVES RETURN TO MICHIGAN

In 1701, four years after the French posts in the Western Great Lakes region had been closed and razed, Antoinne de Cadillac requested the king's permission to build a fort at Detroit. Formerly the French commandant at St. Ignace, he expressed his fear that the increasing **English** presence in the eastern portion of the Western Great Lakes region would prove to be disastrous to the welfare of North American colonial France. Cadillac was particularly concerned, because at that time, English goods were less expensive and better made than French goods. He succeeded in convincing the French king to allow him to construct a major French fort and trading post at the site of present-day Detroit. He then began to encourage tribal groups to settle there. For many of the former Michigan area tribal peoples who had been forcibly relocated to Wisconsin in the 1650's, this was very good news.

Soon there were substantial **Fox, Sauk, Miami, Potawatomi, Ottawa** and **Huron** remnants, as well as **Chippewa**, village settlements in the Detroit area.

THE FRENCH AND FOX CONFLICT

At Detroit, however, the French and the **Fox** soon found themselves involved in conflict. Early on several factors contributed to the dispute. The **Fox** strongly opposed the French idea of extending the fur trade to the **Santee** and the Dakota **Sioux**, who had become enemies of the Fox because of competitory conflict in the same fur trade areas. It also appears that the **Fox** had positively responded to overtures from the **Eastern Iroquois League**, which was historically allied with the English. It seems that the **Iroquois** had informed the **Fox** that the **English** wanted to establish trade relations with them. By that time, English traders were making great efforts to get involved in the fur trade in the Upper Western Great Lakes. The English had a competitive edge because English trade goods at that time were less expensive and better made than French trade goods.

Then, in 1712, the French army commandant at Detroit made a decision involving an intertribal dispute that would cost the French dearly for several decades. The commandant was not Cadillac, rather he was another younger and less experienced man. He had received word that a group of **Fox** and **Mascouten**, for reasons unknown, were intending to attack some **Ottawas** at Detroit. The commandant, without clearing the matter with his superior officers in Montreal, made a decision to launch a **French** attack on the **Fox** village instead. The French and their allies laid siege to the Fox village for nineteen days, during which time the Fox tried unsuccessfully to negotiate a just settlement and surrender. The French siege of the Fox village lasted so long that Fox women and children were dying of thirst as warriors were cut down by French mortars. The Fox finally broke away and were pursued by the French and some of their native mercenaries, eventually losing over 1,000 men, women, and children. The few Fox who escaped fled back into Wisconsin and took refuge with the **Sauk** in the Green Bay area.

At about that same time, trade-related antagonism between the **Mascouten** and some **French** traders came to a head and over 800 Mascouten were killed in a French attack near Detroit. Some French-Indian allies also attacked Mascouten settlements along the Illinois, Michigan, and Ohio border areas.

By 1715 the French had begun to reestablish military and trading posts throughout the Upper Western Great Lakes area. The post at Mackinac, at present-day Mackinaw City, became the center for most French activity in the Upper Great Lakes. Detroit became the center for the Lower Great Lakes. As a result of this renewed and concentrated French activity, native dependence upon French trade goods and economic interests became even more pronounced. In addition to the established posts, many French lived in the native villages as part of the trade network.

Meanwhile, the **French** had determined that they would either exterminate, or capture and send to the West Indies as slaves, the **Fox** who had defied them and taken refuge with the **Sauk** in Wisconsin. In 1730 the French demanded that the **Sauk** village leaders surrender to them the Fox refugees who were living in the Sauk villages. When the Sauk refused, the commander of the French troops at Green Bay led his soldiers to forcibly take the Fox refugees from the Sauk village. The French commander was killed in the attempt. After that, most of the **Sauk** and **Fox** fled from Wisconsin and into an area of present-day Iowa. Finally, in 1737 the French colonial government, in an effort to save face, granted the **Fox** and the **Sauk** a general Crown pardon.

MORE PRESSURE ON THE TRIBAL PEOPLES

In the 1730's the **Chippewa** began to feel pressure from the fierce, fur trade-related competition that had developed between the Montreal-based French and the St. Louis-based French. Fur-bearing animals had become depleted in the coniferous and hardwood forests inhabited by the **Chippewa**. Consequently, they turned to the still game-rich transitional forests and prairie edges and began to migrate from the Chequamegon Bay area southward into the interior headwaters area of the Wisconsin, Chippewa, and St. Croix Rivers between Lake Superior and the Mississippi. They soon found themselves in open conflict with indigenous **Siouan** groups who inhabited the area.

The mid-1740's saw the establishment of permanent **Chippewa** villages in the northwestern and north-central interior of Wisconsin at present-day Lac Courte Oreilles and Lac du Flambeau. The **Chippewa** also pushed into Minnesota against rugged **Santee** and **Dakota Sioux** resistance. Open warfare erupted regularly for a long period of time.

By the mid-1750's, the tremendous pressures from the fur trade had radically shifted tribal settlement patterns, and often as a result, significant cultural differences among most native groups began to disappear. Once important cultural differences had become or were becoming subordinate to European-influenced political and economic considerations.

The **Potawatomi** influence in the trade continued to grow. By the late 1700's, they had major villages and were very influential all along the Lake Michigan shoreline to Chicago, replacing the **Illinois** in the northern Illinois and the Chicago areas. The Illinois were moving further south into the present-day state of Illinois.

THE FRENCH AND ENGLISH WAR AND ITS AFTERMATH

The great war between the French and the English in North America (commonly called the French and Indian War) lasted from 1756 until 1761 and involved tribal peoples fighting on both sides. The war brought major changes to native lives. The French defeat, finalized by the Treaty of Paris in 1763, meant a major readjustment for those tribal peoples who had been longtime French allies.

All French posts were officially transferred to English control, but most of the French civilian, French-Indian mixed (Metis), and American Indian populations remained living near the posts.

The English colonial policy relating to the native tribal peoples was substantially different from that of the French. The rather loosely defined French colonial policy had principally focused on the fur trade and secondarily on missionary activity, as well as, from time to time, on fur trader liaisons with native women. The French policy, however, had a rather strange twist, when one considers a 1755 order sent from the French court at Versailles to Sieur de Vaudreuil de Cavagnal, the governor of colonial New France. The order states that the French king wished to "avoid war with the savages as much as possible." As a result, in an effort directed at "keeping them occupied and weakening them, it has been deemed advisable to take every opportunity to foment and encourage wars between them."[10]

The more formally defined English colonial policy, on the other hand, in addition to focusing on the fur trade, focused on regulating the acquisition of land for colonization and settlement, as well as the acquisition of raw materials from the natural resources of the land. Unlike the French, English interest in native religious practices was relatively limited.

The native tribal peoples suffered greatly because, having become very dependent upon French-supplied trade goods, they found themselves having to deal with English authorities who often despised tribal people and thought of them as being less than human. In addition, under the English, fraudulent trade practices increased in frequency, and the natives developed a growing concern that their lands were about to be seized by English colonists.

THE PONTIAC REBELLION

Fear on the part of tribal peoples that they were about to lose their lands to English colonists precipitated an American Indian rebellion against the English led by an **Ottawa** named Pontiac during the summer of 1763. Pontiac's followers included, in addition to the **Ottawa**, some **Potawatomis, Sauks, Winnebagos,** and **Miamis.** Not many **Chippewas** or **Menominees** assisted Pontiac, largely because of the influence of the mixed-bloods among them, who persuaded them to not antagonize the English. Pontiac's allied force of native tribal peoples initially captured several English forts, including the one at Mackinac, which a number of **Chippewas** and **Sauks** captured by tricking the English commander during a lacrosse game. They persuaded the commander to open the fort gates so that the soldiers, who were watching the game from the wall platforms, did not have to keep climbing down from the walls to throw the ball, which the tribal players kept hitting over the walls, back into play. The tribal players told the English commander that they would have someone from their own group go get the ball when it went over the wall so as not to inconvenience the soldiers watching the game. Once the gates were opened, the Indians took the fort.

Neither Green Bay nor Detroit were captured by the Indians, although Green Bay was abandoned for a time by the English. The tribal peoples were very disappointed when the help that they had expected to receive from the French never arrived. In the end, the English managed to recapture all their posts and to soundly defeat Pontiac and his intertribal allies.

Although Pontiac's rebellion was defeated by the English, it did result in the English Crown adopting a major change in *official* English policy toward the native American Indian peoples in North America. After putting down Pontiac's rebellion, the English government issued the Crown Proclamation of 1763, which declared that all lands west of the Allegheny and the Appalachian Mountains were reserved for the native American Indians. It further required all traders, including the English, to have a English-issued license to do business with the Indians. This was the official policy *de jure*, but the *de facto* situation was often quite different, since the policy was extremely difficult to enforce. In addition, due to the fact that almost anyone could secure a license from the English administrators, competition increased as resources diminished.

The English colonists along the Atlantic coast resented the provisions of the Crown Proclamation, particularly since it deprived them of ready access to lands west of the colonies, thus thwarting their efforts to expand and exploit new resources. This was one of the causes leading to the colonial American Revolution in 1775.

THE AMERICAN REVOLUTION AND ITS AFTERMATH

Once the revolution started, and after a brief period in which both sides urged the native groups to remain neutral, American Indian support and alliances were again solicited by non-Indians. The majority of the Western Great Lakes tribal peoples aligned themselves with the English government against the colonists because they felt the English government posed less of a threat to native lands than the expansion-oriented colonists.

Two notable exceptions to this were tribal groups whose homelands were in the eastern part of the country. One of these exceptions consisted of some of the nations of the once very powerful **Eastern Iroquois League**, including the **Oneida**. The other exception was the combined **Stockbridge** and **Munsee** group, remnants of other once powerful eastern tribal groups. Both the **Oneida** and the **Stockbridge-Munsee** significantly assisted the rebel colonial cause and contributed to the victory of the colonists over England. Many of the **Oneida** and most of the **Stockbridge-Munsee** migrated to and settled in Wisconsin in the 1820's.

A third notable anti-English (but not necessarily pro-colonist) faction was a mixed-tribal group based in the Milwaukee area of Wisconsin. Led by Siggenauk, who was of mixed Chippewa, Ottawa, and Potawatomi ancestry, this Milwaukee-based group significantly frustrated an alleged English military plan to attack the colonies from the Western Great Lakes. Siggenauk met with George Rogers Clark, a colonial army officer, at Kaskaskia during the winter of 1778-79 and soon thereafter committed his Milwaukee area followers against the English. In June of 1777, the English commandant at Mackinac received reports from an English allied trader at Milwaukee stating that agents of Spain had made an alliance with Siggenauk, who was called "Blackbird" by the English.

The reports stated that from his base in the Milwaukee area, Siggenauk was attempting to rally tribal groups from Green Bay to the Mississippi River in an alliance with Spain against England. Spain, eager to provoke trouble for England, its competitor, apparently hoped to gain a greater share of the trade with the tribal peoples, while the English were preoccupied with trying to crush the American colonial rebellion.

Employing periodic and unpredictable attacks on English posts in the Western Great Lakes region, including an assault against St. Joseph, Michigan in 1779, the intertribal group led by Siggenauk did not allow the English sufficient time to organize the alleged planned assault against the colonies from the Western Great Lakes. Very early on, the English placed a bounty on Siggenauk's head—a bounty that was never collected.

When the war ended, the majority of American Indians had again allied with the losing side in a major conflict between European powers. The new United States public now viewed the native tribal lands as conquered and therefore available for expanding settlement and development. The newly emerged United States-"Americans" began to swarm into the lands west of the Appalachians.

Although the English had lost the war, they remained at their Western Great Lakes posts, with the exception of Detroit, and for a time, Mackinac. Stationed at their Western Great Lakes posts, the English continued to monopolize the trade with the tribal peoples, as well as the people of French ancestry, from 1783 until the United States began occupying the Green Bay area in 1816.

THE "SIOUX" ATTEMPT A COMEBACK IN WISCONSIN

In approximately 1806, the **Santee** and some other **Siouan** peoples made one of their periodic intrusions into the Wisconsin area in an attempt to reestablish control over the wild rice areas. **Chippewa** groups, assisted by some **Potawatomi**, soundly defeated the "**Sioux**" at Mole Lake, located in present-day Forest County of northeastern Wisconsin. After that, the "Sioux" never returned in large numbers to Wisconsin; however, warfare between the "Sioux" and the Chippewa continued off and on for many years. Full-scale war was raging as late as 1826. When the United States forced the "**Sioux**" to the Dakota Territory in 1862, over 150 years of bloody intertribal confrontations with the **Chippewa** finally ended.

THE FUR TRADE PEAKS IN WISCONSIN AND THE UNITED STATES ERA BEGINS

The fur trade reached its peak after the end of the colonial revolution with the beginning of the U.S.-"American" period. The American Fur Company, centered at Mackinac with subsidiary main posts at Green Bay and Milwaukee, was founded in 1808. Initially, the company prudently made successful use of experienced French and Metis personnel who had previously worked with the Northwest Company in the region. The Northwest Company had been established in 1779 by independent merchants backed by Montreal capital, and it eventually came to control the Lake Superior and Lake Michigan trade. These traders for the Northwest Company had an excellent rapport already established with the tribal groups at the time of the American Fur Company's arrival in the area. It was not until 1814, however, that the U.S.-"Americans" were strong enough to break the grip of the English Northwest Company on the Great Lakes.

By 1808 the tribal peoples' community life cycles revolved almost exclusively around the fur trade. They spent the winter months trapping the ever diminishing supply of beaver and other fur-bearing animals. Late spring and early summer were spent delivering the furs to the trading posts, especially to the major post at Mackinac. Much of the remainder of the summer was spent gearing up for the next winter's trapping. This cycle continued until the decline of the fur trade during the late 1830's and early 1840's.

By that time, the Metis had become a formidable force in the trade and in native village life. In most cases, they were mixed French and American Indian, although there were a sizable number of mixed American Indian and Irish, American Indian and Scot, and American Indian and Scandinavian (mainly Norwegian and Swede). The Metis were such a formidable force because they were held in higher esteem by the Europeans and the U.S.-"Americans," as they were more European in appearance and in their ways. In addition, because they spoke and could often read and write the English language, they worked as interpreters. This proved to be an important and often financially lucrative role, especially at treaty sessions.

THE WAR OF 1812 AND ITS AFTERMATH:
AMERICAN INDIAN REMOVAL

During the second United States war against the England, the War of 1812, the majority of native tribes allied with the English--the losing side again!

In 1816, with the war over, the U.S. Army landed at Green Bay and rebuilt the fort there. They called it Fort Howard, in honor of a U.S. Army general who had served with distinction against the English in the War of 1812. The U.S. Army also built Fort Crawford at Prairie du Chien to monitor American Indian activities. United States-"Americans" viewed the Wisconsin lands as conquered lands, therefore they were considered to be open to settlement.

Soon several of the tribal groups experienced deceit at the hands of the United States, and the United States almost total disregard for American Indian human rights. The tribal groups were forced to cede their lands to the United States and many, following the Indian Removal Treaty of Chicago in 1833, were forced by the United States Army to move to areas west of the Mississippi.

The early decades of the 1800's also brought American Indian groups who were not indigenous to the Western Great Lakes region into Wisconsin. These groups were removed by the U.S. government from their homelands to reservations in Wisconsin. Many of the **Oneida**, originally one of the tribal nations of the **Eastern Iroquois League**, were relocated to Wisconsin beginning in 1822. The **Stockbridge**, **Munsee**, and **Brotherton**, all remnants of eastern coastal area tribal groups were also relocated to Wisconsin.

In 1835 Wisconsin was officially opened to U.S.-"American" and European immigrant settlement. Land could be purchased for as little as $1.25 an acre at U.S. government land offices; principally at the land office located at Green Bay. Those individuals who could establish a preemptive land claim had first choice of land locations. Preemptive land claims involved often fraudulent claims of having made improvements on a plot of land prior to the land being offered for sale. Most of the preemptive claims that were subsequently recognized were those of U.S.-"Americans" of English ancestry and those of English people directly from England. The legitimate preemptive claims of French, Metis, and American Indian people were generally disallowed or ignored.

In 1836 Nathaniel Hyer wrote from Milwaukee:

We reached the bluff. . . left [east] bank of the Milwaukee River.
The first thing of note, which we observed, was a large number
of small white flags on stakes planted in the ground, which. . .
were to designate Indian graves [there were still thousands of
graves found along the bluffs as late as 1857]. These could be
seen over all parts of the bluff. . . the [Indians] deemed these sig-
nals would protect the sacredness of their burial places from the
encroachments of [the European settlers].[11]

In 1838 the U.S. Army was used to roundup Milwaukee-area American Indians. They were compelled to gather at what was later called "Indian Fields," near the present-day Forest Home Cemetery on the south side of present-day Milwaukee. There they were either loaded into army wagons or forced to walk in a caravan to the Iowa and Kansas Territories west of the Mississippi.

THE FUR TRADE ENDS: MORE DISORIENTATION
FOR THE AMERICAN INDIANS

In the late 1830's and into the early 1840's, with most of the resources exhausted and with some animal species near extinction, the fur trade declined swiftly in importance and then abruptly came to and end. Prolonged overtrapping, coupled with a drastic drop in the demand for furs in the world market due to significant changes in styles and manufacturing technology, proved to be disastrous for the tribal peoples. Because they had become so dependent on the trade, and in the process had lost many of their old traditional ways, tribal peoples had almost nothing to fall back on for subsistence when the trade rapidly declined and then abruptly ended.

In 1848 Wisconsin became a state, ushering in a new era of dramatic changes for Wisconsin's and other Western Great Lakes areas' American Indian people.

The following chapters will provide a more detailed look at specific aspects of the history of most of the tribal groups referred to in this historical overview, beginning with the **Menominee**, the only tribal group presently in Wisconsin that is descended from Wisconsin's ancient, aboriginal peoples.

NOTES

1. The principal source of information for this chapter is John Boatman, "Historical Overview of the Wisconsin Area: From Early Years to the French, British, and American Intrusions," *An Anthology of Western Great Lakes Indian History*, ed. Donald L. Fixico, rev. ed. (Milwaukee: American Indian Studies, University of Wisconsin-Milwaukee), 1989.

2. *NewsLetter*, Archaeological Rescue, Inc., January 1988.

3. *The Milwaukee Journal*, 23 July 1989.

4. *American Indian Culture and Research Journal*, vol. 11, no. 4, 100-103. Mason's statement about cannibalism can be found on page 59 of her book.

5. Walter J. Hoffman, *The Menomini Indians* (Washington, D.C.: Smithsonian Institution, 1896), 36.

6. Ibid., 15.

7. Louise Phelps Kellogg, *The French Regime in Wisconsin and the Northwest*

(Madison: State Historical Society of Wisconsin, 1925), 166.

8. Ibid., 139-141.

9. Personal recollection of the author, who attended this particular religious service at a traditional community on one of the Wisconsin reservations.

10. Reuben G. Thwaites, ed., *Collections of the State Historical Society of Wisconsin*, Vol. 18 (Madison, Wisconsin: State Historical Society of Wisconsin, 1908), 150-153.

11. "Nathaniel Hyer Recalls Frontier Milwaukee 1836," *History of Milwaukee*, A.T. Andreas (Chicago: Western Historical Co., 1881), 159-162.

CHAPTER TWO
THE MENOMINEE

The Menominee, who are descendants of the ancient, indigenous Copper Culture peoples, have been living in Wisconsin longer than any other human group.

The name *Menominee* derives from a widely-used Algonquian word *manomin* ("wild rice") and means "Wild Rice People." The French, after making contact with the Menominee, called them the *Folles Avoines*, meaning the nation of the "Crazy Oats," a reference to the wild rice abundant in their territory. The Menominee called themselves *Mamaceqtaw* (pronounced ma-ma-chay-tau), which means "the people." The Menominee word *Wis-coo-seh* (which later became Wisconsin) means "a good place in which to live."

From the year 800, when the ancestors of the **Winnebago** first entered the Wisconsin area, the Menominee developed and maintained a friendship and close relationships with them. The same was true of Menominee interactions with the **Potawatomi** and some of the other Michigan tribal groups, such as the **Sauk**, who came into Wisconsin in the 1600's.

The original main village of the Menominee was located at the mouth of the Menominee River where the river flows into the bay of Green Bay along the present-day border between Wisconsin and the Upper Peninsula of Michigan. The large village was called Menekaunee (Minikani), now the eastern side of the city of Marinette, Wisconsin.

Other significant Menominee villages existed at the sites of the present-day Wisconsin villages and cities of Wausaukee and Peshtigo in present-day Marinette County; Oconto, Pensaukee, and Little Suamico in present-day Oconto County; Suamico and the Green Bay area in present-day Brown County; the Lake Poygan area in present-day

Winnebago County; the Two Rivers and Manitowoc areas in present-day Manitowoc County; the Sheboygan area in present-day Sheboygan County; the Saukville, Sauk Harbor (Port Washington), Cedarburg, and Mequon areas in present-day Ozaukee County; and several sites in the present-day Milwaukee County area. The Menominee had villages in other areas of eastern and east-central Wisconsin as well. In addition, the Menominee had significant villages in the Stephenson and Escanaba areas of the Upper Peninsula of Michigan.[1]

A large number of Menominee were present in 1634 when the French representative Jean Nicolet stepped ashore at Red Banks, east of the mouth of the Fox River.[2]

The first recorded contact with the Menominee by a non-American Indian after Nicolet's initial contact was that of the French representative Nicolas Perrot who visited the Menominees' large ancestral village, Menekaunee, in 1667. It was Perrot who first introduced some of the Menominee to liquor, an introduction that later was to prove particularly tragic. [3]

As noted in chapter one, in 1679 Claude Allouez, a French Jesuit priest, established the first French Roman Catholic mission, the mission of St. Francis Xavier, at Oka'to (present-day Oconto in Oconto County) where a major Menominee village had been located for a long time.

The Jesuits established a second mission located at another large Menominee village near the mouth of the Fox River, at the present-day city of Green Bay. At this site, the French missionaries deliberately defaced a special "spirit stone" that was recognized and revered by both the Menominee and the Potawatomi. The Jesuits soon established missions in other Menominee village areas at river mouths along the shore of the bay of Green Bay. The French missionary priest Louis Andre spent three months at a Menominee village at Pensaukee, for example; however, he and other missionaries did not have a great deal of success in their efforts to convert these native peoples at that time. Andre spent a total of almost fourteen years with the Menominee and did succeed in teaching them some French songs, which the children in particular liked very much.

It was Andre, in his efforts to establish a rapport with the Menominee at Menekaunee, who benefited greatly from a coincidental weather pattern affecting the migration of fish into the Menominee River from the bay of Green Bay. It seems that the Menominee had become quite despondent because the sturgeon had not entered the Menominee River from the bay. In hopes of attaining Spirit-World assistance in directing the sturgeon into the river, the Menominee had placed one of their spiritually related symbols on a pole next to the river. Andre persuaded the Menominee to allow him to replace the symbol with one of his crosses. (It should be noted that for the tribal peoples the cross was considered a symbol of the Spirits of the Four Winds and balance; however, Andre did not know that.) The morning after the cross was attached to the pole, the sturgeon entered the river, greatly pleasing the Menominee. Andre took the credit, associating the fish migration with his having placed the cross on the pole.[4]

From 1684 until 1831, hardly any missionary contact with the Menominee occurred. An old Menominee is said to have remarked in 1881 that "no black gown" had been seen by his people for more than one hundred years.[5]

Soon after initial contact, the Menominee became quite heavily involved in the fur trade with the French. Perrot and his companions took the first cargo of furs from La Baye (the present-day city of Green Bay) to Quebec as early as 1668.[6]

With the arrival of the French fur traders, the longtime sedentary life of the Menominee began to disintegrate as the tribe began to divide into roving bands organized for the fur trade cycle.

By 1698 the only Europeans the Menominee saw were the French "coureurs de bois," the outlawed "runners of the woods," who were usually in the Wisconsin area against the orders of the French government. By this time, many Menominee women had children with, and were sometimes married to, French traders. By 1718 there were a number of French families living with the Menominee in the area near the fort at the site of the present-day city of Green Bay, as well as across the Fox River along the east shore in an area that was commonly called Munnomonee (Menominee) Town or Shanty Town.

By 1730 many of the Menominee were staunch military allies of the French. Menominee warriors often accompanied French officials to Montreal and Quebec. At that time, the Menominee population was said to be the largest of any tribal group in the region.

It was apparently at that time that a fairly sizeable segment of the Menominee left their ancestral village at Menekaunee and settled near the French trading fort at La Baye (Green Bay).[7]

By 1746 the French de Langlade and Grignon families from Mackinac had arrived and settled at La Baye. As private entrepreneurs, members of these families began to take control of the trade. Members of both families intermarried and had many children with Menominees.

Soon many other French families also arrived, settled, and intermarried with Menominees at La Baye. In addition, since the late 1600's, French fur traders working in the area of Menominee villages located all along the Green Bay shoreline, north through present-day Marinette, Wisconsin and into the area around present-day Escanaba, Michigan, were allying themselves with the Menominees by marrying Menominee women and fathering Menominee children.

The Menominee generally supported the French efforts in the French and English war (French and Indian War), which ended with French defeat in 1761. In particular, the Menominee were strong supporters of Charles de Langlade, a young French Army officer from La Baye who was of mixed French and **Ottawa** ancestry. During the French and English war, no battles took place in Wisconsin; however, Menominees and other Wisconsin tribal peoples accompanied de Langlade to assist French efforts elsewhere, such as in battles that took place in the Ohio valley region.

During one of these military campaigns under the leadership of de Langlade, the Menominee, unawares, returned to their home areas carrying the smallpox virus! That winter, smallpox raged through the Menominee homelands. Within a four year period, the Menominee lost three hundred warriors to smallpox, including most of their war "chiefs."[8]

In 1759 some Menominee warriors unexpectedly attacked the French fort at La Baye in retaliation for the increasing abuse of the Menominee by the French commandant stationed there. According to various accounts of the incident, the Menominees killed between eleven and twenty-two French soldiers. Seven Menominee were taken prisoner by the French and sent to Montreal, where they were imprisoned.[9]

When the French were finally defeated by the English and the English took over the French fort at La Baye, where the majority of the population was either French or French/Indian mixed (Metis), the Menominee did not readily accept the English. Very few English settlers arrived at that time. The Menominee remained close to their French friends and family, usually cooperating with the English only when requested to do so by the French living at La Baye. The English actually occupied the fort, which they called Fort Edward Augustus, for only two years, as they abandoned it at the time of the Pontiac Rebellion in 1763.

The Menominees did not significantly assist Pontiac, largely because the mixed-bloods amongst them persuaded them that it would be a mistake to antagonize the English at that time. In fact, some Menominee warriors assisted the English against Pontiac.[10]

During the colonial revolution against England, the Menominee remained noninvolved except for providing Charles de Langlade with approximately 150 warriors in his campaigns against the colonists. Charles de Langlade, a French-Indian mixed Metis, had been in the French colonial army during the French and English war, but later he accepted an English army commission during the American colonial revolution. Some other Menominee warriors assisted Siggenauk's Milwaukee-based efforts against the English.

In 1776, while the American Revolution raged in the Atlantic coastal region, a nineteen year-old Frenchman named Jacques Vieau arrived in the Western Great Lakes region from Montreal. He was to become significantly involved with the Menominee as both a friend and a relative through marriage.

A descendant of the de Veau family of Marseilles in France, Vieau had been born and raised at Cote de Neige, on the outskirts of Montreal. He, accompanied by his brother Nicolas, had been sent to Mackinac as voyageurs for the Northwest Fur Company. From Mackinac, the brothers were sent to the company's post at La Pointe on present-day Madeline Island in the Chequamegon Bay of Lake Superior. By 1782 Jacques had been put in complete charge of the La Pointe post. Nicolas had moved to La Baye.

In 1786 Jacques also moved to La Baye, where that year he married Angelique, the daughter of Joseph le Roy, a Frenchman, and his wife Marguerite, a daughter of Ah-ke-ne-pa-weh ("Standing Earth"), an important Menominee tribal leader from the La Baye area. Ah-ke-ne-pa-weh, who later was one of the tribal leaders representing the

Menominee at treaty sessions, appears to have been the brother of Kaush-kau-no-weh ("Grizzly Bear"), who long exerted much influence among the Menominee. One of Angelique's maternal uncles (Ah-ke-ne-pa-weh's son) was O-nau-ge-sa, a Menominee leader of the **Potawatomi** at Milwaukee. O-nau-ge-sa had married a daughter of the principal Potawatomi leader at Milwaukee, and it was upon the death of his father-in-law that he, despite being a Menominee himself, became the leader of the Potawatomi there. This is not unusual, since a close relationship developed very early in Wisconsin between the Menominee, who are indigenous to Wisconsin, and the **Potawatomi**, who migrated to Wisconsin from lower Michigan beginning as early as 1630.[11]

Jacques Vieau, who spoke French, Menominee, Potawatomi, English, and apparently also some Winnebago and Chippewa, established his first "jackknife" trading post in 1795 with the help of his companions and family. This "jackknife" trading post, meaning it was put together with whatever materials were immediately available, was located near a mixed Menominee and Potawatomi village at Kewaunee, in present-day Kewaunee County, the site of a large, natural harbor on Lake Michigan.

This is the first example of how the Menominee tribal lineage of Jacques' wife proved to be very advantageous in establishing profitable trade connections. The fact that Angelique's family was renowned and respected in both Menominee and Potawatomi communities helped Jacques quickly become a respected and trusted friend among them. Attesting to his popularity, some of the American Indians, who by that time were calling Jacques "Jambeau" or "Shambo," referred to a creek near the site of one of Jacques' trading posts in the present-day Manitowoc County town of Gibson as "Jambeau Creek."[12]

Jacques Vieau also established trading posts near other Menominee and Potawatomi villages along the lake shore, including those at present-day Two Rivers, at Manitowoc near the rapids, at Sheboygan on the north side of the river at the foot of the rapids, and on the Milwaukee River peninsula in present-day Saukville, Wisconsin. Again, in choosing these locations, Jacques had made good use of his wife's tribal connections.

Jacques Vieau and his entourage finally arrived in Milwaukee harbor between the 18th and the 20th of August in 1795. There, a large number of **Potawatomi**, including relatives of his wife Angelique, as well as some **Sauk** and **Fox** and a few **Winnebago**, warmly welcomed Jacques and his family.

Once in the Milwaukee area, the Vieau's built two log buildings at the foot of a lime ridge approximately one and one-half miles from the mouth of the Menominee River in the present-day Mitchell Park area on the near south side of the city of Milwaukee. One of the buildings was a dwelling for his family; the other was a warehouse. The Vieau family remained at Milwaukee during the winter of 1795, and continued to spend every winter in the area thereafter for about the next three years. Six of the eleven Vieau children were born in Milwaukee, including Louis, who was later to become a "chief" of the **Potawatomi** in Kansas.

Vieau's chief clerk at that time was a man known only by the name "LaJeunnesse," without a first name being given in the available sources. It is possible that LaJeunnesse was a mixed-blood Menominee. At a Menominee tribal council with the English held at Prairie du Chien in 1783, one of the Menominee "chiefs" recorded to have spoken was called "LaJeunnesse." If Vieau's clerk and the Menominee "chief" were one and the same, or if the clerk was an offspring of the LaJeunnesse who spoke at Prairie du Chien, the fact that he had someone of that stature working for him would attest to Vieau's strong influence among the Menominee.[13]

During the War of 1812, the English military commanders in Wisconsin, concerned that the American Indians living in one of the **Potawatomi** villages at Milwaukee might attack English-held positions, requested that Jacques Vieau bring the **Potawatomi** leader and O-pa-hoh, a Menominee leader from Milwaukee, to meet with the commanders and Tomah, another principal Menominee leader (also known as Thomas Carron). A few months later, however, the English commander wrote that he was no longer sure if they should trust Jacques Vieau because he was related to the Milwaukee **Potawatomi** through his wife's family.[14]

As early as 1810, the great Shawnee leader Tecumseh tried to persuade the Menominee to join his intertribal confederation against the U.S.-"Americans," whose increasing encroachment on native tribal homelands was becoming steadily worse. Tomah, a mixed-Menominee leader speaking for the Menominee, told Tecumseh that the Menominee were "fully aware of the injustice of the [U.S.] Americans in their encroachments upon the lands of the [American] Indians," and that the Menominee, too, "feared its consequences, but that [the Menominee] saw no relief for it in going to war." As a result, the Menominee did not assist Tecumseh.[15]

In fact, many of the Menominee, as well as many of the French settlers at La Baye, fought on the English side against the U.S.-"Americans." They followed the lead of an English army officer and fur trader, Robert Dickson. Charles de Langlade, whom the Menominee normally would have followed, had died by that time.[16]

When the war ended in 1815, a United States government trading post and Indian Agency was established at La Baye. It was at this time that the name La Baye was changed to Green Bay. In 1816 the first United States troops landed there and occupied the old fort, renaming it "Fort Howard." The Menominee and other native tribal peoples called the U.S.-"Americans" the "Bostonnais," and/or "Long Knives," in the Menominee language, "Kechemocoman," or "Mokamon." The Menominee leaders at that time officially requested that the United States officials "not molest the French settlers," most of whom were married into the tribe.[17]

In 1818 Jacques Vieau became, for a short while, the principal agent for the American Fur Trade Company. In 1836, distressed that so many of his Indian friends had died during the 1832-33 smallpox epidemic, and disturbed that so many non-French, white settlers were coming into Milwaukee, left Milwaukee to reside permanently on his farm at Green Bay.

That same year, Tomah, one of the principal Menominee leaders at that time, who was also known as Thomas Carron, died on Mackinac Island. He had traveled to nearby Drummond Island, which had remained in English control, to collect "presents" (clothing, blankets, knives, kettles, etc.) that he expected the English would pay him for supporting their efforts in the recent war. He was told, however, that the English would no longer be providing "presents," and that the U.S.-"Americans" who had won the war were now in charge of his people and their lands. Angry and quite despondent, he went to Mackinac Island, got hold of some bad liquor, drank to excess, and died of acute alcohol poisoning. Later, John Lawe of Green Bay (the area where

Tomah was born and raised) had a monument erected over Tomah's grave, honoring Tomah as the "Grand Chief of the Folle Avoine [Menominees]." The city of Tomah, Wisconsin is also named in his honor.[18]

In September of 1991 while on Mackinac Island for the purpose of presenting a scholarly paper to the International Fur Trade Conference held at the Grand Hotel, this author learned, quite by accident, that the hotel had been built on the site of the old American Indian burial grounds. This means that Tomah's remains may very well lie beneath that structure, an ostentatious symbol of the affluence of the dominant society.

In 1817 at the site of present-day St. Louis, Missouri, the Menominee were compelled to agree to a treaty in which they pledged their friendship to the United States. They were additionally made to confirm to the United States, by right of conquest, any cession of land made previously by them to the French, English, or Spanish governments. At that time, some Menominees began to protest that U.S. government representatives were creating "chiefs" in order to get Menominee leaders to "sign" the treaties. Actually, most Menominees could neither read nor write, and "signing" meant touching the pen that was used to make their "mark," often an "X," on the documents.[19]

The Menominee people, victims of their times, decimated by disease and, increasingly, by alcohol abuse, were seemingly leaderless in 1827 when presidential representative Lewis Cass became angry with the apparent lack of a "head leader" among the Menominee. Needing someone to deal with in negotiating land cessions, he arbitrarily confirmed the title of "sachem" (an east-coast Algonquian term for leader) on Ishkish (later called Oshkosh), the leader of the Lake Poygan band of the Menominee. Lake Poygan is located in present-day Winnebago County, west of Lake Winnebago. This occurred during a discussion at Buttes des Morts concerning a dispute that had developed between some Menominee and **Winnebago** groups and the **Oneida** and **Stockbridge** peoples, who had recently arrived in the area from the eastern United States at the instigation of the U.S.-"Americans." Menominee protests and accusations that the United States was "creating chiefs" grew stronger at that time.

In 1831 while meeting with U.S. government officials in Washington,

D.C., Menominee leaders were compelled to cede all of their lands east of Green Bay, Lake Winnebago, and the Milwaukee River to the United States, a total of more than three million acres. Included were 500,000 acres, located on the east side of the Fox River in the Green Bay area, to be used for the "New York Indians," meaning the **Oneida**, the **Stockbridge**, and the **Munsee**, as well as a group called the "St. Regis tribe." At that time, all of these tribal groups were being compelled by the United States to migrate to Wisconsin from their homelands in New York and other areas along the Eastern Seaboard.

The United States agreed "to pay" the Menominee $25,000, in increments of $5,000 annually, with the first payment to be made in August of 1831. The money, when paid to the Menominees, was to be used "as the President of the United States may direct."

In this same treaty, "a tract of land," the size of which is unspecified, located on the west side of the Fox River at the center of which was the site of the present-day city of Neenah in Winnebago County, was "set apart" and "designated for their [the Menominees'] future homes, upon which their improvements as an agricultural people [were] to be made." The "reservation" was made "for the purpose of weaning them from their wandering habits." The United States government employed five non-Indian farmers for a period of ten years, at $500 per year, to teach the Menominee farming. The United States agreed that the Menominee "shall be at liberty to hunt and fish on the lands they have ceded to the United States. . . until it be surveyed and offered for sale by the President."[20]

In 1832 the Treaty of 1831 was amended at Green Bay, Wisconsin and the Menominee were compelled to agree to cede 46,080 acres of their original lands along the eastern side of Lake Winnebago to the United States for use by the **Stockbridge** and **Munsee tribes**. The 500,000 acres located on the east side of the Fox River in the Green Bay area which the United States, just the year before, had designated for the use of the "New York Indians," including the **Stockbridge** and the **Munsee**, was now designated as being for non-Indian settlement. In addition, the Menominee were compelled to agree to cede still another 23,040 acres of their original lands for use by the "Brothertown Indians" (**Brothertons**), other mixed-tribal remnants, who were also being removed from the eastern coastal area of the United States. The

Menominee in return were awarded "presents in clothing," valued at one thousand dollars, as well as five hundred bushels of corn, ten barrels of pork, ten barrels of flour, and other unspecified goods.[21]

A disastrous smallpox epidemic swept through the Menominee tribe, which was already in great disarray, in 1834. U.S.-"American" authorities reported that most of the Menominee were, by that time, mixed-bloods, with **French**, or **Potawatomi**, **Winnebago**, **Chippewa**, **Sauk**, or **Ottawa** ancestry.[22]

In 1836 at the Treaty of the Cedars conducted at Cedar Point, located on the shore of the Fox River near Green Bay, the United States forced the Menominee to cede an additional 4,184,320 acres, including the land in the Appleton/Kaukauna area of present-day Outagamie County that had been specifically reserved for them in the 1831 treaty. The Menominee were told that in return for the land, the United States would pay them $400,000, at the rate of $20,000 a year for a period of twenty years. In addition, the government agreed to pay the Menominee, each year for twenty years, $3,000 worth of provisions, including tobacco, 30 barrels of salt, and $500 per year for farming equipment. The government also agreed to build two blacksmith shops and employ two blacksmiths to work with the Menominee. Furthermore, the government agreed to "pay the just debts" that the Menominee owed to non-Indian merchants and traders, which had been recorded on an official list and totaled $99,710.50. The government additionally agreed to pay to the Menominees' "relatives and friends of mixed blood" a total of $80,000, to be divided amongst them.[23]

The 1836 treaty further stipulated that the Menominee released the United States government from its obligations to the Menominee made under the Treaty of 1831 and the Treaty of 1832, except those obligations pertaining to the government paying farmers and blacksmiths to work amongst the Menominee. In return, the government agreed to invest $76,000 of Menominee money held in trust by the United States "in some safe stock" until such time that the president of the United States saw fit to use it for the benefit of the tribe.[24]

In 1837 Frederick Marryat, a retired English navy captain wrote the following about the plight of the Menominee and other tribal people after having traveled through Wisconsin. Relating to the alleged purchases of the native tribal lands by the United States authorities, Marryat wrote, "they [the American Indians] are compelled to sell; the purchase money being a mere subterfuge, by which it may appear as if their lands were not wrested from them, although in fact, it is."[25]

In 1838 when United States Army troops rounded up and forced Milwaukee area American Indians to journey to the Kansas and Iowa Territories, five of Angelique and Jacques Vieau's eleven Menominee-French Metis children went with the American Indians. All eleven Vieau children are officially listed on **Menominee** and/or **Potawatomi** tribal rolls. Andrew Vieau became one of the principal founders of the present-day city of Green Bay. Amable and Peter Vieau were among the founders of Muskego in Waukesha County, Wisconsin.[26]

By 1838 the Menominee had been severely decimated by European diseases, the worst of which was smallpox. The Menominee population was reduced to an estimated 3,000 people by that time.[27]

In 1848, the year that Wisconsin became a state, the Menominee were forced to cede all of their remaining lands in Wisconsin to the United States with the Treaty of Lake Pow-aw-hay-kon-nay (present-day Lake Poygan). They were informed that in exchange for this land cession they could have 600,000 acres of land in the Crow Wing River area of Minnesota (which at that time was occupied by the "**Sioux**," who had not been consulted concerning this decision). The government also agreed to "pay" the Menominee the sum of $350,000, to be allocated under the conditions set forth as follows: The "chiefs" were to receive $30,000 of the $350,000, to be divided amongst them, as soon as they demonstrated to the government that they were prepared to remove the Menominee to Minnesota. The actual cost of removing the tribe from Wisconsin was to be paid with an allocation of $20,000 from the total amount.[28]

After the Menominees had been in Minnesota for one year, they were to receive another $20,000 from the original amount. In addition, $15,000 of the original amount was to be used to establish a manual labor school and erect a grist and sawmill on the Minnesota reservation. Another $25,000 was to be used for paying a miller and blacksmiths. An additional $40,000 of the original amount was to be distributed to the Menominee "mixed bloods." What remained of the original $350,000 was to be paid in ten equal annual installments beginning in 1857.[29]

The Menominee requested that the "mixed-blood" payment be distributed at Lake Poygan, but the U.S. government said that it would take place instead at the fort at Green Bay in 1849. The U.S. government then placed an advertisement in the *Green Bay Advocate* newspaper stating that all persons claiming to be of partial Menominee blood should sign a special register, which would be at Green Bay's Hotel Astor. The Menominee leaders stated that they wished to see and speak with those claiming to be of partial Menominee ancestry; however, the government decided that they should only be allowed to see the Astor list. That was quite useless, as most of the Menominee leaders could neither read nor write.

The formula for the distribution of the "mixed-blood" money was as follows: Fifty dollars was to be given to each individual whose name was included on the Astor Hotel list. It appears that there were more than 700 names on an initial list. There are approximately 267 names on the final list; however, many of the names are followed by the notation "& sons" or "& children" or "wife and children." Some names are not legible at all. The majority of the surnames on the final list are French names. The balance of the $40,000 that remained after each of the individuals were given their fifty dollars, approximately $26,000, was to be divided in equal shares among fifty specified individuals. All but approximately four of the fifty individuals specified had French surnames. Those four appear to have had English surnames.[30]

There have been non-substantiated allegations made in the past that approximately $35,000 of the original $40,000 was disbursed to relatives of the interpreter of the 1848 treaty. The term "49er," said in a derogatory manner, has often been used to refer to individuals whose ancestors allegedly benefited from the 1849 Menominee "mixed-blood" payment. Some Menominees say that the recipients of the payment relinquished their Menominee tribal rights; however, there is no legal basis for that conclusion.

In 1849, the same year as the "mixed-blood" payment, a cholera epidemic further decimated and demoralized the Menominees.[31]

Oshkosh, from the Lake Poygan Menominee group, when informed by representatives of the United States government that he was expected to lead all of the Menominee out of Wisconsin and into Minnesota, refused to act. The U.S. Army, otherwise occupied, did not enforce the removal order at that time. Some Menominees were heard to exclaim, "Why doesn't he [the U.S.-"American," or "Kechemocoman" (a derogatory epithet meaning "great or long knife")] go himself in such a fine country!"[32]

By 1852 the Menominee, who had lost all their ancestral lands but had refused to leave Wisconsin, were in the process of being allocated what was to be a temporary reservation along the upper Wolf River in north-central Wisconsin, a large tract of land that was considered at the time to be virtually worthless to the U.S.-"Americans" and the increasing number of immigrant settlers. In November of 1852, the Menominee were compelled by U.S. authorities to leave the areas of Wisconsin where they had been living and travel to the temporary reservation located north of Shawano County in central Wisconsin. By that time, many of the Menominee were literally starving. It appears that it was the intention of United States authorities to gather the Menominees in one place and eventually remove them from the state.[33]

In 1854 at a treaty session conducted at Keshena Falls on the Wolf River in Wisconsin, the Menominee were compelled to give up any claims that they might still have against the United States for any reason, including all those arising as a result of any previous treaty with the government. In return the Menominee were to receive the 235,000 acre reservation created in 1852, which until this point the United States had viewed only as a temporary home for the Menominee. The government also agreed to build and operate for the Menominee a manual labor school, a blacksmith shop, a grist mill, and a sawmill. The United States also agreed to pay the Menominee $242,686, to be paid in fifteen annual installments beginning in 1867, provided that the payments were to be used for such projects, including "civilization," as the president of the United States saw fit.[34]

At that time, many Menominee leaders (called "chiefs" by the U.S. government), including Oshkosh and Keshena, refused to agree to the treaty, complaining that those Menominee leaders who did agree and had their "marks" affixed to the document did so under threat of U.S. annihilation of the Menominee tribe and militarily enforced removal to lands west of the Mississippi. In response, the United States Senate refused to ratify the treaty, thereby making the removal of the

Menominee under the direction of the U.S. Army appear imminent. Faced with that reality, both Oshkosh and Keshena put their "marks" on the treaty, all the while stating that they were "compelled to do so."[35]

One of the first locations on the reservation that was settled by the Menominee beginning in 1852 was the area of Keshena and Keshena Falls in the southern portion of the reservation where some Menominee were already living prior to the major relocation of the Menominee into that area. It was part of the fringe area of the territory that the Menominee had considered their homeland for a very long time. The Wolf River at Keshena, and the small lakes to the east, teemed with fish. The location was also near the abundant wild rice supply at Shawano Lake. From Keshena and Keshena Falls, the Menominee began to spread out into the Moshawquit Lake and other lakes areas. The first arrivals of relocated Menominees were mostly from the Lake Poygan area, but they were soon joined by Menominee bands from the Menominee River, Peshtigo River, and Oconto River villages, as well as by those from the Green Bay area. With the incoming Menominees came people of French ancestry who chose to continue to live with their Menominee friends and neighbors.[36]

Those "chiefs," such as Carron, Lamotte, Kinepoway (also spelled Akinebui), and Oshkiqhinaniu, who had become Christians prior to this time, tended to locate the peoples from their bands along the east side of the Wolf River in the Keshena area. Soon, however, Kinepoway (Akinebui) moved with his band to an area northwest of Keshena, which became known as the West Branch settlement. The followers of the old, non-Christian, Menominee religion divided into two groups. One, led by leaders such as Oshkosh and Shawano, settled along the west bank of the Wolf River. The others, led by leaders such as Keso, settled further north up the Wolf River at a place that became known as Wayka Creek. The Menominee River Band also mostly stayed in the Keshena area, while the Peshtigo River Band settled northeast of there. The Oconto River Band settled quite some distance north and east of Keshena, near a branch of the Oconto River. Their settlement became known as South Branch. Still later, a group of Menominee who were still following the old pre-Christian Menominee religion, wanting to be far from the increasing Christian and United States influence, moved far to the northwest and formed the settlement that became known as "the pagan settlement," eventually called Zoar.[37]

It was not long after the bands arrived on the reservation that they began to break up. Barely two years had gone by when in 1856, the Menominee were compelled to give up 46,080 acres in the southwest corner of their reservation. The government then allocated that acreage for a reservation for the Stockbridge and the Munsee tribal peoples. The United States agreed to pay the Menominee for the land at a price of 60 cents per acre ($27,648) in whatever installments and for whatever purpose that the president of the United States saw fit, provided that the Menominee give up their use of liquor.[38]

In 1855 the United States government constructed several U.S. Indian Agency buildings at the reservation's Keshena settlement, and an Indian Agent took up residence there. The duties of the agent included disbursing annuity payments (installment payments on the full amount that the United States had agreed to pay in return for lands ceded at treaty sessions); directing employees, such as the millers, farmers, and blacksmiths, which the government had authorized under the treaties; regulating trade activity; and supervising the tribal peoples in general. Four of the Indian Agents appointed between 1855 and 1870 were investigated and replaced as a result of charges brought against them by tribal leaders.[39]

Almost as soon as the Menominee settled on the reservation, Wisconsin land surveyors arrived, and not long thereafter, non-Indian timber interests began efforts to gain control over the Menominees' rich pine forests.[40]

Also at that time, the Menominee Tribal Council began to formally complain to government authorities that "whites" were seducing Menominee women.[41]

In the nineteenth century, the U.S. government had two principal objectives relating to the Menominee. One, already largely accomplished by 1855, was to remove and resettle them away from the areas in their old homeland that were rapidly being settled by Euro-Americans and recently-arrived European immigrants. The second objective was to get the Menominee to cease their largely nomadic, hunting life-style and become sedentary farmers. This meant that not only did the government have to train the Menominee to become farmers, but that the government also had to provide the Menominees with food (usually pork, flour, and grain, often vermin infested) until sufficient agricultural crops were ready for harvest. A serious setback occurred almost immediately, when in 1856 the Menominees' wheat crop was destroyed by disease and when an unusually early frost occurred on August 24th, which destroyed their corn and potato crops. The same conditions repeated themselves the next year, and by the third year, the Menominee, many of whom had returned to their old fishing, hunting and gathering life-style in an effort to help stave off starvation, ate the seed grain provided for planting by the government.

Further complicating all of this was the fact that the light, sandy soil in the Keshena area was not conducive to long-term farming, and the more productive soil was in the heavily timbered, but also stony, ridges where clearing without proper equipment was not possible.[42]

More problems occurred after 1858 when Oshkosh died. Struggles over the question of who would be "head chief," combined with disagreements between the Christian and the "pagan" factions as well as among the more than eleven bands, combined with efforts by non-Indians and mixed-bloods to gain more and more control, resulted in still greater tribal disorganization and misery. By 1863 the U.S. Commissioner of Indian Affairs reported to the U.S. Congress that the approximately 2,000 Menominee on the reservation, with "thousands of acres of wet and worthless marsh," were living in "almost hopeless poverty."[43]

The winter of 1863 was very severe, and most of the Menominees' livestock died. Drought followed during the next summer, destroying most of the Menominees' crops. The U.S. government Indian Agent reported that, in his opinion, the Menominee wanted to farm, and given the appropriate opportunity, they "would soon become good farmers." However, he added, "the entire reservation is almost utterly worthless [for farming]."[44]

By 1868 there were approximately two hundred small, usually one room, log houses on the reservation, a significant increase over the only seventy-five such houses that existed six years prior. Clearly, the traditional wigwam house was being abandoned, especially by the Christian Indians. In addition, horses and oxen had largely supplanted the birch bark canoe as the principal form of non-pedestrian transportation. Roads had been cut from Keshena, northeast to South Branch, northwest to

West Branch, and west to the **Stockbridge** and **Munsee** reservation. In addition, an "elaborate" military road had been cut north from Shawano, through Keshena, and then along the east side of the Wolf River (presently Wisconsin Highway 55). There is evidence that the road was really built at the request of lumbering interests.[45]

Meanwhile, although there had been a school operating on the reservation for almost fifteen years, the U.S. government Indian Agent reported in 1867 that "very few can boast even a limited acquaintance with the English language, and still fewer can read or write it." The dispersal of Menominee families away from the Keshena area contributed to this situation, as did the serious ongoing conflict over educational policy between government authorities and missionaries.[46]

A Catholic priest known as Father Bonduel had lived very briefly at Keshena, where he oversaw the construction of a chapel not long after the reservation was first established; however, he soon left, and until 1880, the only priests the supposedly-Christian Menominees saw were those who visited irregularly.[47]

By 1867 the Menominee population had decreased from the previous approximately 2,000, to approximately 1,800, largely due to smallpox, dysentery (disease of the lower intestinal tract), and other illnesses such as pneumonia. In addition, many Menominee were suffering as a result of the abuse of alcoholic beverages. When a non-Indian was arrested and brought to an area district court charged with the offense of having brought liquor onto the reservation, the judge dismissed the case and severely criticized those who had brought it before him, stating "it was no use to stop the traffic [of liquor on to the reservation]."[48]

Another increasingly serious problem involved a practice allowed by the U.S. government since 1863, when the government gave permission to lumbermen to cut "dead and down" timber on the Menominee reservation. More and more, the Menominees complained to the government Indian Agent that non-Indian lumbermen were cutting green, standing timber instead. In 1868 great fires raged through areas of standing timber, and it was alleged that the fires had been started by non-Indians intent on making it easier for them to take the standing timber illegally.[49]

By the 1870's, the Menominees were beginning to learn that a group of non-Indian lumber interests, called the "Pine Ring Lumber Barons" by scholars and others, was apparently in league with some members of Congress, and this group was taking steps to obtain the Menominee forests.[50]

In 1872 the first temporary lumber camp operated by the government Indian Agent, using exclusively Menominee laborers, was opened. Prior to this time, all commercial lumbering, both legal and illegal, had been done by non-Indians. The government, however, soon changed its policy and forbade the Menominee to conduct their own lumbering.[51]

In 1875 after the closing of the small, local schools at the South Branch and West Branch settlements, as well as the closing of the Keshena day school, a central boarding school with an initial enrollment of seventy-six was opened at Keshena. The boarding school, involving the removal of Menominee children from their homes for a large part of the year and placing them under the control of non-Indians, was part of a government effort aimed at detribalization and, perhaps, de-Indianization.[52]

In 1880 the U.S. government established an Indian Police office and Court, employing American Indians, on the Menominee reservation. This was part of an increasing effort on the part of the federal government to further undercut and destroy the rapidly eroding authority of the traditional band "chiefs."[53]

It was in 1880 that the Franciscan Order of the Catholic Church, assisted by the Sisters of St. Joseph, took over the Catholic mission on the Menominee reservation. They reorganized the main parish at Keshena and created new branch parishes at the South Branch and West Branch settlements.[54]

During the summer of 1881, some members of the **Potawatomi** and the **Chippewa** tribes introduced what became known as the Big Drum religion to a small group of Menominee. The religion, as it gained more followers, became known among some of the Menominee as the Dream Drum, with its followers being called the Society of Dreamers. Both the Catholic priest and the Indian Agent began to utilize groups of Catholic Menominees in an attempt to disrupt and breakup the "drum services." The agent even sent for a detachment of U.S. Army troops, who promptly arrived and remained on the reservation for several weeks in order to keep the newly introduced religion from growing stronger and gaining converts. It was at that time also that most Catholic

Menominees broke almost totally away from any remnants of the old traditional Menominee ways. Other Menominees, wishing to retain the old ways, moved to the "pagan" settlement at Zoar, where the inhabitants tended to be more closely associated with traditionalist members of the **Potawatomi** tribe.[55]

In 1882 the U.S. government again gave the Menominees permission to engage in lumbering, and as the lumbering activity expanded, the seemingly futile farming activity declined even more rapidly.[56]

During 1883, the Franciscans started a small Catholic boarding school at Keshena. The Sisters of St. Joseph were in charge of instruction at the school. The number of Menominee children attending either the Catholic boarding school and the government boarding school increased substantially when the U.S. government made school attendance compulsory for all American Indian children between the ages of six and eighteen. The boys curriculum centered around carpentry, shoemaking, blacksmithing, and farming. The girls were taught mainly "housework," sewing, baking, and knitting. By that time, the U.S. government also had expressly forbidden the use of tribal languages in the schools; all instruction was to take place in English. This, too, was an integral part of the government's detribalization, de-Indianization policy. The Menominees at the Zoar community continued strenuously to resist these government efforts and refused, whenever possible, to allow their children to attend the schools. U.S. authorities had also deemed the practice of the old medicinal ways and many of the traditional tribal ceremonial dances to be illegal, with violators subject to arrest by tribal police and punishment through the Court of Indian Offenses.[57]

In 1886 a hospital was opened on the reservation at Keshena. It was staffed by a physician and three Catholic nuns who acted as nurses.[58]

In 1887 the United States Congress passed the General Indian Allotment Act, which slowly, but effectively, divided communally held Indian reservation lands into smaller and smaller pieces of private property, many of which were eventually lost to non-Indians. The Menominee reservation, however, was spared from the allotment process as a result of a combination of "some bureaucratic slip-ups and tribal opposition [to allotment in general]."[59]

In 1888 the Menominee were again ordered by the U.S. government to stop logging even the downed timber. The U.S. Attorney General had ruled that the American Indians had the right of "occupancy only" on reservations, and that only the United States had title to the natural resources, including the timber. A year later, the government reversed itself once more and again gave the Menominee permission to log dead and downed timber on their reservation. Meanwhile, non-Indian lumber interests increased their pressure on the government to allow them to log the reservation.[60]

Then in 1890, the United States Congress authorized a sustained-yield logging operation, which included allowing the Menominees to cut standing timber on the Menominee reservation. The legislation specified that the logging was to be done under annual contracts in specified areas and was not to exceed a specified maximum number of board feet. The logging also had to be done under the supervision of non-Indian logging superintendents. After the individual Menominee logging contractors' and other expenses had been paid, the balance of the profits from the sale of the timber was to be divided as follows: One-fifth was to go into a fund for hospital and "poor relief" on the reservation. The remaining four-fifths was to go into a tribal trust fund held and managed by the U.S. government.[61]

Each year thereafter for many years, between approximately fifteen and twenty million board feet of timber was cut and banked on the Wolf and Little Oconto (at South Branch) Rivers, then driven down river to the mills of various buyers. By 1905 the "Menominee Log Fund" in the U.S. Treasury totalled more than two million dollars, making the Menominee, at least on paper, one of the wealthiest tribes in the United States.[62]

Meanwhile, in 1890 the U.S. government authorities had called the principal Menominee leader Neopit Oshkosh, and the other Menominee leaders, to Washington, D.C., where they were told that they must formally surrender their titles to leadership of the tribe. Given no other choice, they completed another major step toward the federal government's objective of detribalization and de-Indianization, by agreeing to the dissolution of traditional tribal leadership roles in favor of government-approved ones.[63]

In 1906 the Menominee proposed to the U.S. government that instead of sending their timber elsewhere to be milled, they should be allowed to mill it on their reservation, realizing the profit for themselves. That same year, a railroad track was constructed through the Menominee reservation, with a depot located at the site of the proposed mill.[64]

In 1908 the Menominees' request was granted, and the tribe was authorized to construct a sawmill at the proposed site on the west bank of the Wolf River approximately twelve miles northwest of Keshena. There, the milling village of Neopit developed. The mill was initially intended to create employment for tribal members thereby providing a means to maintain their own livelihood. The Neopit mill operators "hired any Indian willing to work," and it soon became evident that "the Menominee took pride in earning their own way." It was not long thereafter that the Menominees' mill began to show a profit. After a time, the profits were sufficient for small annual payments to be made to each member of the tribe.[65]

During the winter of 1919-1920, the Menominee were once more ravaged by disease, this time in the form of a terrible influenza epidemic, which killed most of the remaining traditional Elders.

In 1928 the report to the United States Congress made by the Meriam Commission, which had been appointed to study the status of American Indian tribes and make a report to the Congress, specifically singled out both the Klamath tribe of Oregon and the Menominee tribe of Wisconsin as approaching eligibility to have their reservation-trust relationship with the federal government terminated. Interestingly enough, both had major stands of excellent, virgin timber on their reservations.

Because the Menominees' logging and lumber mill activities required them to enter into contracts, the tribe sought and was granted permission from the U.S. government to develop a form of elective government, consisting of a ten-person board that acted in an advisory capacity to the federal Bureau of Indian Affairs administrators on the reservation. This board was responsible to the tribal council. Because the Menominees already had this unique and functional tribal structure, when the opportunity for self-government was extended to American Indian tribes across the United States in 1934 under the provisions of the U.S. government's Indian Reorganization Act, the Menominee did not elect to participate in that part of the act because they saw no need to create a new governmental structure. The Menominee tribe did, however, elect to participate in the portion of the act that allowed them veto power over their budget, in effect requiring U.S. Bureau of Indian Affairs officials to be responsive to the tribal will in matters relating to the budgets for tribal business.

The Menominee peoples' life-styles by that time "ran the gamut from a small group of strongly Indian oriented people to a small elite of strongly white oriented people, with the mass of people operating at various points between these two extremes." The "Indian oriented" families tended to depend significantly on the more traditional means of sustenance, hunting and fishing, sometimes supplemented by various part-time jobs, which provided some small amounts of cash. A large number of Menominees worked periodically at unskilled or semi-skilled jobs. At "the elite end of the scale" were people in higher paying skilled trades or lower level managerial positions.[66]

In 1934 the Menominee tribe began a lawsuit alleging federal mismanagement of their forest resources. The case dragged on for many years. Finally, in 1951, the United States Court of Claims held that the Menominee tribe was entitled to approximately $7,600,000 from the federal government. When the accrued interest was added to the judgement amount, the Menominee award totalled almost ten million dollars. The Menominees decided that the award amount should be dispersed as follows: Each of the approximately 3,200 persons officially enrolled as members of the tribe at that time were to receive $1,500. The remaining $5,200,000 was to be used by the tribe for community improvements and new economic development.

As late as September of 1950, St. Joseph's Boarding School in Keshena was still operating. A Menominee woman recalled, in 1992, that she was only four years of age when she first entered the boarding school on the reservation in September of 1950. In October of that year, she turned five. That was the last year for the boarding school, because the following year it was converted into a day school.

In 1953 the United States Congress, by passing House Concurrent Resolution 108, set the stage for disaster for the Menominee people. That resolution set forth the general policy designed to terminate federal responsibility for American Indian affairs and demonstrated the intent and mood of the Congress regarding American Indians' long-term needs.

Simply put, termination meant that the particular American Indian tribe subject to termination would no longer be legally recognized as an American Indian tribe, reservation lands would no longer be held in federal trust (the tribe would no longer have a reservation), and tribal members would no longer be, legally, American Indians.

House Concurrent Resolution 108 stated that "as rapidly as possible" and "at the earliest possible time," Indians "should be freed from federal supervision and control and from all disabilities and limitations specifically applicable" to them. The resolution ignored the rights guaranteed to American Indian tribes by the United States government in treaties and contractual agreements. The resolution did direct the Secretary of the Interior to examine "all existing legislation. . . and treaties" relating to tribes in several states, including the Menominee of Wisconsin, and to report his recommendations to the Congress by January 1, 1954.[67]

Although the Meriam Report of 1928 had singled out the Menominee tribe as one of two tribes in the United States that were approaching eligibility to cut federal ties, the U.S. Bureau of Indian Affairs had made no significant effort to prepare the Menominee for managing their own affairs. The equipment in the Menominees' lumber mill had been allowed to deteriorate, no new attempts to diversify products or increase production had been suggested or encouraged, and no serious effort had been made to phase the Menominee themselves into full administration of the reservation and its assets.

Meanwhile, the Menominees' 1951 court award was being held in the federal treasury, pending Congressional approval for disbursement. It soon became apparent to the Menominees that if they wanted their money, they would be forced to pay a stiff price for the Congressional approval--acceptance of their termination as an American Indian tribe.

In June of 1953, then Senator Arthur V. Watkins from Utah, the leader of the Indian-termination movement in the Senate, made a special trip to the Menominee Reservation, where he predicted dire consequences should the Menominee people not agree to termination. When the Menominees voted the next day, and the votes were counted, it was found that 169 had voted to accept termination and five had voted against it. Most Menominees did not vote on the matter at all. Many Menominee who lived away from the reservation had not received timely notice that the vote was to be taken, and no provision was made for absentee ballots. This author knows of individual Menominees who at the time were serving with United States armed forces. Those individuals mailed their votes in opposition to termination back to the reservation; however, their votes were never counted.

At the present time, many who admit to having voted for termination insist that they were led to believe they were merely voting to request release of their $1,500 per capita payments, since a single vote was taken on the combined issues of termination and the per capita payments. Others admit that they voted for termination because they were in fear of Watkins' threats and hoped that their acceptance of termination would give the tribe some advantage in negotiating on the specific terms. Many people who cast no ballot had stayed away from any meetings about termination because staying away was an acceptable traditional way to express disapproval. In addition, a significant number, being neither able to read nor write, did not know enough about the issue to comfortably take part in a decision-making process with which they were quite unfamiliar. No matter what the individual Menominees thought they were voting for or against, "they could not possibly have made an informed decision because most of the details of the termination plan for transfer of the reservation to state jurisdiction and for management of its assets were developed after passage of Public Law 83-399, which was even discussed and amended after the Menominees' questionable 'agreement' to termination had been secured."[68]

There are two matters relating to this issue on which most Menominees appear to agree. The first is that termination was never their idea. The second is that no matter what they said or did, Senator Watkins had made it clear that the U.S. government would eventually terminate them regardless of their desires.

The United States Congress "acted with unusual, perhaps even unprecedented, haste in approving this highly experimental legislation--which would affect the lives and property of more than 3,200 Menominee--on the basis of an equivocal mandate from less than ten percent of the tribe's eligible voters." In addition, the Congress "simply chose to disregard" the decision of a Menominee General Council meeting that was held after the June 1953 vote. At that general council meeting, where another vote was taken, 197 Menominees, including many of the 169 who had voted earlier, "now voted unanimously to forego their per capita payments if their price was to be termination."[69]

By June 17, 1954, Congress had passed Public Law 83-399 to terminate the Menominee. The Menominee tribal roll was closed ninety days after that. The termination was to be effective in 1958; however the effective date was, later, postponed to 1961 because all of the intricate details involving the transfer of jurisdiction from the federal government to the Menominees (who were no longer to be, legally, American Indians) and the state of Wisconsin could not be taken care of in time.

Before termination became final, it was learned that the Bureau of Indian Affairs had made an error in calculating annual payments to the tribe from mill profits. Prior to the discovery of this error, the Congress, operating on the assumption that the tribe had far more in the U.S. Treasury than it actually did, had decided that the tribe must pay half of the expenses of implementing the termination, as well as all its own legal costs. As a result, by the time that the termination became final in 1961, the Menominees were operating at a substantial annual deficit.

In 1961 the Menominee Reservation was transferred to Wisconsin's jurisdiction as a new county called Menominee County. The land and assets of the Menominee (no longer legally an American Indian tribe) were converted into a corporation called Menominee Enterprises. The one major industry, the logging and the lumber mill, was in serious financial straits. The state of Wisconsin devised contractual arrangements whereby a neighboring county, Shawano, was to provide educational and law enforcement services not available in the new county. These "arrangements soon became a source of Indian-white tensions, since the Menominee were subject to officials in whose election they had no voice."[70]

Menominee Enterprises, the corporation set up to manage the land and other assets of the former reservation, "allowed tremendous power to be concentrated in the hands of a few people, nearly half of whom were not Menominee and were not directly answerable to the Menominee people." The corporate plan provided for each of the 3,280 individuals who had been officially enrolled in the Menominee Indian tribe as of 1954 to receive a bond with a face value of $3,000, paying four percent interest and reaching maturity in the year 2000. Each of those same individuals also received 100 shares of stock in Menominee

Enterprises. The bonds were negotiable, with Menominee Enterprise having the first option to buy, but the stock was nonnegotiable until 1973 and had paid no dividends to that date.[71]

Because there were a large number of minors, as well as individuals who were judged to be incompetent for one reason or another, among the 3,280 individuals who had been officially enrolled in the Menominee Indian tribe as of 1954, a major Milwaukee trust company was chosen to act on behalf of these minors and "incompetent" shareholders. The bank and trust company, therefore, maintained control of a significant portion of Menominee shareholders' votes pertaining to corporate matters. In addition, because most of the corporate power was vested in the Menominee Enterprise Voting Trust, the control of the corporation and its assets "was almost automatically exclusionary of all but a certain kind of business mentality drawn from white expertise outside the tribe."[72]

Even some of the former tribe's members who held offices in the corporation from 1961 to 1971, the first decade of termination, appeared to view the many increasingly dissatisfied Menominee people as "impractical, 'unacculturated,' and even radical 'left-wingers'."[73]

The new county's only major industry and source of employment, the sawmill, which "had been left in a dangerously antiquated condition by the BIA," was subject to the criticism of "costly experts who were hired to help put the corporation on a profit-making basis." The experts suggested that "in view of the depletion of the tribal treasury and the lack of capital for expansion, that the inefficiently large labor force [of the saw mill] be cut back." The result of that action was to lay many people off, perhaps permanently, dumping them onto already strained welfare rolls.[74]

In an attempt to distribute the tax burden and retire the bonds with a minimal outlay of cash, Menominee Enterprise officials encouraged individual Menominees to buy their families' traditional home sites, which had been held, prior to termination, in tribal trust. The officials suggested using the bonds for this purpose. With unemployment mounting, many who bought land in this manner soon found that they could not pay their taxes and faced foreclosure. Economic necessity, coupled with sociocultural problems, forced some people to sell their bonds for whatever cash they could get rather than apply them to land purchase.

Then, as if things weren't bad enough, Menominee Enterprises decided it could not allocate money from the corporation's limited budget to bring the hospital up to state requirements. This meant that a portion of the 1951 judgment money that had been invested in the hospital had been wasted. Following the closing of the hospital, tuberculosis, long under control on the reservation, suddenly reached epidemic proportions again. The terminated Menominee were no longer eligible to receive services from federal Indian health facilities because they no longer belonged to a federally recognized American Indian tribe.

In an attempt to raise needed tax revenue, Menominee Enterprises began to lease land located on a few of the many small lakes in the county, as well as on scattered sites along the Wolf River, to non-Indians for summer homes. There were also some, perhaps many, Menominees who also wished to take advantage of the lease arrangement, which included a reasonable schedule of payments. The Menominees, however, were allegedly told that they could not lease the property, but rather that they would have to purchase it, even if the property had been used by their family for generations. The purchase price and payment schedule was more than many Menominees could reasonably afford.

Then, "as the tax situation became more oppressive and the corporation more desperate for cash, the [non-Indian] lessees were quietly allowed to buy the land outright."[75]

The most serious trouble "erupted with the publicizing of The Lakes of the Menominees project, involving more than 5,000 acres of artificially created lake to afford maximum shoreline frontage and access for some 2,500 projected lots."[76] The project began with the preparation for and creation of a relatively large lake called "Legend Lake," which was created by destroying several small natural lakes. In 1967 Menominee Enterprises entered into a partnership with one of the major recreational land developers in Wisconsin. Menominee Enterprises was to provide the land, and the developer was to provide initial costs and expertise in building dams, digging lake basins, and promoting sales. The developer was to get five percent off the top of all land sales and the remainder was to be divided equally between Menominee Enterprises and the developer after promotion and sales expenses were deducted. Menominee Enterprises would also gain more taxpayers for the county as a result of the development.

Menominee opponents of the Legend Lake project countered that the new taxpayers' demands for services would exceed any advantage offered by the expanded tax base. They also noted that as the project developed, water levels of surrounding lakes had been noticeably affected and they insisted that the general ecology of the region would be seriously affected as well.

The developers and Menominee Enterprises appear to have ignored the devastating societal impact of the project on the Menominee people living on the former reservation, "over half of whom were on some form of public assistance and who had a high rate of unemployment." The completed project, by its very nature, would result in an "invasion" of relatively affluent non-Indians "who could afford prime recreation and retirement home sites." The Menominees' immediate, intermediate, and long-range future held "the dismal prospect of affluent whites taking advantage of a cheap Indian labor pool of domestics, handymen, and sometimes colorfully costumed natives [as] land sales hype exploited the Indian presence as a tourist attraction."[77]

Promotional brochures, newspapers, and other advertising, largely arranged for by the developer, featured "artists' renditions of the befeathered brave paddling his canoe in the moonlight on the Lakes of the Menominees," and/or standing with his hand out welcoming the non-Indian. "This was a far cry from the kind of viable cultural identity that once allowed the Menominee to say 'our forest', 'our mill', 'our hospital'. . . in the same breath with 'our powwow'."[78]

Opposition to termination and its immediate aftermath began before its effective date in 1961 and escalated immediately thereafter. An organization called CAMP, meaning Citizens for the Advancement of the Menominee People, kept the opposition to termination alive. One of its most vocal leaders was a non-Indian woman who had been a nurse in the Menominees' hospital prior to its closing. She was married to a Menominee and had raised her several children in a cabin located in the Keshena Falls area of the reservation. Almost constantly writing to local, state, and federal politicians, as well as to newspapers, she was largely responsible for keeping the issue before the general public.[79]

At that time, a journalistic investigatory team from one of the major television networks spent several days filming and talking with

Menominees on the former reservation about termination and its immediate effects on their lives. Some of the Menominees who were filmed and interviewed were traditional Elders, including one who had lived in the Zoar community most of his life, but who, at the time, was living with his wife at Rabbit Ridge in the Keshena area. When the television crew went to his home to meet him, the door to his home was open, the interior of the house appeared to be in disarray, and no one seemed to be at home. One of the reporters saw some rustling in some overgrown bushes across the road from the house. Investigating, they found the elderly woman hiding with her small grandchildren partly hidden under her apron, like a mother hen with her chicks.

Asked what had happened, she replied that some men had been drinking and had come into the house, began to fight, and there had been some shooting. Asked where her elderly husband was, she replied that he had walked to Keshena to the county offices, as he had been doing each day since he received a letter from there. Asked what the letter said, she replied that neither of them knew because neither could read well enough to decipher what was said in the letter. The television crew, after making arrangements to see that she and the children were all right, proceeded to Keshena and to the county office building. There they found the elderly man standing, with his hat in his hand, in a room housing the county's social services department. Asked why he hadn't taken one of the chairs that were available in the room while he waited to be taken care of by the staff person, he replied that the receptionist hadn't invited him to sit down. For him to have sat down in this place, which was unfamiliar to him, without being asked, was not in compliance with his traditional upbringing. When the television crew asked to see the letter that had prompted his daily walk from Rabbit Ridge, they quickly saw that it was a form letter sent to all residents stating that a dentist would be available on certain days to check the condition of one's teeth. When the individual who was serving as the guide for the television crew asked the non-Indian receptionist why the old man hadn't been taken care of after having shown up at the office several days in a row, the receptionist replied that "these people have to learn to be more assertive and ask." Such assertiveness also would have been considered improper from the traditional perspective. The guide then, responding with dismay and anger, picked up a glass ash tray and threw it against the wall, shouting that the department director had better get out there and take care of this old man or he, the guide, would make the director wish that he had. This incident and others like it were filmed and recorded by the television crew as the guide introduced them to other Menominees.

The film and audio tape from the several days of investigatory reporting on the former reservation (Menominee County) were never shown or heard anywhere. They were destroyed, apparently at the insistence of powerful individuals from the non-Indian dominant society who stood to lose much if the public saw and heard what the television crew had learned. One of the principal reporters from a Milwaukee television station, who had been an integral part of the network investigatory team, was fired at approximately that same time.[80]

Also at that time, a small group of American Indian Movement supporters were active on the former reservation—a fact that is today little known to most people, both on and off the reservation. On one occasion, the group threw Japanese-made "Indian-items" out the front door and onto the parking lot of a tourist-oriented gift shop in Neopit. A Roman Catholic nun who was working in the gift shop was told that none of the group would hurt her, all she had to do was hold the door open. That same gift shop also featured very high priced, rare, authentic Menominee ceremonial garb and ceremonial items. Those ceremonial items had been obtained by a Catholic priest from the elderly widow of a Menominee "drum chief." The priest had told her that he was dismayed and saddened that she, an apparently good Catholic who attended mass daily, still had those "things of the devil religion," which had belonged to her husband. The priest told the elderly woman that he believed she would feel much better if she gave those "devil items" to him for proper disposal. Not wanting to offend him, she complied. He then put them in the gift shop and sold them to wealthy tourists for exceedingly high prices.[81]

The small group of American Indian Movement supporters also periodically went around the lake development and river lease areas and knocked the "Indians keep out" signs off the trees--signs that had been placed there by the developers who wished to attract affluent non-Indians to the properties. On one of those properties, an elderly Menominee woman was confronted by several non-Indians while she was spreading some blankets on the ground in preparation for a picnic with her grand-children. The particular property, on the shore of one of the lakes, had been utilized by her family for a very long time prior to termination. When she explained this to the non-Indians, who were demanding that she pick up her things and leave, and when she furthermore assured them that all she wanted to do was hold a picnic for her grandchildren, the non-Indians became verbally abusive, stating that they had leased that property from the developers and Menominee Enterprises. When the woman still resisted leaving, they shouted at her, "Look squaw [considered a derogatory word by many tribal peoples], this is now our property, get off before we throw you off." The elderly woman left.[82]

Organized resistance to the things that were taking place on the former reservation lands, then and now comprising Menominee County, began in late 1969. The organized resistance began with one of the daughters of the woman who had been among the most active and vocal leaders of the anti-termination CAMP group.[83]

The young Menominee woman, a college student at the time, became very angry "at the high-handed treatment she received at the annual [Menominee Enterprises] stockholders' meeting after [she asked] for a more detailed financial breakdown of the corporation's activities than was provided in published reports distributed to the certificate holders."[84] The young woman turned for help to Wisconsin Judicare, a federally-funded agency that had been established a short time before this to serve the state's northern counties, including the new Menominee County. Judicare soon found itself with an expanding group of Menominee clients and began to provide legal assistance that the Menominee as a group had long needed, but heretofore could not afford.

In the spring of 1970, a spontaneous protest demonstration against the Legend Lake project was sparked when white land owners forced a group of Menominee to leave an accustomed picnic spot.[85]

By the time that the summer of 1970 had begun, various anti-termination and anti-Menominee-exploitation efforts, including those of the remnants of the old CAMP group on the former reservation, as well as those of groups in both Milwaukee and Chicago, "had coalesced" into an organization called "DRUMS," meaning Determination of Rights and Unity for Menominee Shareholders.[86] The DRUMS organization "revived the concept of the tribal council of the pre-termination days," as they held a series of meetings on the former reservation. They also facilitated effective communication with Menominees who did not live in Menominee County, as well as with non-Indians who were against termination and with other Menominee supporters, through the publication, distribution, and mailing of news-letters.[87]

DRUMS members and supporters also picketed the development project's land sales office in Menominee County, as well as at restaurants in Milwaukee and other cities "where prospective Legend Lake property buyers were treated to steak dinners and a sales pitch." DRUMS members and supporters also picketed at the offices of the First Wisconsin Trust Company in Milwaukee, which handled the affairs of Menominee minors and "incompetents."[88] DRUMS also conducted "a massive, well organized march from Menominee County to the state capitol in Madison where then governor Patrick Lucey [a supporter of Robert Kennedy's national political efforts] agreed to visit Menominee County to view the situation at first hand," resulting in his giving support to the cause of restoration, which called for an end to termination and a return to legal tribal and reservation status.[89]

With the help of Judicare, occasionally assisted by the American Civil Liberties Union, DRUMS became involved in a great deal of intensive and continuing litigation against Menominee Enterprises. This activity on the part of DRUMS "was met with swift and fierce retaliation from [Menominee Enterprises]. . . [in the form of] statements in the press condemning DRUMS, and in various counter-suits."[90]

DRUMS' agenda included reversing termination, thereby returning the Menominees and their lands to federally recognized tribal status, reopening the Menominee tribal roll, restoring the Menominees to their pre-termination eligibility for Bureau of Indian Affairs services, and returning to a political and economic structure that allowed the Menominees to take charge of and administer their own affairs. DRUMS also vowed to "undo the Legend Lake project" as much as possible.[91]

By that time, the artificially-created Legend Lake was being called "Leaky Lake" by some individuals, and it was believed by others that it would eventually cause flooding in Keshena.

By late summer in 1970, many Menominee Enterprises officials realized that they "could no longer dismiss opposition as the outlook of only a small handful of dissidents." By the time of the next Menominee Enterprises stockholders' meeting in December, termination would have been in effect for ten years. At that meeting, the stock certificate holders "would have the opportunity of voting to abolish the Voting Trust, thereby gaining direct control in the election of [Menominee Enterprises] management."[92]

In the elections held at meetings several times thereafter, the Voting Trust, which had maintained direct control over Menominee Enterprises for the last ten years, was retained. This situation continued largely as a result of the fact that a vote to discontinue the Voting Trust required fifty-one percent of all the shares of the corporation. One-third of the votes to retain the Voting Trust, and thereby keep things as they were, was cast as a bloc by the First Wisconsin Trust Company, based in Milwaukee. The company controlled the votes of the minors and "incompetents." "The votes of the minors alone, had they been cast as many of their parents' votes were cast, would have provided the necessary majority of 51 percent of the shares to abolish the Voting Trust."[93]

These efforts on the part of DRUMS to end the Voting Trust resulted in Menominee Enterprises deciding to change the composition of the trust in an effort to win enough support to keep it in effect. An integral part of the change included increasing the number of members of the Voting Trust from seven to eleven. At the next voting meeting, DRUMS managed to get two young Menominee women elected. Both of them were college educated.

DRUMS members who had been lobbying in Washington, D.C. saw some of their efforts bear fruit when then President Richard Nixon publicly repudiated the termination policy as a mistake that created rather than solved problems. DRUMS continued to point to the deteriorating socioeconomic condition of the Menominee people as evidence that termination had resulted in disaster.

Late in the fall of 1971 at an election held to fill four positions on the Menominee Enterprises Voting Trust, the two DRUMS incumbents were reelected, and in addition, two more DRUMS members won seats on the Voting Trust. Surprisingly, one of the DRUMS members was elected chair of the Voting Trust.

By that time, both the Wisconsin state government and the federal

Bureau of Indian Affairs appeared to be in agreement with the majority of the Menominee people, as well as a growing number of Menominee Enterprises officials, that termination should be reversed and the Menominee peoples and their lands restored to federal status. The Menominees' ten year experience with the experiment called termination had proven to be disastrous in its consequences. Wisconsin's U.S. Senator William Proxmire and Wisconsin's 7th District Congressman David Obey also supported the concept of restoration and began drafting appropriate legislation, utilizing the active input of attorneys from the national Native American Rights Fund, and even more significantly, from the Menominee peoples themselves.

Fortunately, "unlike the termination proceedings which had been held behind closed doors with the mass of Menominee people kept in ignorance, work on the Restoration Bill involved public meetings and open discussion with the Menominee people." The legislation calling for restoration of the Menominee peoples and lands was introduced in both houses of the United States Congress on April 22, 1972.[94]

In May of 1973, the U.S. House of Representatives Sub-Committee on Indian Affairs held hearings on the former Menominee reservation in an effort to provide Menominees with an opportunity to convey their views to the Congress. In addition, three bus-loads of Menominees later went to Washington to attend and put forth testimony at the Sub-Committee's hearing there.

By the summer of 1973, with restoration nearly in sight, dissension developed within the DRUMS organization. The dissension resulted, in part, "because so much of the action. . . had shifted to Washington, D.C. . . [after the prior tremendous activity in Wisconsin] the bulk of the DRUMS membership was left with little to do and felt their contribution to the cause was no longer appreciated." Many members also appear to have grown resentful of the Menominee women, who as leaders of DRUMS and the restoration effort, were the focus of much media publicity.[95]

When DRUMS progressed from direct, mass action against Menominee Enterprises and succeeded in putting DRUMS representatives into positions of power in the management of the corporation, "the enemy was no longer clearly defined." Confrontational tactics, which had been essential to get public and legislative attention, while at the same time providing deep personal satisfaction to many of the participants who found themselves finally able to do something on their own behalf, now appeared to be viewed as no longer appropriate by the DRUMS members on the corporate board. Those individuals were increasingly criticized by rank and file DRUMS members, who said that the DRUMS members on the corporate board were beginning to sound and behave "like the old guard [Menominee Enterprises officials], compromising true DRUMS objectives."[96]

An example of this may be seen in the situation that developed when, although the DRUMS members on the Menominee Enterprises board "moved quickly to halt the Lakes of the Menominees project before more land was lost, they voted to renew the contract with the State of Wisconsin to lease a stretch of the Wolf River for a public campground. Now in a position to understand that the corporation's financial condition was even more precarious than they had suspected, they felt the substantial revenue from the state was essential to the tribe's economic survival until and after restoration was an accomplished fact."[97]

The Menominee Restoration Act (Public Law 93-197) passed overwhelmingly in the Congress and became law with President Nixon's signature on December 22, 1973; however, it was not to take effect until 1975 in order to give the Menominees and the government adequate time to prepare for both the return of the land in Menominee County to federal trust status and for the official recognition of the Menominees as American Indians once again.

The first task facing the Menominee people, following the provisions of the restoration legislation, was to elect a nine member Restoration Committee, which would serve as an interim government. The Restoration Committee would also have the responsibility of developing a constitution, to be submitted to the members of the Menominee Tribal Nation for approval.

In addition, the Restoration Committee would have the responsibility of conducting an election of regular tribal officers, updating the tribal enrollment list, and finding "ways to dismantle and restructure the corporation to benefit the Menominee while also conforming to applicable Wisconsin securities laws."[98]

Problems relating to health, employment, education, and "the general atmosphere of social malaise," all either exacerbated or created by termination, also had to be addressed.[99]

One of the women who had led the fight against termination and for restoration was elected chairperson of the Restoration Committee; however, "the nominating process had been marked by acrimonious allegations of a new elite replacing the one DRUMS had overcome." In addition, as the Restoration Committee worked on the complex tasks mandated for them in the Restoration Act, the members "were increasingly subjected to criticism. . . [including] that they were taking too much time knuckling under to legalities and technicalities instead of striking out boldly against the white power structure. . . as DRUMS had done at the start." A primary concern of the members of the committee was to ensure that the Menominee people obtained a government that benefited from "federal protection without federal domination." They wanted to be sure that the Menominee would be truly self-determining, "with a constitution going far beyond the limited powers they had exercised prior to termination and avoiding the constraints still hampering [other tribes, organized under the provisions of the 1934 Indian Reorganization Act]."[100]

Meanwhile, a new group composed principally of "young militant activists began to take the lead in criticizing the Restoration Committee." Apparently inspired by "pan-Indian confrontations and take-overs" that had occurred elsewhere in the United States since 1970, the new group attracted some DRUMS activists who felt that they had not been provided an opportunity to share in the fruits of restoration. Some of these individuals appeared to be particularly resentful of those DRUMS members who had served on the former Menominee Enterprises board and who were then serving on the Restoration Committee.[101]

The Restoration Committee "disclaimed accusations that they did not communicate with the people, pointing out how their scheduled information and discussion meetings were broken up by yelling and name calling [and] they also noted bitterly that it was not their fault if their critics would not bother to read their monthly news-sheet designed to keep the tribe apprised of their work."[102]

The Restoration Committee members, "confident that they still had majority tribal support. . . [appeared to have] underestimated the strength their opposition could muster against them."[103]

When New Years Day 1975 dawned, most Menominees were sur-
prised, even shocked, to learn that on New Years Eve an armed group of
about thirty individuals, calling themselves the Menominee Warrior
Society, had entered and occupied a vacant Roman Catholic Alexian
Brothers novitiate building located near Gresham in Shawano County,
just outside the Menominee reservation. The reader should note that
the militant group, which included some non-Menominees, was not a
traditional Menominee societal institution. They announced that they
had claimed the facility in the name of the Menominee tribe for use as a
hospital and an alcohol and drug detoxification center.

Almost immediately, as news media representatives began to swarm
into the Gresham area, "vicious but usually latent anti-Indian attitudes
in Shawano County became quickly manifest with armed whites
demanding that the governor deal severely and summarily with the
Indians." The Wisconsin governor responded by calling in a member
of the **Stockbridge** tribe, who already was a state employee, to serve as
a negotiator in the dispute. The governor also ordered units of the Wisconsin National Guard to replace Shawano County law enforcement
officers at the task of patrolling the novitiate and keeping the peace. The
American Indian Movement (commonly known as "AIM") sent
members to assist the Menominee "Warriors." In addition, nationally
known figures, such as Marlon Brando, the motion picture actor, put in
brief but well-publicized appearances as they identified with the
"Warriors" and their cause. The "Warrior" occupation of the buildings
lasted for a period of thirty-four days and drew extensive national, and
even international, media coverage.[104]

The Restoration Committee, whose resignation the "Warriors" had
demanded, denounced the occupation as "a meaningless farce insofar
as the building was not on reservation land and would be a white
elephant for the financially strapped tribe to remodel and maintain as a
hospital, particularly since plans were already well underway to provide
a new medical facility on the reservation."[105]

The Restoration Committee neglected to note that the building was
on land that, prior to 1856 when it was given by the United States to the
Stockbridge and the **Munsee**, was a part of the original Menominee
Reservation created between 1852 and 1854.

In the minds of the "Warriors' white and intertribal partisans... the

Restoration Committee [had] demonstrated what the Warriors claimed to be the case: the Committee had no feeling for 'traditional' Indians and had sold out to the white establishment in citing fancy legalisms to discredit the occupation and reject the idea of obtaining the novitiate for the tribe."[106]

Thirty-four days after it began, the occupation ended. There had been no loss of life or even serious injury. Many of the members of the menominee Warrior Society were immediately arrested and jailed by Shawano County officials as they left the novitiate property. Their arrests were contrary to the "Warriors'" understanding of the agreement they had reached with state officials.

The "Warriors" had decided to leave the novitiate buildings only after the Roman Catholic order of Alexians agreed to turn the property over to the tribe "after studies were made to develop an acceptable plan for its use." That never happened. On July 9th of the following summer, "the Alexians summarily negated their agreement with the Warriors," thereby fanning "smouldering discontent on the reservation [which burst] literally into flame with fire-bombings of white owned property, attempts to burn Restoration Committee members' homes, and acts of personal violence, including some deaths."[107]

These "Warriors" demonstrate the severe "frustrations and damaged egos" of many young Menominees and are examples of "the tragic legacies of termination." Anyone born between June 17, 1954, when the official Menominee roll was closed, and 1975, when restoration became effective, were not legally considered to be Menominee. These people grew up "subject to discriminaton and a sense of helplessness as schooling and law enforcement in Menominee County had been turned over to Shawano County, where there was widespread prejudice against Indians."[108] In addition, they had "heard their elders deplore, and saw for themselves, how the tribal estate was desecrated and bargained away by the white business community serving as advisors and administrators to the tribe." Some came from families that "had tried to make their way in urban areas after termination [only to learn that, often] the experience. . . [was one of] simply exchanging rural poverty for city slums." The militant "Warriors," many of them young, in their often desperate quest for a positive sense of Indian identity, had taken on the identity of a "Warrior Society."[109]

During 1975, the Trust and Management Agreement that restructured the old Menominee Enterprises corporation, the name of which had been changed to Menominee Tribal Enterprises, Inc., was completed, and Menominee tribal lands were converted back to American Indian Reservation status. The following year, the new constitution and by-laws, "unprecedented in Indian affairs in the great degree of tribal self-determination" were approved by the tribe. The restored Menominees and their reservation are excluded from the provisions of U.S. Public Law 280 that was passed in 1953 as part of the federal policy of termination and was meant specifically to phase out federal law enforcement and judicial responsibilities to American Indian tribes in five states, including Wisconsin. Because the 1975 Menominee Restoration legislation did not include the Menominee under the provisions of U.S. Public Law 280, the Menominee are the only tribal group in Wisconsin with their own court, judges, and law enforcement.[110]

Now, after almost two decades since restoration to federally recognized tribal status, the Menominee are still in the process of recovering from the disastrous effects of termination and are continuing to rebuild their community. Besides having a viable new housing program, a modern health facility, and a viable school system, which includes their own high school, the Menominees' mill and forestry enterprise is an increasingly productive operation.

According to the 1990 United States census figures, the uniquely combined Menominee Reservation and Menominee County had a total population of 3,395 Menominee Indian people living there, with 1,628 of those being female. A total of 447 Menominees were under the age of five and 177 were over the age of sixty-five. The median age was reported to be 21.4.[111]

Also at that time, according to the U.S. census figures, there were 1,176 Menominee Indian housing units on the reservation (in the county), but only 901 of them were occupied. Of those, 475 were owner-occupied and had an average value of $40,900. The rest were renter-occupied, with the average monthly rent being $120. There were 699 family households, with 293 of these being headed by a female.[112]

In August of 1992, the Legend Lake seven mile flowage had approximately seven hundred and fifty "upscale vacation homes" constructed on its shores.[113]

In October of 1992, with an estimated 4,000 of the approximately 7,000 Menominees currently on the official tribal roll living in the combined Menominee Reservation and County, the area was described as "the poorest in Wisconsin."[114]

Suffering from "rampant alcoholism, terrible violence, high rates of teen pregnancy, child abuse, and unemployment," the area was described as "an angry place," where "surrounding whites resent what they consider the special and unfair privileges [of American Indians, many of whom they view as being] lazy [and who, they believe] ought to quit being Indians and assimilate into America's proverbial melting pot. Many [American] Indians, in turn, distrust whites. . . ." Most of the Menominees not living on the reservation were living in the cities of Milwaukee, Chicago, Green Bay, and Madison.[115]

Since the late 1980's, the Menominees have supplemented their income producing activities with a financially successful Las Vegas-style gaming operation located at the south end of Keshena. The gaming operation includes a casino and a large bingo hall, which in the 1991 fiscal year contributed more than four million dollars to the tribal budget, amounting to two-thirds of that budget. Also on the positive side, the gaming operation, employing 460 people at the present time, has helped reduce unemployment on the reservation from 29 percent in January of 1991 to 16 percent in October of 1992. The Menominees' forestry and sawmill business employed approximately 300 people as of October 1992. Although the Menominees are often objects of prejudice and discrimination in the surrounding non-Indian communities, the Menominees contribute an estimated twenty five to thirty million dollars to the economies of those communities for items such as clothing, cars, utilities, restaurants, entertainment.[116]

NOTES

1. Felix M. Keesing, *The Menomini Indians of Wisconsin: A Study of Three Centuries of Cultural Contact and Change* (Madison, Wisconsin: University of Wisconsin Press, 1987), 54-55. This is a reprint of an original edition published in Philadelphia in 1939 by the American Philosophical Society. Keesing spelled the name of the tribal nation "Menomini." I prefer to spell the nation's name as

the tribal peoples themselves spell it, "Menominee." This, as well as some of the other information in this chapter, is also from the oral traditions of the Menominee Elders Pauees and Wallace Pyawasit who taught me in the 1960's and 1970's, and who also officially recognized and accepted me in a traditional Naming Ceremony in 1976 at the Zoar village on the Menominee Indian Reservation in Wisconsin.

2. This and much of the other information in this chapter is from John Boatman, "Historical Overview of the Wisconsin Area: From Early Years to the French, British, and American Intrusions," *An Anthology of Western Great Lakes Indian History*, ed. Donald L. Fixico, rev. ed. (Milwaukee: American Indian Studies, University of Wisconsin-Milwaukee), 1989.

3. Keesing, 54-55.

4. Ibid., 59-61.

5. Ibid., 62.

6. Ibid., 56.

7. Ibid., 71, 76-77.

8. Ibid., 74.

9. Ibid., 74-75.

10. Ibid., 84-85.

11. John Boatman, "Jacques Vieau: A Son of Montreal and A Father of European Wisconsin--Another Perspective on the French and Native Peoples," delivered on May 22, 1992 at an International Conference of the French Colonial Historical Society held at McGill University in Montreal, Quebec, Canada, in conjunction with events marking the 350th Anniversary of the Founding of Montreal. Copyright Reserved by John Boatman in March 1992. The family name is spelled "Vieaux" in "Memoir of Charles de Langlade," by Joseph Tasse, in *Wisconsin Historical Collections*, vol. 7, (Madison, Wisconsin: State Historical Society of Wisconsin, 1876), 177; as well as "Veaux" in "Lawe and Grignon Papers, 1794-1821," *Wisconsin Historical Collections*, vol. 10 (Madison, Wisconsin: State Historical Society of Wisconsin, 1888), 137.

12. "Narrative of Morgan L. Martin," *Wisconsin Historical Collections*, vol. 11 (Madison, Wisconsin: State Historical Society of Wisconsin, 1888), 387. Jacques was also called "Jean" in "Lawe and Grignon Papers, 1794-1821," 137; "The Fur Trade in Wisconsin," vol. 19, 400-401; "Fur Trade in Wisconsin," *Wisconsin Historical Collections*, vol. 20, 360; Index to volumes 1-20, *Wisconsin Historical Collections*, 532; as well as "Narrative of Andrew J. Vieau, Sr.," *Wisconsin Historical Collections*, vol. 11.

13. "Fur-Trade on the Upper Lakes: 1778-1815," *Wisconsin Historical Collections*, vol. 19, 305-306; "Papers from the Canadian Archives 1778-1783," *Wisconsin Historical Collections*, vol. 11, 170; "Narrative of Andrew J. Vieau, Sr."

14. "Lawe and Grignon Papers, 1794-1821," 98-103; Samuel A. Storrow, "The Northwest in 1817," *Wisconsin Historical Collections*, vol. 6 (Madison, Wisconsin: State Historical Society of Wisconsin, 1872), 154, 176; "Dickson and

Grignon Papers, 1812-1815," *Wisconsin Historical Collections*, vol. 11, 271, 296-297.

15. Keesing, 91.

16. Ibid., 91-92.

17. Ibid., 92.

18. James W. Biddle, "Recollections of Green Bay in 1816," *First Annual Report and Collections of the State Historical Society of Wisconsin, Volume I*, (Madison, Wisconsin: State Historical Society of Wisconsin, 1855), 54-58.

19. "Treaty With The Menominee, 1817," *Treaties and Agreements of the Indian Tribes of The Great Lakes Region* (Washington, D.C.: Institute for the Development of Indian Law, 1974), 10; Keesing, 129-130.

20. "Treaty With The Menominee, 1831," *Treaties and Agreements of the Indian Tribes of The Great Lakes Region* (Washington, D.C.: Institute for the Development of Indian Law, 1974), 24-28, 42; Keesing, 131.

21. "Treaty With The Menominee, 1832," *Treaties and Agreements of the Indian Tribes of The Great Lakes Region* (Washington, D.C.: Institute for the Development of Indian Law, 1974), 39-41.

22. Keesing, 102.

23. "Treaty With The Menominee, 1836," *Treaties and Agreements of the Indian Tribes of The Great Lakes Region* (Washington, D.C.: Institute for the Development of Indian Law, 1974), 43-44.

24. Ibid., 44.

25. Frederick Marryat, "An English Officer's Description of Wisconsin in 1837," *Collections of the State Historical Society of Wisconsin, Volume 14*, ed. Reuben G. Thwaites (Madison, Wisconsin: 1898), 138-139.

26. Les and Jeanne Rentmeester, *The Wisconsin Creoles* (Melbourne, Florida: Les and Jeanne Rentmeester, 1987); "List of Mixed Blood of the Menominee Nation," *The Green Bay Advocate*, 28 June 1849.

27. Gustave de Neveu, "A Menominee Indian Payment in 1838," *58th Annual Report of the Wisconsin Historical Society*, trans. Emily B. de Neveu (Madison, Wisconsin: State Historical Society of Wisconsin, 1910), 153.

28. "Treaty With The Menominee, 1848," *Treaties and Agreements of the Indian Tribes of The Great Lakes Region* (Washington, D.C.: Institute for the Development of Indian Law, 1974), 73-75.

29. Ibid.

30. "List of Mixed Blood of the Menominee Nation," *Green Bay Advocate*, 28 June 1849.

31. Keesing, 102.

32. Ibid., 140.

33. Ibid., 142.

34. "Treaty With The Menominee, 1854," *Treaties and Agreements of the Indian Tribes of The Great Lakes Region* (Washington, D.C.: Institute for the Development of Indian Law, 1974), 78-79.

35. Keesing, 142-143.

36. Ibid., 148-152.

37. Ibid., 148-152, 181.

38. "Treaty With The Menominee, 1856," *Treaties and Agreements of the Indian Tribes of The Great Lakes Region* (Washington, D.C.: Institute for the Development of Indian Law, 1974), 92-93; Keesing, 150.

39. Keesing, 152-153.

40. Ibid., 153.

41. Ibid.

42. Ibid., 154-156.

43. Ibid., 149, 157-159.

44. Ibid., 159.

45. Ibid., 160-161.

46. Ibid., 163.

47. Ibid., 164.

48. Ibid., 166-167.

49. Ibid., 168.

50. Nancy O. Lurie, "Menominee Termination and Restoration," *An Anthology of Western Great Lakes Indian History*, ed. Donald L. Fixico, rev. ed. (Milwaukee: American Indian Studies, University of Wisconsin-Milwaukee, 1989), 145.

51. Keesing, 173, 182-183.

52. Ibid., 174-175.

53. Ibid., 176.

54. Ibid., 187.

55. Ibid., 180-181.

56. Ibid., 183-184.

57. Ibid., 187-189, 191.

58. Ibid., 190.

59. Lurie, 145.

60. Keesing, 185.

61. Ibid., 186.

62. Ibid.

63. Ibid., 192-193.

64. Ibid., 187, 222.

65. Lurie, 145-146; Lewis Meriam, et al., *The Problem of Indian Administration* (Baltimore: Brookings Institute, 1928), 516.

66. Lurie, 146-147. George Spindler and Louise Spindler, *Dreamers Without Power: The Menomini Indians* (New York: Holt, Rinehardt and Winston, 1971).

67. Lurie, 148-149.

68. Ibid., 151-152.

69. Ibid., 152.

70. Ibid., 155.

71. Ibid., 156-157.

72. Ibid., 157.

73. Ibid.

74. Ibid., 157-158.

75. Ibid., 160.

76. Ibid.

77. Ibid., 163.

78. Ibid.

79. The author vividly remembers on several occasions sitting and visiting with and learning from this remarkable woman, Connie Deer, in her cabin.

80. The author, at that time a student at the University of Wisconsin-Milwaukee, was that guide. I was approached by some Milwaukee area television people and told that the network wished to do a special investigatory news report on the termination of the Menominee people and its immediate aftermath. I agreed to act as an unpaid guide on the former reservation for the television crew, introducing them to Menominees who might have special perspectives on the situation—perspectives that otherwise might never be revealed to the general public. Because the film and audio tape were destroyed, they never were.

81. This author was with the small group of American Indian Movement supporters and witnessed the events described. They were also related to the author by the elderly woman described.

82. This incident, and many more like it, were related to the author by this elderly woman, and by many other Menominees at that time.

83. Lurie, 163-164.

84. Ibid.

85. Ibid., 164.

86. Ibid. For a detailed history of the DRUMS organization, see Nicholas Peroff, *Menominee Drums: Tribal Termination and Restoration, 1954-1974* (Norman: University of Oklahoma Press, 1982).

87. Lurie, 164.

88. Ibid., 164-165.

89. Ibid., 165.

90. Ibid.

91. Ibid.

92. Ibid., 166.

93. Ibid., 166-167.

94. Ibid., 170. To help fund its work, while at the same time publicizing the Menominee cause, the committee published a book detailing the injustices of termination and the need for restoration. See: Deborah Shames, ed., *Freedom with Reservation: The Menominee Struggle to Save Their Land and People* (Madison: National Committee to Save the Menominee People and Forests, 1972).

95. Lurie, 171-172.

96. Ibid., 173.

97. Ibid., 173-174.

98. Ibid., 174-175.

99. Ibid., 175.

100. Ibid., 175-176.

101. Ibid., 176.

102. Ibid.

103. Ibid., 177.

104. Ibid., 177-178.

105. Ibid., 178.

106. Ibid., 179.

107. Ibid., 179-180.

108. Ibid., 180. Richard Kenyon, "A Tribe in Transition," *Wisconsin: The Milwaukee Journal Magazine*, 25 October 1992, 15.

109. Lurie, 180; Kenyon, 15.

110. Lurie, 180-181; Louise Spindler, "Menominee," *Handbook of North American Indians, vol. 15, Northeast*, ed. Bruce Trigger (Washington, D.C.: Smithsonian Institution, 1978), 708-724.

111. "Summary Population and Housing Characteristics: Wisconsin," Table 17, *Selected Population Characteristics for American Indian and Alaska Native Areas: 1990* (Washington, D.C.: U.S. Department of Commerce, Economics and Statistics Administration, Bureau of the Census, U.S. Government Printing Office), 369.

112. "Summary Population and Housing Characteristics: Wisconsin," Table 18, *Selected Housing and Household Characteristics and Land Area for American Indian and Alaska Native Areas: 1990* (Washington, D.C.: U.S. Department of Commerce, Economics and Statistics Administration, Bureau of the Census, U.S. Government Printing Office), 370.

113. *Milwaukee Sentinel*, 30 August 1992.

114. Kenyon, 12-14.

115. Ibid.

116. Ibid., 17-18.

CHAPTER THREE
THE WINNEBAGO

The Winnebago are probably descendants of the ancient Oneota peoples who migrated into Wisconsin from the area of present-day Illinois and Indiana beginning in approximately A.D. 800. It appears that these people left their home region and came north into Wisconsin in order to escape domination by the politically and economically complex society of peoples scholars call the Mississippian Cahokians. The Oneota established farming settlements in the area around Lake Winnebago, Butte des Morts, Winneconne, as well as at Lake Poygan. The Oneota and later their descendants, the Winnebago, peacefully shared the area with the indigenous **Menominee**, who were in the region when the Oneota arrived.[1]

The Winnebago language and their original culture is quite distinct from that of the Algonquian speaking tribal peoples of the Great Lakes region, such as the Menominee. The Winnebago speak a "Siouan language, quite closely related to the Chiwere language spoken by the Iowa. . . and Missouri [tribal peoples], [and is] remotely related to the [language] of the Dakota."[2]

The Winnebago gradually spread northward and eastward from the Lake Winnebago, Butte des Morts, Winneconne, and Lake Poygan region into the area around the mouth of the Fox River at Green Bay. Some Winnebago legends place their origin at Red Banks, which is approximately ten miles northeast of the mouth of the Fox River. Wherever the Winnebago settled, they continued to share the territory and live peacefully with the **Menominee**.

Prior to 1634 when the first European entered Wisconsin, the Winnebago people called themselves "Ho-chun-gra." In the English language, there are several different translations for this word. One of the translations is "people of the big voice." Another is "people of the big fish," possibly referring to the sturgeon that once abounded in the waters near their village areas. The word "Winnebago" is actually an Algonquian language derivative, probably from the Potawatomi word *Win-pye-ko*, which means "people of the dirty water." This refers to the muddy water of the lower Fox River where a large group of Ho-chun-gra lived. The French called the Winnebago the "Gents Puants" (later "Puans"), translated as "stinkards." This descriptive term was based on the fact that each year in the heat of summer, dead fish rotted in the muddy Fox River water where the river connects with Lake Winnebago. The French also called the bay of Green Bay "the bay of the Puans" and also sometimes referred to Lake Michigan as "Puans Lake."

Charles le Roy, Sieur de Bacqueville de la Potherie, in his *Histoire de l'Amerique Septentrionale* which, as previously noted, was based on Nicolas Perrot's manuscripts from the period 1667 to 1680, wrote: "The Puans [Winnebago] were masters of this Bay [Green Bay], and to a great extent of the adjoining country. This nation was a populous one. . . . and spared no one. . . . The Malhominis [Menominee] were the only tribe who maintained relations with them. . . . They [the Winnebago] declared war on all nations they could discover. . . ."[3]

Potherie's statement suggests that de Champlain may have sent Nicolet to arrange a peace with the Winnebago, whom the French had initially believed were either Chinese or tributary peoples of the Chinese. It was important that peace be assured so that French trade plans were not threatened and interrupted. Nicolet may have arrived in the Green Bay area while the Winnebago were still dominant but maintained their principal villages upriver in the Lake Winnebago area. Nancy Lurie stresses that based on available evidence, "the primary purpose of his journey was to establish peace with the Winnebago."[4]

We know that Nicolet's first shore landing was not at a Winnebago village, since the account of his visit states that when he was two days' journey from the Winnebago, he sent out an envoy. Champlain's map of 1632 also suggests that the Winnebago were living near Lake Winnebago at the time of Nicolet's arrival.[5]

The *Jesuit Relations* reports that upon learning of the arrival of Nicolet, the Winnebago "dispatched several young men to meet the

Manitouiriniou." The word *Manitouiriniou* is an Algonquian word, more likely to have been used by the Jesuits than a word from the Winnebago language. The Jesuits were, by that time, already quite familiar with Algonquian languages, but not at all familiar with that of the Winnebago. Nicolet was probably met by a mixed group of Menominee, Winnebago, and some Potawatomi.[6]

In their travels to other areas, the Winnebago apparently had, for a long time before Nicolet's arrival in Wisconsin, spurned trade with the French or any other European group they encountered. The Franciscan Recollet Brother Gabriel Sagard in his 1632 account *Le Grand Voyage du Pays des Hurons* reported that the French had learned this fact from the Ottawa in the 1620's, well before Nicolet's voyage.[7]

Shortly after Nicolet's visit to the Green Bay area, a smallpox epidemic ravaged the sedentary, mainly agricultural Winnebago. By the time the French agent, explorer, and interpreter Nicolas Perrot arrived in 1667, the Winnebago population had been severely reduced. Demographers estimate that the once populous Winnebago then numbered approximately 450-600 people, including approximately 150 warriors. The causes of the severe population decline included, in addition to the disease epidemics, frequent attacks by a union of tribes led by the **Ottawa** in retaliation for the deaths of some Ottawa envoys of the French. In addition, Winnebago legend tells of losing approximately five hundred warriors, who apparently perished in a fierce storm while they were on either the bay of Green Bay or Lake Winnebago. Lurie states that "their might of thirty years before as well as the causes of their reduced condition were still fresh memories [when Perrot arrived]."[8]

After the arrival of the **Fox** in Wisconsin during the 1650's, the Winnebago became involved with them in territorial wars. As the Winnebago population became even more severely depleted, a group of **Illinois**, pitying their plight, sent the Winnebago some food supplies. The Winnebago responded by killing the Illinois who delivered the food. Then, fearing that the main force of the Illinois would retaliate, the Winnebago took refuge on Doty Island on the north end of Lake Winnebago. The Illinois, however, decided to wait until winter to advance over the ice, only to find that the island village was deserted. The Winnebago had left for their winter hunting villages. Pursuing them overland, the Illinois killed or captured all of the Winnebago they encountered. Some Winnebago traditions substantiate Perrot's accounts of this period, describing the treachery of some of their own people in the Illinois incident. Because of their treacherous acts against the Illinois, the Winnebago believed they had brought upon themselves "spirit-world" punishment in the form of war, plague, famine, and near annihilation. The Winnebago, according to the available evidence, were brought to the brink of extinction.[9]

The Winnebago avoided extinction at that time, however. As the Winnebago territory became deluged with Algonquian remnants from Michigan who were fleeing the Eastern Iroquois League, the Winnebago gradually began to intermarry with them, thereby recouping their population losses. In the process, the Winnebago borrowed many cultural traits from the Michigan Algonquians.

By the beginning of the eighteenth century, the Winnebago had begun to settle more and more along the Rock River of southern Wisconsin, as well as in the southwestern region of the state, in an effort to avoid contact as much as possible with the Europeans.

The Winnebago provided some support to the French in the French-English war (commonly called the French and Indian War), which ended in 1761. They also provided some support to Pontiac's intertribal effort against the English in 1763. During the American colonial revolution, they also helped support the intertribal effort against the English. During the War of 1812, however, the Winnebago provided some support to the English against the U.S.-"Americans." After the war of 1812 ended with a United States victory in 1816, U.S. troops built Fort Crawford at Prairie du Chien, partly to keep a watchful eye on the activities of the Winnebago.

It was that same year that a Winnebago leader, Neokautah, began to levy a toll charge to anyone who wished to use the Fox River upstream or downstream from his village located on Doty island. Doty island is located at the point where the Fox River meets Lake Winnebago at the lake's northwestern end. Since travel on that portion of the river was essential to those from the area who were coming from or going to Green Bay, Neokautah, who proved to be a truly enterprising business man, became known as "the keeper of the Fox River valley."

Also in 1816, at their Wisconsin River village located near Prairie du Chien, the Winnebago were compelled to agree to a treaty pledging their friendship to the United States and confirming to the United States any cession of land made previously by the Winnebago to the French, English, or Spanish governments. As was the case with the Menominee and other tribal groups, most Winnebagos could neither read nor write, and "signing" a treaty meant touching the pen that was used to make their "mark," often an "X," on the documents.[10]

In 1820 European and U.S.-"American" lead miners began to swarm into the Winnebago area of southern and southwestern Wisconsin.

In 1827, as a result of a series of indignities and assaults against the Winnebago people, particularly Winnebago women, by U.S.-"American" miners and illegal settlers, the Winnebago tribal council delegated a warrior named Red Bird to take what they believed to be justifiable revenge. Red Bird and his two companions attacked a house near Prairie du Chien, killing and wounding several people. The United States government in response threatened a general military reprisal against the entire Winnebago nation unless Red Bird and his companions surrendered. They did surrender themselves to the U.S. Army and were sentenced to be hanged. A number of American settlers were favorably impressed by Red Bird's eloquent surrender speech that pointed out the legitimate tribal grievances against the miners and others which had led the Winnebagos to seek revenge. Some local, U.S.-"American" officials suggested that a Winnebago delegation go to Washington, D.C. to plea for clemency on behalf of Red Bird and his companions. A Winnebago delegation left for Washington, not knowing that the United States government planned to use the Red Bird incident as an opportunity to seize the lead mining area.[11]

When the delegation arrived in Washington, they were told that the lead region was the real source of the trouble, and that they could have Red Bird and his companions back if they would remove themselves from the lead mining area. In addition, they were told that they would be justly compensated for the land. Even though the members of the delegation emphasized that they were not authorized to cede any lands, they were pressured into "signing" a treaty in 1829. This provided for the first large Winnebago land cession, approximately one-half of the Winnebagos' southern Wisconsin lands.[12]

The delegation returned to Wisconsin only to learn that while they were in Washington, Red Bird had died in the U.S. prison where he was being held. Immediate pressure was then put on the Winnebago to cede the remainder of the fertile farmland between Madison and Lake Winnebago. In 1832 they were compelled to cede the land in another treaty "signing," but were told that they could keep the northern lands between the Wisconsin River and Black River Falls. In addition, they were told that they were to be granted a reservation on the Turkey River in Iowa territory (an area then inhabited by the **Sioux** and other tribes). The Winnebago who went there soon found themselves to be the targets of hostilities from those groups.[13]

Lumbering interests soon began to pressure the United States government to remove the Winnebago from all of their remaining Wisconsin lands. In 1835 when the United States officially opened Wisconsin lands to white settlement, the Winnebago protested, stating that they did not wish to give up more lands or leave Wisconsin. In response, the United States government called for another Winnebago tribal delegation to come to Washington. In 1837 the Winnebago tribal council sent twenty men to Washington, D.C., making it clear to these men that they had no authority to sign any treaty or cede any land. In Washington, however, the delegation was told that they could not return home to Wisconsin unless they "signed" the treaty set before them. They "signed" under protest so that they would be allowed to return home. They told the United States government that the tribe could not be expected to abide by the treaty, since they did not have council authority to sign it. The United States government had assured them at that treaty signing session that they would have eight years to vacate Wisconsin lands and remove to west of the Mississippi River. According to the written account of an official observer at the 1837 Treaty session: "As each man went up and put his 'mark' on the treaty, he repeated the words (in English) 'Eight' years. The treaty actually reads 'Eight Months.'"[14]

The delegation believed that they were actually buying time to renegotiate a more acceptable treaty--one that was properly authorized by the tribal council. Later, the interpreter at the signing admitted that he had been directed to deceive the delegation. The Winnebago people back in Wisconsin were extremely angry and upset. The members of the delegation insisted that they had been misled. The situation created a permanent split in the tribe. One faction believed they should remove from Wisconsin and make the best of an obviously bad situation. The other faction refused to leave Wisconsin. In 1840, three years after the treaty had been "signed," many of those who had refused to leave were force marched from Wisconsin by U.S. troops. Some escaped and remained fugitives in Wisconsin for about twenty-seven years thereafter. Some who had left, voluntarily or involuntarily, later sneaked back to Wisconsin and joined the fugitives.

In 1865 those who had remained outside of Wisconsin received a reservation in Nebraska after having been removed from several settlements in Minnesota and South Dakota. In 1874 U.S. troops were utilized for one last forced removal of the Winnebago from Wisconsin. In this removal, the Winnebago were not allowed to take their belongings. Children were separated from parents. People died of exposure to the elements and from malnutrition, and women were molested by soldiers.[15]

At that same time, many Winnebago people fled into forested areas of central and west-central Wisconsin, where they often lived the lives of fugitives.

Finally in the 1880's, the United States government granted non-trust status homesteads of up to forty acres each to some of the Wisconsin Winnebago. Many of these homesteads were later lost by the individual Winnebago families to non-American Indians due to non-payment of county property taxes.

In 1934 some of the Winnebago leaders made an effort to formally organize under the provisions of the federal Indian Reorganization Act. Some Winnebago factions, however, resisted, "because they feared that the [federal] government would not act promptly on pending [Winnebago] land claims."[16]

In 1949 the Winnebago in Wisconsin elected a formal claims committee, and finally in 1961, the Wisconsin Winnebago Business Committee was formed. During the Kennedy administration years, the U.S. government acquired additional trust-status land for the Winnebago in Wisconsin.

For some time now, the Winnebago, like many of the other Wisconsin area American Indian tribal groups, have been supplementing their tribal income through the operation of gambling casinos, such as the Ho Chunk casino located near Baraboo in eastern Sauk County. The casino operation, however, has also been a source of considerable turmoil and serious division among the Winnebago people.

The Winnebago, as of 1982, had approximately 4,116 acres in Wisconsin. Of that amount, only approximately 290 acres was tribally owned trust land, with the remaining balance being divided into individual allotments scattered over a wide area. Although 290 acres are officially trust lands, held in trust for the Winnebago by the United States government, the trust lands are not a contiguous reservation such as that of the Menominee and some of the Chippewa groups.[17]

According to the 1990 United States census, the approximate population of those Winnebagos living on "reservation and trust lands" in Wisconsin was as follows: (It should be noted that the following figures only reflect the Winnebago population living on "reservation and trust lands." Population figures for Winnebagos *not* living on "reservation and trust lands" were unavailable.) A total of 700 Winnebago people were living on "Wisconsin Winnebago Reservation and Trust Lands." Of these, 282 were female. A total of 73 of these people were under the age of five, and 38 people were over the age of sixty-five. The median age was reported to be 20.5.

The Baraboo area of eastern Sauk County had approximately 105 Winnebago people living on "reservation and trust lands" there. The Black River Falls area of central Jackson County had approximately 308 Winnebago people. The La Crosse area of La Crosse County reported only nine Winnebago people living on "reservation and trust lands." The Mauston area of south central Juneau County had approximately 92 Winnebago people. The Tomah area of east central Monroe County had approximately 88 Winnebago people. The Wausau area of central Marathon County also had only nine Winnebago people reported.[18] The Wisconsin Rapids area, located on both sides of the Wisconsin River in eastern Wood County and the Nekoosa area of southeastern Wood County, together had a total of approximately 42 Winnebago people living on "reservation and trust lands." The Wittenberg area, located in far west central Shawano County near the Marathon County border, had approximately 27 Winnebago people. There were also nine Winnebago reported as living in Crawford County and eleven in Clark County. Population figures for the Wisconsin Dells area, located on the east side of the Wisconsin River in northwest Columbia County, were not available.[19]

During the summer months, some aspects of the traditional Winnebago culture may still be seen as part of the "Stand Rock Indian Ceremonial" in the Wisconsin Dells recreation area.[20]

NOTES

1. An excellent source of information about the Winnebago is Nancy Lurie, "Winnebago," *Handbook of North American Indians, vol. 15, Northeast*, ed. Bruce G. Trigger (Washington, D.C.: Smithsonian Institution, 1978), 690-707. See also Nancy Lurie, "Winnebago Protohistory," *Culture in History, Essays in Honor of Paul Radin*, ed. Stanley Diamond (1960), 791-792.

2. Lurie, *Handbook*, 690.

3. Lurie, "Winnebago Protohistory," 795-796.

4. Ibid., 798.

5. Ibid., 799.

6. Ibid., 799, 801; Arthur C. Neville, "Historic Sites About Green Bay: The Landfall of Nicolet, 1634," *Green Bay Historical Bulletin*, vol. 2, no. 3 (1926), 2.

7. Lurie, "Winnebago Protohistory," 791; as well as a personal note to author, 13 February 1987.

8. Lurie, *Handbook*, 691.

9. Ibid., 691-693.

10. "Treaty With The Winnebago, 1816," *Treaties and Agreements of the Indian Tribes of The Great Lakes Region* (Washington, D.C.: Institute for the Development of Indian Law, 1974), 9-10.

11. Lurie, *Handbook*, 697-698.

12. Ibid.

13. Ibid., 698-699.

14. *Wisconsin Historical Collection*, vol. 7 (Madison, Wisconsin: Wisconsin State Historical Society, 1876), 393.

15. Lawrence Onsager, "The Removal of Wisconsin Winnebago Indians," unpublished manuscript, 1981, (per verbal communication with Nancy O. Lurie, February 1987).

16. Susette Daugherty, et al, "The History of the Hochungra People (Winnebago Tribe) of Wisconsin," *Wisconsin Woodland Indian Project Curriculum* (Rhinelander: Rhinelander School District, Wisconsin Department of Public Instruction and the Great Lakes Inter-Tribal Council, 1982), 16.

17. Ibid., 17.

18. "Summary Population and Housing Characteristics: Wisconsin," Table 17, *Selected Population Characteristics for American Indian and Alaska Native*

Areas: 1990 (Washington, D.C.: U.S. Department of Commerce, Economics and Statistics Administration, Bureau of the Census, U.S. Government Printing Office), 369.

19. "Summary Population and Housing Characteristics: Wisconsin," Table 18, *Selected Housing and Household Characteristics and Land Area for American Indian and Alaska Native Areas: 1990* (Washington, D.C.: U.S. Department of Commerce, Economics and Statistics Administration, Bureau of the Census, U.S. Government Printing Office), 370.

20. Daugherty, 20.

CHAPTER FOUR
THE POTAWATOMI

As noted in chapter one, some Potawatomis were at Red Banks when Nicolet landed there in 1634. The Potawatomi (originally pronounced, by them, "bo-de-wah-do-mi"), along with the **Ojibwe**, or **Chippewa**, and the **Ottawa**, were once part of a much larger group called *Anishinabe* or *Anishinaabeg*. That word has been variously spelled and translated. One of the translations is "The People Who Came From Beyond Where the Sun Rises." Other translations include "Original Man," "The People," and "Human Being." According to a number of legends, the Anishinabe were originally inhabitants of the gulf of the St. Lawrence River region. The legends go on to state that a very long time ago, before the arrival of Columbus in the Caribbean region, the Anishinabe, including the **Potawatomi**, **Chippewa**, and **Ottawa**, migrated to the Western Great Lakes area, dividing at the Straits of Mackinac. The Potawatomi migrated south into the present-day lower Michigan where, according to their legends, they became the "keepers of the [ceremonial] fire" for all three of the tribal groups.

The French made their first contact with the Potawatomi shortly after 1641 in lower Michigan. At that time, the Potawatomi had already begun to remove themselves from the lower Michigan area because of **Eastern Iroquois League** attacks, some Potawatomi having migrated into the Green Bay area of Wisconsin prior to 1634. In 1641 many more Potawatomi were migrating northward and northwestward through the Straits of Mackinac area of Upper Michigan and then south into Wisconsin, where they joined the Potawatomi who had migrated earlier.

In Wisconsin, the Potawatomi initially settled on present-day Rock, Washington, Detroit, and Plum islands, all located off the north end of the Door Peninsula where the bay of Green Bay meets Lake Michigan.

The *Jesuit Relations* referred to the islands as "the islands called Huron," apparently referring to the fact some **Huron** remnants, fleeing the **Eastern Iroquois League**, had made their home there for a time. The name for those islands found on early maps was "the Potawatomi Islands." Present-day Washington Island was called "Wa-se-ki-ga-ne-so," by tribal peoples, referring to the fact that it could be seen from a distance because its cliffs reflected the sunlight. U.S.-"Americans" named it "Washington" after 1816 in honor of the Washington, the lead vessel of the United States Navy ships that brought the first U.S. troops to the Wisconsin area in 1816. The ship had stopped there for a time in the natural harbor. Present-day Rock Island had been called Menominee Island by the local natives. Present-day Detroit Island, for a time, was referred to as Ottawa Island, because a band of **Ottawa** lived there for a time.[1]

The Potawatomi also settled in the present-day Door County and Kewaunee County areas, especially on the Door Peninsula, as well as on the small islands in the bay of Green Bay directly offshore from the present-day Peninsula State Park. In addition, the Potawatomi settled on Manitou Island located in the middle of the bay of Green Bay. The name of that island was changed after 1816 to Chambers Island in honor of U.S. Army Colonel Talbot Chambers, who was one of the commanders of the first U.S. troops to arrive in Wisconsin.[2]

Other Potawatomis were migrating southward and westward following the Lake Michigan shoreline, across northern Illinois, into Wisconsin, where they also began settling along the lake shore. In both of these Wisconsin regions, the Potawatomi, like the **Winnebago** before them, got along peacefully and intermarried with the indigenous **Menominee**.[3]

By 1667 the Potawatomi, who by 1648 had become serious rivals to the **Ottawa** middleman role in the French fur trade in the Michigan area, were heavily involved in the French fur trade based at Green Bay where Nicolas Perrot had formed a series of alliances with tribal peoples living in the area. By that time, a large Potawatomi village was also located near present-day Kewaunee.

After Perrot left the Green Bay area, another French trading expedition arrived under the leadership of Louis Jolliet. Jolliet's traders stirred up tribal animosity and quarreled with tribal leaders over payment for furs. As a result, a Potawatomi delegation traveled to Sault Ste. Marie, complained about the activities of the French, Green Bay-area traders, and requested that a "Black Robe" visit the area to arbitrate their grievances. In response to the Potawatomi request, Claude Allouez, a French Jesuit priest, returned with them to the Green Bay area. While in northeastern Wisconsin, he established the first French mission, the mission of St. Francis Xavier, at Oka'to (present-day Oconto in Oconto County), where a major **Menominee** village had long been located. A combined Potawatomi and **Sauk** village was also located there when Allouez arrived.

The Potawatomi influence in the fur trade continued to grow. By the late 1700's, they had established major villages and were very influential all along the Lake Michigan shoreline, from Green Bay south to Chicago. In the northern Illinois and Chicago areas, they had by that time replaced the original **Illinois**, who had moved further south.

During the French and English War, which ended with an English victory in 1761, the Potawatomi generally allied themselves with the French. They also were allied with Pontiac against the English in 1763.

By 1769 the Potawatomi were trading extensively with the Spanish at St. Louis. This annoyed the English; however, except for the support they gave Siggenauk based at Milwaukee, the Potawatomi loosely allied themselves with the English against the North American colonists during the colonial revolution.

After the colonial victory and the subsequent creation of the United States, the Potawatomi strengthened their alliances with the English and, again, except for those in the Milwaukee area, sided with the English against the U.S.-"Americans" in the War of 1812. Despite the fact that the United States won this second war with England, many Potawatomi continued to maintain their English loyalty for quite some time.

In late October of 1832, while participating in a treaty session with the United States held at the Tippecanoe River in the present-day state of Indiana, the Potawatomi were compelled to cede to the United States all of their lands in the Illinois, Indiana, Michigan, and Wisconsin regions. Eighty-eight Potawatomi individuals were granted "reservations" ranging in size from one-quarter section to sixteen sections of land. A section consists of 640 acres of land. Most of those individuals, however, only received a parcel of land consisting of one section.

Fourteen of those individuals receiving "reservations" had French surnames.[4] One name appears with the notation "a chieftess" after it.

The United States agreed to pay to the Potawatomi a sum of $15,000 each year for twelve years ($180,000), in addition to $32,000 "in goods" to be paid as soon as the goods could be gathered together. An additional $10,000 in goods was to be paid the following spring. The United States also agreed to pay the "just debts" that the Potawatomi owed to traders totalling $20,721.[5]

In September of 1833, Jacques Vieau, who, as noted in chapter two, had married into the **Menominee** tribe and was related by marriage to Potawatomis from Milwaukee, traveled to the rapidly growing village of Chicago hoping to take advantage of the treaty stipulation relating to the payment of debts owed to traders. Several individuals owed him for trade goods. While he was there, San-gau-nau-nee-bee (meaning "Sour Water"), a Potawatomi village leader from the St. Joseph's River area of southwestern lower Michigan, walked into Vieau's temporary trading shanty and walked over to a big keg of plug-style tobacco in the shanty. He took about six pounds out and turned to walk away with the tobacco. Vieau said to him, in the Potawatomi language, "What are you going to do with that?" San-gau-nau-nee-bee turned and replied, "I am going to use it." Vieau responded, "It doesn't belong to you!" Angered, San-gau-nau-nee-bee, again, began to leave with the tobacco saying, "What of that? I am an Ogima ("Chief") and can do as I please!" Vieau then stood up, threatening, "You can, can you?" San-gau-nau-nee-bee immediately pulled out a long knife; however, before he could do anything with it, Vieau lunged forward and with his two hands grabbed San-gau-nau-nee-bee by his neck and his breechclout and threw him out of the shanty, the plugs of tobacco scattering in all directions. San-gau-nau-nee-bee hurried over to a group of American Indians who stood watching nearby. Vieau followed him.

One of the other Potawatomi leaders, Che-po-i, whose name means "the corpse" (probably so named because his nose was cut off clear to the bridge), looked at Vieau, shook his finger at him and said loudly, "Jacques Vieau, we have always heard you were a popular man, a benefactor of our peoples, feeding them when they were hungry; but today you have lost all, you have spoiled yourself, by doing that which we saw you do to the noble San-gau-nau-nee-bee. Never again will you have our favor!" Jacques looked him in the eye and asked, "Who are you, talking with such authority?" Che-po-i replied, "I am Che-po-i, the head man of the St. Joseph River band of Potawatomi." Jacques, not backing down an inch, said, "If I was such a looking man as you are, Che-po-i, I should consider that the name you bear suits well. You, who wants to show so much authority, go where you lost your nose and find it; only then will you be fit to come here to Chi-ca-go and make such fine speeches!" Immediately the large crowd of American Indians, who had gathered around upon hearing the confrontation between Che-po-i and Vieau, burst into vociferous applause. Che-po-i, glaring fiercely at the impudent French man, sat down in chagrin.[6]

The preceding account of the experience of Vieau at Chicago, in which he dared to deal in such a way with these Potawatomi leaders when he was most certainly and vastly outnumbered, is further testimony to the great advantage accrued to French and other non-native traders who married into powerful tribal families. It should also be noted, however, that Vieau, although he was seventy-six years of age at the time, stood approximately six feet tall and weighed about two hundred and twelve pounds. Temperate when it came to alcoholic beverages, he usually had a happy and sociable disposition and was well-liked by tribal peoples in general.[7]

That same year, 1833, following the Treaty of Chicago that stipulated the removal of several tribes to the region west of the Mississippi, American army troops forced many of the Potawatomis out of Wisconsin and into Kansas Territory. Some avoided this forced removal by fleeing north into Wisconsin's still densely forested regions.

In 1838 the U.S. Army was again deployed to roundup Milwaukee area American Indians, including many Potawatomi. From Milwaukee, they were forced to migrate to the Iowa and Kansas territories west of the Mississippi. One of those who made the journey was the eighty-eight year old leader Onausissah, who was compelled to walk with his followers all the way to the present-day Council Bluffs, Iowa area from his village along the Milwaukee River in the present-day Waubeka area of Ozaukee County. While that was happening, another related Potawatomi leader named Waupaca, not knowing of the forced marches, was engaged in preventing the massacre of some Euro-American settlers at the site of the present-day city of Waupaca, named later in his honor.

Five of Angelique and Jacques Vieau's eleven **Menominee**-French Metis children went with the Milwaukee-area tribal peoples when the United States Army troops rounded them up and forced them to journey to the Kansas and Iowa Territories. One of their sons, Louis Vieau, later became a "chief" of the **Potawatomi** in Kansas, where the Potawatomi, heavily influenced by the cultures of the prairie and plains tribal peoples, eventually became known as the Prairie Potawatomi.

In 1868 a more assimilated faction of Potawatomis, who had previously accepted allotments of land and then lost them, were moved to the Oklahoma Territory and became known as the Citizen Band of Potawatomi.

As late as 1885, some Potawatomis who had escaped forced removal from Wisconsin were frequenting a trading post located at Waubee Lake in present-day Oconto County. These and other Potawatomis who had managed to stay in Wisconsin despite the federal government's forced-removal policy, became known as the Forest Potawatomi, to distinguish them from the Prairie Potawatomi who were living on a reservation in Kansas. These Forest Potawatomi were simply squatters on land in northern Wisconsin that no one else wanted at the time.

By 1913 most of these Potawatomi, joined by others who had clandestinely returned to Wisconsin from elsewhere, were settled in various areas of present-day Forest County. That year, the United States Congress enacted legislation that granted them some non-trust parcels of Forest County land located at Stone Lake, south of Crandon, as well as west of Wabeno.

As late as 1920, there were still some Potawatomi families located at Kewaskum in northern Washington County. In addition, there were approximately ten Potawatomi families, many of whom had returned to Wisconsin from the Kansas region, settled in the McCord area of Oneida County. The McCord area Potawatomi community, however, gradually dispersed in the 1930's. Another Potawatomi group migrated northeastward into Michigan's Upper Peninsula, where they settled in what became known as the Hannahville Potawatomi community near present-day Escanaba.

Still another Potawatomi group, initially consisting of approximately one hundred Prairie Potawatomi who had returned to Wisconsin, settled in various areas of central Wisconsin's Wood County. They are federally recognized as American Indians, however, they are listed on the tribal roll of the Potawatomi reservation in Kansas.

In September of 1981, Wisconsin's Forest Potawatomi community finally received a $600,000 payment from the federal government that had been promised to them in 1921. The payment was a partial payment for the amount owed to them under the provisions of their 1832 treaty with the United States. Tribal officials stated that each member of the tribal community under the age of sixty would receive $1,300; while each member over the age of sixty would receive $1,700. The balance was to be "set aside for tribal development."[8]

By 1982 the largest segment of the Wisconsin Forest Potawatomi community was located in the Wabeno area of southeastern Forest County. Together with the Stone Lake (called Lake Lucerne on road maps) community, which is located a few miles southeast of Crandon, the Potawatomi had approximately 11,000 acres.[9]

According to the 1990 United States census figures, 279 Potawatomis lived on the Potawatomi "reservation and trust lands," totaling 18.6 square miles (11,904 acres) in Forest County, Wisconsin. One hundred twenty-one persons of that total were female. Thirty-six of those people were under the age of five, and eleven were over the age of sixty-five. The median age was reported to be 19.7.[10]

Also according to the 1990 U.S. census figures, there were 84 housing units in the Potawatomi community, with 75 of them occupied. Of that number, 55 were owner-occupied, and all had an average value of $18,500. There were 56 family households, with 22 of these being headed by a female.[11]

Recently, a tract of city of Milwaukee land was put into federal trust for the Wisconsin Forest Potawatomi. The Potawatomi operate a large bingo hall on the land, supplementing their tribal income with the profits from its operation. Originally, before the 1831 treaty, this area had been part of the Menominee lands, which the Menominee shared with the Potawatomi.

NOTES

1. Conan Bryant Eaton, *The Naming*, (1981) 1, 7-12, 29-30; *Rock Island*, (1979) 1, 51; *Washington Island 1836-1876*, (1980) 2; all part of "A Part of the History of Washington Township," *The Island Series* (Washington Island, Wisconsin: Conan Bryant Eaton/The Island Series).

2. Robert E. Gard and L.G. Sorden, *The Romance of Wisconsin Place Names* (New York: October House, Inc., 1968), 21.

3. A principal source of the information on the Potawatomi is James A. Clifton, "Potawatomi," *Handbook of North American Indians, vol. 15, Northeast*, ed. Bruce Trigger (Washington, D.C.: Smithsonian Institution, 1978), 725-742. This is supplemented by information from my notes taken during the time I was a student of Nancy O. Lurie at the University of Wisconsin-Milwaukee in the 1960's. Other sources include Ives Goddard, "Mascouten," *Handbook*, 671; Jim Daniels and Harry Ritchie, Potawatomi Elders from the 1982 Forest County Potawatomi Elderly Group, as well as Billy Daniels, written by Shelley Oxley, "The History of the Potawatomi Indians of Wisconsin: Keepers of the Fire," *Wisconsin Woodland Indian Project Curriculum* (Rhinelander: Rhinelander School District, Wisconsin Department of Public Instruction and the Great Lakes Inter-Tribal Council, 1982). The reference to the traditional pronunciation of the name, as well as the aspects of the ancient history of the Potawatomi is from pages 3 and 7 of the teacher information sheet contained within the curriculum.

4. "Treaty With The Potawatomi, 1832," in *Treaties and Agreements of the Indian Tribes of The Great Lakes Region* (Washington, D.C.: Institute for the Development of Indian Law, 1974), 35-36.

5. Ibid.

6. John Boatman, "Jacques Vieau: A Son of Montreal and a Father of European Wisconsin--Another Perspective on the French and Native Peoples," Copyright Reserved March 1992. The information relating to Jacques Vieau's 1833 Chicago experience is from the "Narrative of Peter J. Vieau," *Wisconsin Historical Collections*, vol. 15 (Madison, Wisconsin: State Historical Society of Wisconsin, 1900), 460-461. The narrative, as published, was based on an interview with Peter J. Vieau conducted by Reuben G. Thwaites, the secretary and superintendent of the State Historical Society of Wisconsin and editor of the Wisconsin Historical Collections.

7. "Narrative of Peter J. Vieau," 458.

8. *Rhinelander Daily News*, 18 September 1981, found in Oxley, "Keepers of the Fire," 26.

9. Oxley, "Keepers of the Fire," 23.

10. "Summary Population and Housing Characteristics: Wisconsin," Table 17, *Selected Population Characteristics for American Indian and Alaska Native Areas: 1990* (Washington, D.C.: U.S. Department of Commerce, Economics and Statistics Administration, Bureau of the Census, U.S. Government Printing

Office), 369.

11. "Summary Population and Housing Characteristics: Wisconsin," Table 18, *Selected Housing and Household Characteristics and Land Area for American Indian and Alaska Native Areas: 1990* (Washington, D.C.: U.S. Department of Commerce, Economics and Statistics Administration, Bureau of the Census, U.S. Government Printing Office), 370.

CHAPTER FIVE
THE FOX AND
THE SAUK

The Fox, another member of the Algonquian language and culture group, originally made their home in the region of present-day southern Michigan and northwest Ohio. They came into Wisconsin fleeing **Eastern Iroquois League** attacks in the mid-1600's.

The Fox called themselves "Mes-kwah-ki-ha-ki" (much later pronounced and spelled Mesquakie), which means "Red Earth People." The **Chippewa** peoples referred to the Mes-kwah-ki-ha-ki as the "Otakamik," which means "People of the Other Shore," because the Mes-kwah-ki-ha-ki were originally settled along the shores of the Great Lakes opposite **Chippewa** settlements. Later, the English and the U.S.-"Americans," as well as newly arriving European immigrants to Wisconsin, pronounced this Chippewa word "Outagamie." The French called the Fox the "Renards," the French word for fox. This is probably a result of the French confusing the name of the Fox Clan of the Mes-kwah-ki-ha-ki with the name for the entire nation.[1]

Initially after their arrival in Wisconsin, the Mes-kwah-ki-ha-ki (herein after to be referred to as the **Fox**) were involved in several territorial battles with the **Winnebago**; however, by 1665, with territorial matters apparently somewhat settled, the Fox, seeking furs for the trade, began to range as far as the Chequamegon area in northern Wisconsin. There they found themselves in territorial conflict with the **Santee** and other "Siouan" groups. Most of the Fox then withdrew to and settled in the region upriver from the mouth of the present-day Fox River. The Fox River was formerly called the Neenah River by the indigenous **Menominee**. Its name was changed sometime after the Fox had begun to settle there.

By 1677 the Fox had also settled along the lower Wolf River. It was not long before the Fox had established and developed a fairly large village near present-day Neenah in Winnebago County.

In 1701 when the French constructed a major fort and trading post at the site of present-day Detroit and began to encourage tribal groups to settle there, many of the former Michigan area native peoples who had relocated to Wisconsin in the 1650's returned to Michigan, including a large number of Fox.

Soon, however, the French and the Fox found themselves involved in conflict. Several factors contributed to the conflict that developed. One was the fact that the Fox had strongly opposed the French idea of extending the fur trade to the **Santee** and Dakota **Sioux**, who had become enemies of the Fox due to competition over the same fur trade areas. It also appears that the Fox may have responded positively to trade overtures from the **Eastern Iroquois League**, which historically was allied with the English. Then, in 1712 the French army commandant at Detroit received word that a group of Fox and **Mascouten**, for reasons unknown, were intending an attack on some **Ottawas** at Detroit. The commandant, without clearing the matter with his superior officers in Montreal, made a decision to launch a French attack on the Fox village instead.

At the beginning of the attack, the leader of the Fox village climbed upon a wall and called out in French, "What does this mean? . . . Thou didst invite us to come live near thee [referring to Cadillac's earlier invitation]. . . . and yet thou doest declare war against us!"[2]

The French and their tribal allies laid siege to the Fox village for nineteen days, during which time the Fox tried unsuccessfully to negotiate a surrender. The French siege of the Fox village lasted so long that Fox women and children died of thirst as warriors were cut down by French mortars. The Fox finally broke away and were pursued by the French and some of their native mercenaries. Over 1,000 Fox men, women, and children were killed. The few Fox who escaped fled back into Wisconsin and took refuge with the **Sauk** in the Green Bay area.

The original homeland of the **Sauk**, another tribe of the Algonquian language and culture group that had fled into Wisconsin during the mid-1600's, was the region of lower Michigan near the mouth of the Saginaw River where it flows into Saginaw Bay of Lake Huron.

Calling themselves "Asa-ki-wa-ki," meaning "People of the

Outlet," referring to their ancestral home at the mouth of the Saginaw River, they were first mentioned in French records around 1640. The first actual European contact with them, however, was not until 1667, when the French missionary priest Claude Allouez met them at their village in the Green Bay area of Wisconsin.[3]

The French called the Asa-ki-wa-ki the "Saki," while the English called them the "Saukies." This name was later shortened to "Sauk," the word that will be used for this tribal group in this text. In 1667 Allouez called them "Ousaki." This word much later became "Ozaukee," the name of the Wisconsin county north of Milwaukee County.

Because of the close relationship between the Sauk and the Fox during the French period, and especially at the time of U.S.-"American" takeover, the U.S.-"Americans" referred to them as if they were one tribe, calling them the "Sac n' Fox."

In 1716 the French, apparently determined to demonstrate to other tribal groups that they would not allow the **Fox** or any other tribal group to defy them, sent a relatively large military unit to Wisconsin in pursuit of the Fox who had escaped the Detroit area. The French, however, soon found that this objective was easier stated than accomplished, as the **Fox** and their **Sauk** allies continued to thwart the French.

In 1730 a large group of **Fox** set out from Wisconsin with the intention of taking refuge with the **Seneca**, a tribe of the **Eastern Iroquois League**. Apparently the **Seneca** had invited the Fox group to live in the Seneca homeland located in the New York area. Units of the French military, however, assisted by a large group of their intertribal allies, overtook the Fox group southeast of Lake Michigan. The French military commander reported the complete annihilation of that particular group of Fox.

Embarrassed by the apparent defiance that the remaining **Fox** had shown, the French decided that those who remained must either be exterminated or sent as slaves to the West Indies. Consequently, the French demanded that the **Sauk** village leaders at Green Bay surrender to the French the Fox refugees living among them. When the **Sauk** leaders refused to surrender the refugee **Fox** to the French, the commander of the French military force at Green Bay was sent to remove the Fox refugees from the Sauk village. He was killed trying to force his way into the Sauk village. After that, most of the **Sauk** and **Fox** fled from Wisconsin into present-day Iowa.

Finally in 1737, the French government, embarrassed by their failed efforts, granted the **Fox** and the **Sauk** nations a general Crown pardon.

Skeptical, but by then strengthened by their growing alliance with the **Sauk**, a few of the **Fox** returned to Wisconsin. The **Sauk**, refusing to return to the then French-dominated area near Green Bay, settled along the Rock River in southern Wisconsin and northern Illinois, as well as along the lower Wisconsin River in Wisconsin. Another group of **Sauk** also settled at an old **Menominee** village site in present-day Ozaukee County (the site of the present-day village of Saukville).[4]

Late in the eighteenth century, most of the **Sauk** and the few **Fox** remnants living in Wisconsin relocated to the area along the Mississippi River between the Rock River in northern Illinois and the Des Moines River in Iowa. The principal center of their settlement was where the Rock River joins the Mississippi.

In 1804, hearing that they were expected to deal with the relatively new United States rather than with the English, whom they had dealt with since the French defeat in 1761, a small delegation of **Sauk** and **Fox** remnants traveled to St. Louis where William Henry Harrison, the governor of the U.S. Indian Territory, awaited them. There they learned that U.S. authorities were quite angry because of the recent actions of some warriors from their tribes.[5]

The United States representatives demanded that they agree to a treaty ceding to the United States most of the lands upon which they had previously lived in Michigan and Wisconsin. In return, they were to receive both the friendship and the protection of the United States in the Iowa and Illinois lands where they were living at the time. In addition, they were to receive $2,234.50 worth of "goods" immediately, as well as $1,000 worth of "goods" each year thereafter. The United States also agreed that it would "never interrupt [the] tribes in the possession of the lands which they [continued to] rightfully claim, but will on the contrary protect them in the quiet enjoyment of the same. . . against all other white persons who may intrude upon them." The treaty specifically stated that "if any citizen of the United States or other white person should form a settlement upon lands which are the property of Sac [Sauk] and Fox tribes, upon complaint being made thereof to the

[U.S.] superintendent or other person having charge of the affairs of the Indians, such intruder shall forthwith be removed."[6]

During the War of 1812, warriors from both **Sauk** and **Fox** villages fought on the side of the English against the U.S.-"Americans." At the conclusion of that war, both the **Sauk** and the **Fox** were compelled to reaffirm the provisions of the 1804 treaty.

In order to keep a close watch on the activity of these groups, especially in the area where the Rock River joins the Mississippi River, the United States constructed Fort Armstrong on Rock Island, located in present-day Illinois, eighty miles south of the present-day Dubuque, Iowa.

During the War of 1812, a **Sauk** named Keokuk had emerged as a leader, and when the war ended, Keokuk became convinced that further resistance against the increasingly powerful United States was futile.

He was opposed by an older, quite distinguished warrior named Black Hawk. Black Hawk was the principal leader of a faction of the **Sauk** who believed that eventually the English from Canada would come to the assistance of the Sauk in their growing difficulties with the United States.

After the difficulties between the United States and the **Winnebago** tribe arose in 1827 as a result of the lead miners swarming onto Winnebago lands in southwestern Wisconsin, the governor of Illinois demanded that the United States government remove from Illinois any tribal peoples still living there. In response, U.S. authorities promised in the spring of 1828 to remove the **Sauk** and remnant **Fox** from Illinois by the following year. That federal promise resulted in approximately twenty white families going ahead and settling on **Sauk** lands while the Sauk were away at their winter hunting camps west of the Mississippi. These non-Indians were squatters and had no legal right to settle on the Sauk land. They hoped to stake out their claims to good land before the area was officially opened for settlement.

When the spring of 1829 arrived, the **Sauk**, along with the remnant **Fox** who were living with them, followed Black Hawk back to their villages in northern Illinois. There they found the non-Indian squatters planting fields and occupying the tribal lodges, including Black Hawk's own lodge. The Sauk, protesting to U.S. authorities, brought with them an elderly Sauk man who had been at the 1804 treaty session at St. Louis.

He emphatically denied having ceded any land north of the Rock River to the United States. The federal authorities in Illinois simply refused to consider this position.

Black Hawk then traveled to meet with the English at their fort across the river from Detroit. He returned to northern Illinois confident that the English, as well as a group of **Winnebago**, would assist the Sauk if conditions grew worse. The summer of 1830 passed without bloodshed in the Rock River area. When autumn arrived and the Sauk and Fox departed for their winter hunt, they hoped conditions would be better in the spring when they came back.

In the spring of 1831, however, members of the Illinois militia opened fire on some of the Sauk and Fox, upon which Black Hawk retreated to the west side of the Mississippi River with his people. There they set up their camp under a white flag, hoping that it would show that they did not wish to fight the U.S.-"Americans."

Meanwhile, one of Black Hawk's assistants returned from Canada and reported that again the English had pledged their support to the Sauk and Fox efforts aimed at preventing the United States from evicting them from their lands.

Then in April of 1832, upon the invitation of one of the **Winnebago** leaders, Black Hawk's group crossed the Mississippi River from Iowa and began to ascend the Rock River. Their destination was a Winnebago village about forty miles upriver. Arriving there, they remained for several days, discussing the anticipated arrival of English troops to help them in their struggles with the U.S.-"Americans."

By April 28th, Black Hawk had led his people further upriver, hoping to gain support and food from the **Potawatomi**. That same day, the Illinois militia, having raised 1,700 men for federal service, pledged them to the command of General Henry Atkinson. In addition, 340 more regular federal troops arrived and were placed under the command of Colonel Zachary Taylor, the future president of the United States. On May 9th, the army begin to ascend the Rock River.

Meanwhile, Black Hawk had been told by the **Potawatomi** that they could spare no food for his followers. In addition, he learned that there was no evidence that English help in the form of food, supplies, or men, was on the way.

Black Hawk and a small party of warriors then set out to try to contact the troops and arrange for safe passage back down the Rock River. On May 14th, three young, unarmed warriors carrying a white flag approached an encampment of 275 Illinois militiamen who were under the command of Major Isaiah Stillman. The encampment was located along the river approximately fifteen miles south of present-day Rockford, Illinois. It was the intention of the three to inform the soldiers that Black Hawk wished to lead his people peacefully back down the Rock River and across the Mississippi. The militiamen, who were generally a drunken and disorderly group, disregarded the white flag and seized and killed the three young warriors. Five other warriors, who had been sent by Black Hawk to observe what was happening, were pursued by the militiamen and two were also killed. The remaining three warriors returned to Black Hawk and reported what had happened. Enraged, Black Hawk, who at that time was no longer a young man (he was between sixty-five and seventy-one years of age), led forty warriors to the militia encampment. Seeing the large group of warriors, the militiamen fled, and in the confusion and panic, eleven soldiers and two tribal warriors were killed. The incident came to be known as the Battle of Stillman's Run.[7]

Having failed to communicate their intention to negotiate a surrender, Black Hawk realized that they had to try to head northwest and escape over the Mississippi River. Black Hawk's group found itself forced into a ten-week ordeal during which they attempted to elude the militia while fighting off starvation. The situation became increasingly more desperate. The **Sauk** and remnant **Fox** had demonstrated their ability to elude the troops, but as a result of continually moving their camp sites, hundreds of women, children, and elderly were near starvation. They proceeded north along the Rock River through the area of present-day Rockford, Illinois and through present-day Beloit, Janesville, Fort Atkinson, Johnson Creek, and Hustisford, all in southern Wisconsin, before they turned west through the present-day Madison area and from there northwest to present-day Sauk City on the Wisconsin River.

The U.S. troops, who finally caught up with Black Hawk's people as they were preparing to cross the Wisconsin River, found ample evidence that Black Hawk's people were starving. Bark had been peeled from trees and holes where found where Black Hawk's people had grubbed for roots.

At the Wisconsin River, some of the warriors were assigned the task of trying to hold off the advancing troops while the others constructed rafts with which to cross or flee down the river. Although they held off the troops until most of the people had either crossed the river or had started down river under cover of darkness, the warriors forming the rear guard suffered many casualties. An estimated seventy were killed by the soldiers. The U.S. troops had less than ten casualties.

The U.S. commander decided to wait for reinforcements before pursuing Black Hawk's followers further since his men had only one day's food left and they had no tools with which to construct boats. The first night, while they were waiting, they heard one of Black Hawk's men call out to them from a nearby hill. Although he was trying to deliver another surrender message, the troops did not understand because they had no interpreter with them. Black Hawk's effort to surrender failed again.

A week went by before the waiting troops were joined by General Atkinson's main force. The army then crossed the river approximately twenty miles downstream from where the **Sauk** and **Fox** had crossed. Black Hawk's people should have had an insurmountable lead on the troops by that time; however, severely weakened by weeks with little food and with many wounded, their progress had been excruciatingly slow. As a result, the army was rapidly gaining on them when they reached the Mississippi near the mouth of the Bad Axe River in present-day Vernon County on August 1, 1832.

Those **Sauk** and **Fox** who had successfully made it down the Wisconsin River to the point where it joined the Mississippi River found that the commandant at Fort Crawford in present-day Prairie du Chien had blockaded the mouth of the Wisconsin with two chartered steamboats armed with artillery and troops, and accompanied by more soldiers on a flat boat. Most of the native people were shot or drowned during the confrontation that followed. In addition, some American Indian mercenaries paid by the army were engaged in running down fugitive Sauk and Fox in the area. The mercenaries brought thirty-four prisoners to the fort; most of them women and children. At least nine other prisoners were killed as evidenced by scalps brought to Fort Crawford.

Meanwhile, the troops who had caught up with the main group of

Black Hawk's followers at the site of present-day Victory, Wisconsin, were literally firing on anything that moved. The event turned into a massacre. Most of the Sauk and Fox were killed as they tried to escape. Approximately fifty did escape, however, following Black Hawk northward.

In late August, a group of American Indians, tempted by a reward of $200 and twenty horses, took Black Hawk prisoner and delivered him to the army at Fort Crawford. During the entire "Black Hawk War," only seventeen soldiers were killed and only twelve were wounded. An estimated fifteen-hundred **Sauk** and **Fox** men, women, and children were killed. Many of the men and women killed were elderly.

On September 21, 1832 at Fort Armstrong located at Rock Island, Illinois, the remaining **Sauk** and **Fox** were compelled to agree to a treaty in which they ceded all of their remaining lands to the United States except for a 400 square mile (256,000 acres) reservation in Iowa west of the Mississippi and bisected by the Iowa River. For the six million acres of Iowa land fronting the Mississippi River ceded by the **Sauk** and **Fox**, the estimated worth at that time being more than seven million dollars, the United States agreed to pay $660,000 in installments over a thirty year period, as well as to provide a blacksmith, a gunsmith, and an annual supply of tobacco and salt.[8]

Black Hawk, who as previously noted was between sixty-five and seventy-one years of age at the time, was put in chains and taken to an army prison located at St. Louis. The next spring, after spending the winter in prison, he was put into a circus wagon and taken on display throughout major eastern United States cities, after which he was returned to Iowa.

In 1836 the United States government compelled the **Sauk** and **Fox** to cede the entire 256,000 acre reservation in Iowa that they had been guaranteed in the 1832 treaty session. The United States' justification for the action was that the Sauk and Fox were "desirous of obtaining additional means of support" and needed "to pay their just creditors."

The United States agreed to pay $30,000 to the **Sauk** and **Fox** in June of 1837, as well as $10,000 a year for ten years. In addition, the United States government also agreed to pay the debts owed by the Sauk and Fox to non-Indian traders and other businessmen. Those debts were calculated to total $48,458.87. The United States also agreed to provide two hundred horses to the Sauk and Fox at the same time as the June 1837 treaty payment. The treaty also specifically stated that the Sauk and Fox could no longer hunt or fish on the ceded land.[9]

Black Hawk, the elderly leader of the **Sauk** and **Fox** who had led the resistance against their removal and the loss of their homelands, died in Iowa in 1838. After his death, his body was boiled by relic seekers who wished to get the skin and flesh off the bones quickly, after which his bones ended up on display for a time in a dentist's office in Quincy, Illinois. Later, Black Hawk's remains were transferred to a museum in Burlington, Iowa; however, the museum and the bones were destroyed by fire in 1858.[10]

In 1842 the United States government compelled the **Sauk** and **Fox** to agree to still another treaty, in which they specifically ceded "to the United States forever, all of the lands west of the Mississippi River, to which they have any claim or title, or in which they have any interest whatever." The United States agreed "to assign a tract of land suitable and convenient for Indian purposes [to the Sauk and Fox] for a permanent and perpetual residence for them and their descendants. . . [the] tract of land shall be upon the Missouri River, or some of its waters."[11]

By 1865 the combined **Sauk** and **Fox**, which had an estimated population of 6,500 in 1825, had been reduced by the effects of war and disease to fewer than 1,000 people. In February of 1867, about half of these people "assented to a treaty through which they exchanged their lands [along the Missouri River] in Kansas for a 480,000-acre tract in the Indian Territory [mostly in the present-day state of Oklahoma]."[12]

NOTES

1. The principal source of the information on the Fox is Charles Callender, "Fox," *Handbook of North American Indians, vol. 15, Northeast*, ed. Bruce Trigger (Washington, D.C.: Smithsonian Institution, 1978), 636-647. This is supplemented by information from my notes taken during the time I was a student of Nancy O. Lurie at the University of Wisconsin-Milwaukee in the 1960's.

2. Louise Phelps Kellogg, *The French Regime in Wisconsin and the Northwest* (Madison: State Historical Society of Wisconsin, 1925), 280-281.

3. The principal source of the information on the Sauk is Charles Callender,

"Sauk," *Handbook of North American Indians, vol. 15, Northeast,* ed. Bruce Trigger (Washington, D.C.: Smithsonian Institution, 1978), 648-655. This is supplemented by information from my notes taken during the time I was a student of Nancy O. Lurie at the University of Wisconsin-Milwaukee in the 1960's.

4. Wallace Pyawasit, Menominee Elder who died in November 1981. Personal communication to the author.

5. For a much more detailed account of the war that is usually called "The Black Hawk War," see William T. Hagan, "The Black Hawk War," *An Anthology of Western Great Lakes Indian History,* ed. Donald L. Fixico, rev. ed. (Milwaukee: American Indian Studies, University of Wisconsin-Milwaukee, 1989), 119-143.

6. "Treaty With The Sauk and Foxes, 1804," *Treaties and Agreements of the Indian Tribes of The Great Lakes Region* (Washington, D.C.: Institute for the Development of Indian Law, 1974), 3.

7. Richard L. Kenyon, "Hearing the Echo of Black Hawk," *The Milwaukee Journal,* Wisconsin Section, 15 September 1991, 20.

8. "Treaty With The Sauk and Foxes, 1832," *Treaties and Agreements of the Indian Tribes of The Great Lakes Region* (Washington, D.C.: Institute for the Development of Indian Law, 1974), 33-35.

9. "Treaty With The Sauk and Foxes, 1836," *Treaties and Agreements of the Indian Tribes of The Great Lakes Region* (Washington, D.C.: Institute for the Development of Indian Law, 1974), 46-47.

10. Kenyon, 17.

11. "Treaty With The Sauk and Foxes, 1842," *Treaties and Agreements of the Indian Tribes of The Great Lakes Region* (Washington, D.C.: Institute for the Development of Indian Law, 1974), 68-71.

12. Arrell Morgan Gibson, *The American Indian: Prehistory to the Present* (Lexington, Massachusetts; Toronto: D.C. Heath and Company, 1980), 404.

CHAPTER SIX
THE KICKAPOO,
THE MASCOUTEN,
AND THE MIAMI

The **Kickapoo**, many of whom came into Wisconsin fleeing the **Eastern Iroquois League** invasions into their homeland in the mid-1600's, were first mentioned in the French records in 1640. At that time, they were more commonly known by the name that the **Huron** tribal peoples called them, "On-ta-rah-ro-non," which means (in the English language) "Lake People." The **Kickapoo**, who were living in the general area of southeast Michigan and northwest Ohio, called themselves "Kii-kaa-poa," a name whose meaning is uncertain. Cultural and linguistic evidence links them to the **Fox**, **Sauk**, and **Mascouten**, as well as to the **Shawnee** of Ohio.[1]

The **Mascouten**, whose name may derive from an Algonquian word for prairie people, "Mas-ko-te-wi," were located in the southwestern part of lower Michigan prior to European contact. They were referred to by the **Huron** as "the Fire-Keepers," and at one time may have been a division of the **Potawatomi**. The Mascouten also fled Eastern Iroquois League invasions into their homeland in the mid-1600's, and many came into Wisconsin at that time.[2]

Before contact with the Europeans, the **Miami** lived at the southern end of lower Michigan, in northern Illinois, as well as in the northern Ohio area. There is some evidence that they and the **Illinois** were once one group, with separation occurring near the time of European contact. Many Miamis also came into Wisconsin fleeing the Eastern Iroquois League in the mid-1600's.[3]

In Wisconsin, the **Kickapoo**, **Mascouten**, and **Miami** shared a large village located along the Fox River near present-day Berlin, Wisconsin in the far northeastern corner of Green Lake County.

The **Kickapoo**, who became involved in the fur trade very early, were also located in encampments along the Rock River into present-day Illinois, as well as along the Illinois River. They tended to resist missionary efforts and were sometimes overtly hostile to the French.

By the 1680's, many of the **Miami** had relocated back to their pre-European contact homeland areas, where they were joined by many **Mascoutens**.

In 1712 at about the same time that the French-initiated hostility between the French and the **Fox** was taking place, a trade-related antagonism between the **Mascouten** and French traders came to a head, and over eight hundred Mascoutens were killed in a French attack near Detroit. In addition, some French-Indian allies also attacked Mascouten settlements along the Illinois, Michigan, and Ohio border areas.

When the English defeated the French in 1761, the **Mascouten** and the **Miami** tended to support the English; however, the **Kickapoo** transferred their allegiance to the Spanish based at St. Louis. By the time that the new United States was formed, most of these three tribal peoples had voluntarily left the Wisconsin area and resettled in the Illinois and Indiana areas.

The **Mascouten** and the **Miami** were almost totally absorbed by the **Kickapoo** by 1813, after which the United States forced them into the Indian Territory (which later became Oklahoma). In order to avoid United States domination, some of the **Kickapoo** fled to and established communities in Mexico.

NOTES

1. The principal source of the information on the Kickapoo is Charles Callender, Richard K. Pope, and Susan M. Pope, ''Kickapoo,'' *Handbook of North American Indians, vol. 15, Northeast*, ed. Bruce Trigger (Washington, D.C.: Smithsonian Institution, 1978), 656-657, 662-667. This is supplemented by information from my notes taken during the time I was a student of Nancy O. Lurie at the University of Wisconsin-Milwaukee in the 1960's.

2. The principal source of the information on the Mascouten is J. Joseph Bauxar, ''History of the Illinois Area,'' 599, and Ives Goddard, ''Mascouten,'' 668-672, both in *Handbook of North American Indians, vol. 15, Northeast*, ed. Bruce Trigger (Washington, D.C.: Smithsonian Institution, 1978). This is supplemented by information from my notes taken during the time I was a student of

Nancy O. Lurie at the University of Wisconsin-Milwaukee in the 1960's.

3. The principal source of the information on the Miami is Charles Callender, "Miami," *Handbook of North American Indians, vol. 15, Northeast,* ed. Bruce Trigger (Washington, D.C.: Smithsonian Institution, 1978), 681-682, 686-689.

CHAPTER SEVEN
THE CHIPPEWA

The Ojibwe or Ojibway tribal people living in the United States at the present time are most often called by the name **Chippewa**. As noted in chapter four, they originally called themselves Anishinabe or Anishinaabeg. As also noted in that chapter, Anishinabe has been variously spelled and translated. They were first called Chippewa by English-speaking peoples. The word Chippewa is an English rendering of the word "ocipwe," the word referring to their style of moccasin, which has a puckered seam at the toe. They continue to be called Ojibwe, Ojibwa, or Ojibway by traditionalists on both sides of the United States-Canadian border. In this chapter, they will be referred to by their most commonly known name: "Chippewa."[1]

As also noted in chapter four, according to a number of their legends, the Chippewa were originally inhabitants of the gulf of the St. Lawrence River region. Some of the legends state that a very large intertribal group of **Chippewa**, **Potawatomi**, and **Ottawa** migrated to the Western Great Lakes area a long time before Columbus arrived in North America, dividing at the Straits of Mackinac. Some scholars, however, believe that the first Chippewa migration to the Western Great Lakes area did not occur until the late 1500's and into the early 1600's. The scholars contend that the motivation for the migration was to flee an outbreak of epidemic disease raging through their original home region.

According to the legends, as well as according to some archaeological and ethnological evidence, the migrating Chippewa stopped several times for extended periods along their migration route. One of the stops was at present-day Sault Ste. Marie along the Michigan and Canada border. The final stop, where the Chippewa established a large village, was at the island called "Mo-nin-gwa-ne-kah-ning" (The Place of the Yellow Hammered Flicker), located off the south shore of Lake Superior in the Apostle Islands group. The island, now known as Madeline Island, was renamed in the early 1800's in honor of the daughter of the local leader of the Crane Clan of the Chippewa who married the French trader Michael Cadotte. She had been named Madeline at her Christian baptism.[2]

According to some legends, the Chippewa, after having lived at Mo-nin-gwa-ne-kah-ning for a very long time, abandoned their village because of the acts of an evil shaman living on the island. They then returned to the rapids of the St. Mary's River area.[3]

The first European mention of the Chippewa is in the Jesuit Bartelmy Vimont's account of Jean Nicolet's 1634 voyage, recorded in the *Jesuit Relations* six years after Nicolet's voyage took place.[4] At that time, the Chippewas' major settlements were at Mackinac Island, St. Ignace, and Sault Ste. Marie. In addition, they appear to have had some fishing camps located along the southeast shore of Lake Superior.

The French called them the *Saulteur* (People of the Rapids) because of their large village located at the rapids (*Sault*) of the St. Mary's River where Lake Superior enters into Lake Huron.

In 1641 a group of Chippewa attended a ceremonial feast of the dead at a **Huron** village located in the Georgian Bay area. There they met some French Jesuit missionaries and invited the missionaries to accompany them back to their "Gitchi-gami" (Lake Superior) settlements.

In 1679 after the Chippewa and the **Santee** agreed to a truce in the hostility that had developed between them as a result of increasingly intense competition for natural resources, especially for furs necessary for trade with the French, the Chippewa established villages at Chequamegon Bay, in the Apostle Islands, and at Keweenaw Bay, all in the Lake Superior southern shore region. Their Chequamegon Bay villages, located along the shore, were their first Wisconsin settlements.

In 1693 Pierre Le Sueur, an officer in the French army, arrived at Chequamegon Bay and established the first permanent French settlement on the southwest point of Madeline Island. There the French built Fort La Pointe, which they abandoned in 1700 but reconstructed in 1718.

When the French army captain Paul le Gardeur, Sieur de St. Pierre, arrived at La Pointe in 1718 to reconstruct the fort, he found starving Chippewas, who for some reason had either forgotten or were not able to pursue their pre-fur trade subsistence activities.

In the 1730's, feeling intense pressure from the fierce fur trade-related competition that had developed between the various tribal groups in the region, which was exacerbated by an intense rivalry between the Montreal-based French and the St. Louis-based French, the Chippewa thrust south and southwest into the **Santee** home region of Wisconsin. Soon the Chippewa were active along the headwaters of the present-day Chippewa, St. Croix, and Wisconsin Rivers. There they found themselves involved in warfare with the **Santee** and other Siouan groups over competition for the increasingly scarce fur-bearing animals and other natural resources.

In 1745 the Chippewa established their first permanent inland settlements in Wisconsin. These settlements were located on the shore of Ottawa Lake in northwestern Wisconsin (now called Lac Courte Oreilles) and at Lac du Flambeau (the Lake of the Flames) in north-central Wisconsin. Lac du Flambeau was so-called by the French because the native practice of night fishing with torches created the illusion that the lake was on fire.

The Chippewa also pushed into Minnesota against rugged **Santee** and **Dakota Sioux** resistance. Open warfare erupted regularly for a long period of time as a result.

During the French and English wars in North America, the Chippewa generally allied with the French and did not readily accept the English after the French defeat in 1761.

Other than the episode of joining with the **Sauk** in tricking the English at Mackinac, the Chippewa did not ally themselves with Pontiac in 1763 against the English. Their neutrality, which seriously hurt Pontiac's effort, is attributed to the strong influence of the French interpreter at Sault Ste. Marie, Jean Baptiste Cadotte. Cadotte, who was half Chippewa and half French, was the son of a French army officer named Cadeau. Cadotte also married a Chippewa woman. Like many other French and Metis men who had married into or had other strong ties with the Chippewa tribe, Cadotte was firmly against an attack on the English because of his own interests and investment in the trade. He apparently told the Chippewa leaders that the power of the French in their lands was gone forever, and that they must cooperate with the English or risk English military reprisal and loss of all trade goods.[5]

In 1770 the Chippewa and **Siouan** groups became engaged in a fierce battle in the area of the St. Croix River falls. The Chippewa, who by that time were equipped with some European guns and ammunition, severely defeated the **Sioux** there and ended any further significant **Santee** and other Siouan presence in northwestern Wisconsin.

The Chippewa also had light birch bark canoes, which were far more adaptable than the awkward dugout canoes possessed by the Sioux. In addition, by that time, the bulk of the Sioux had already begun a westward migration, attracted by trading posts that had been established by the French in the lower Minnesota valley, and by the developing horse and buffalo culture, which had reached the northeast plains. With the Chippewa occupation and settlement of the former Santee homelands in Wisconsin and in the border area of Minnesota, the Chippewa became more fragmented, and bands came together less frequently thereafter.

By the time that the colonial revolution had broken out on the East Coast of the present-day United States, a few individual Chippewas had settled in various places in Wisconsin, such as at Green Bay and points south, including at the **Menominee** and **Potawatomi** villages at Milwaukee. The Chippewa were relatively non-involved in the colonial revolution.

When the colonial revolution ended and the new United States nation came into being, the Northwest Fur Company, based in Canada and still under English control, dominated the Lake Superior and northern Wisconsin region trade. The Chippewa became even more dependent on the trade during that time period, and dialects of the Chippewa language were used as the *lingua franca* (a common language used among peoples with varying native languages) of the trade for quite some time.

In February of 1806, a United States Army lieutenant named Zebulon Pike was sent by the U.S. government to meet with the Chippewa leaders. He told them that the United States, which had defeated the English in the colonial revolution, wanted them to stop showing their allegiance to the English, to stop seeking presents from the English, and to give up the medals and English flags that they already had in their possession. He also told them that English rum and other alcoholic beverages were banned from that time forward. In addition, he told them that they must no longer fight with the **Sioux**. At that time, Pike wrote to his superior officers telling them that unless they sent him a significant number of troops, there was no way he could enforce anything he had told the Chippewa. Shortly after Pike's departure from the Chippewa region, conditions returned to what they had been prior to his arrival, and in addition, new hostilities between the Chippewa and the **Sioux** broke out in the Wisconsin-Minnesota border region. Bands of **Sioux** reentered Wisconsin and attempted to regain control of their former wild rice areas. They were soundly defeated by combined Chippewa and **Potawatomi** forces in the area of present-day Mole Lake (Forest County), after which they never again tried to enter Wisconsin in large numbers or for organized hostile purposes.

In 1808 representatives of Tecumseh, the Shawnee intertribal leader from the Ohio region, tried to convince the Chippewa leaders to join the intertribal effort to drive the Europeans and U.S.-"Americans" from the native lands. Again, as was the case with the Pontiac effort, Metis individuals such as members of the Cadotte family, fearing an interruption of the fur trade and loss of profits, convinced the Chippewa that it would be a mistake to join the intertribal effort.

During the War of 1812, the Chippewa refused to assist the English, despite repeated requests from the English for Chippewa help against the U.S.-"Americans."

With the end of the war and the U.S. victory, the Chippewas found themselves having to deal with John Jacob Astor's American Fur Company, as well as with U.S.-"American" lumbermen, miners, farmers, and town builders, all of whom began to intrude onto the Chippewa lands.

On August 19, 1825, at Prairie du Chien, the Chippewa were compelled by the United States military to agree to a treaty in which they pledged to remain at peace with the **Sioux**, as well as with the **Sauk** and the **Fox**. In addition, the Chippewa were required to "acknowledge the general controlling power of the United States."[6]

In 1827 the United States government compelled the **Menominee** to recognize the southern border of the Chippewa lands as running northeast from the Plover River portage (in the present-day Stevens Point, Portage County area) to a point on the Wolf River that was equidistant from Shawano and Post Lake (in present-day Langlade County near the Oneida County-Forest County border), and from there to the falls of the "Pashaytig River" (the present-day Peshtigo River), and north from there to the junction of the Burnt-wood and Menominee Rivers (in present-day Marinette County), and from there northeast to the bay of Green Bay.[7]

These borders designated by the United States government in this treaty were to have serious ramifications relating to the Chippewa treaty rights turmoil of the 1980's and 1990's, as federal courts accepted the legal validity of "treaty-recognized title," meaning "congressional recognition of specific land areas belonging to the Indians," in this case the Chippewa of Wisconsin.[8]

The 1830's saw the demise of the fur trade upon which the Chippewa had become so very dependent. In 1835 the American Fur Company began to channel its efforts into a new economic enterprise, commercial fishing. Quickly, the Chippewa became heavily involved in that effort from their villages located on the south shore of Lake Superior.

In 1836 the separate territory of Wisconsin was created from the Wisconsin portion of the old territory of Michigan.

The following year on July 20, 1837, Henry Dodge, the governor of the Wisconsin Territory, as well as the federal superintendent of Indian affairs for the territory, presided over a treaty session held at the St. Peter's Indian Agency located at the mouth of the Minnesota River. The United States government, bowing to intense pressures from U.S.-"American" economic interests to open the rich white pine and other timber areas to logging and development, compelled the Chippewa to cede to the United States between nine and ten million acres of land in the St. Croix River and Chippewa River regions of Wisconsin. In return for the land "abounding in Pine timber," the United States agreed to pay $70,000 to non-Indian traders to settle Chippewa debts, another $100,000 to Chippewa mixed-bloods, and additionally promised to pay to the Chippewa $35,000 in cash and goods each year for a period of twenty years.[9]

On the seventh day of the treaty session, which lasted ten days, two Chippewa leaders told Governor Dodge through an interpreter, "We wish to hold on to a tree where we get our living, and to reserve the streams where we drink the waters that give us life." The official recorder of the treaty session proceedings, after recording the above quote exactly as translated by the interpreter, wrote, "I presume it to mean that the Indians wish to reserve the privilege of hunting and fishing on the lands and making sugar from the Maple." On the eighth day, one of the Chippewa leaders again told Governor Dodge that the Chippewa "wish to reserve the privilege of making sugar from the trees, and getting their living from the Lakes and Rivers, as they have done heretofore. . ."[10]

The reader who wishes to understand what may really have happened should bear in mind, as Ronald Satz so correctly points out, that the early nineteenth century Chippewa "often understood words and events in different terms than their white counterparts. . . ."[11]

Satz continues:

"There was no single word in the nineteenth century Chippewa language for fishing, so it is very likely that the convenient catch-all [Chippewa] word meaning 'general foraging' with any kind of a device for any purpose was used by interpreters to translate the meaning of the treaty wording 'hunting' [and] 'fishing'. . . . such substitutions could render an Indian's understanding very different from a white person's understanding of treaty stipulations. . . . [Furthermore] since oral rather than written communication was the typical mode of Indian negotiations, the final written document. . . was not as important to [the Chippewa] as their understanding of the verbal agreements. . . [therefore, the Chippewa] left treaty negotiations with understandings based on the dialogue that had taken place while whites left with a written document. . . ."[12]

The actual words in the official Treaty of 1837 regarding those rights reserved by the Chippewa (which have come to be called usufructuary rights by the courts) are:

The privilege of hunting, fishing, and gathering the wild rice, upon the lands, the rivers and the lakes included in the territory ceded, is guaranteed to the Indians, during the pleasure of the President of the United States.[13]

The reader should note that only wild rice, not timber, is specifically named in the actual treaty. In addition, the duration of the usufructuary rights is specifically stated as being "during the pleasure of the President of the United States."

Shortly after the treaty session had ended, Reverend William T. Boutwell, who was an official witness to the session, reported that dozens of timber speculators were already at work choosing cut sites and beginning the construction of timber mills.

United States government ignorance and apparent carelessness about the real needs of the Chippewa (as well as the needs of other tribal peoples) often led to the purchase of treaty payment goods that were ridiculously inappropriate. For example, the United States shipped a number of saddles and bridles to Chippewas who had no horses and who, furthermore, had no need for them in the heavily forested areas. Sometimes guns, but not ammunition, were shipped to the tribal peoples. Some of the guns were so defective that they exploded when fired, crippling the native hunter.[14]

Soon, the Chippewa lands were clear-cut by loggers and then sold by unscrupulous land speculators to a steady flow of unsuspecting European immigrants who had just arrived off the ships from the East Coast. The immigrants soon found that not only was much of the land unsuitable for agriculture, but also that the game animals were near the point of extinction as a result of years of overtrapping and recent over-kill to feed logging crews.

Henry Schoolcraft, the first U.S. government Indian agent assigned to the Chippewa, wrote that he was particularly disturbed to find that the Chippewa had been seduced into frittering away their land for only temporary ends, with no provisions having been made for their permanent welfare.

On October 4, 1842 at La Pointe on Madeline Island, the Chippewa were compelled to cede their remaining Wisconsin lands to the United States. That treaty states that "the Indians stipulate for the right of hunting on the ceded territory, with the other usual privileges of occupancy, until required to remove by the President of the United States. . . ."[15]

Before the year 1849 had ended, the United States government learned that the newly formed legislature of the Minnesota Territory had passed resolutions favoring revocation of the usufructuary rights provided to the Chippewa in both the 1837 and the 1842 treaties.

Revocation of the usufructuary rights by the president of the United States was allowed by both treaties. Consequently, on February 6, 1850, President Zachary Taylor, who had once served as commandant at forts in both Wisconsin and Minnesota, signed an executive order revoking those rights. The order also ordered the removal of all Chippewa from the Upper Peninsula of Michigan, Wisconsin, and the ceded portions of Minnesota, to non-ceded lands in Minnesota. Copies of the signed order were sent to the Indian agents stationed at Chippewa agencies. This unilateral action on the president's part was in compliance with both treaties, as written and signed.[16]

The Chippewa resisted the removal order and were aided by a vigorous lobbying effort on the part of members of the Wisconsin legislature, church groups, and regional newspapers who were all against the forced removal. President Taylor died unexpectedly on July 9, 1850. He was succeeded by Vice President Millard Fillmore, and months passed without any removal action being started. Then, in an effort to lure the Chippewa from Michigan and Wisconsin to a non-ceded region of Minnesota, the annual treaty payment site was moved from La Pointe to Sandy Lake located on the east bank of the upper Mississippi River. In autumn of 1850, several thousand Chippewa traveled there only to find that no provisions had been made for them, and that the promised payment money had not been allocated by the U.S. Congress. Without food and provisions, the Chippewa were not prepared to spend the winter in Minnesota. After waiting there six weeks, to no avail, they made their way back to Wisconsin. It has been estimated that over four hundred Chippewas died of illness, hunger, and exposure to the elements during the ordeal.[17]

In 1852 President Millard Fillmore rescinded President Taylor's removal order. Two years later, in September of 1854, reservations for some of the Chippewa bands in Wisconsin were delineated.

One of the reservations delineated in 1854 was a reservation located east of present-day Ashland in Ashland County in northern Wisconsin. Presently called the Bad River Reservation, it was delineated for a portion of the band of Chippewa that traces its ancestry back to the Loon Clan of the Chippewa. Their first settlement on the south shore of Lake Superior was in the area on the mainland across from Madeline Island at the junction of the present-day Bad River (originally called, by the

Chippewa, the "River of the Swamp") and the White River. In 1841 a Protestant Christian missionary, Reverend Leonard Wheeler, arrived among the Bad River Chippewa and tried to change their way of life from his base in the village of Odanah.[18]

In 1981 the Chippewa of Bad River, called the *Bad River Band of Lake Superior Chippewa*, were operating a successful fish hatchery. In 1990 the reservation consisted of approximately 122,880 acres and had approximately 1,070 Chippewa inhabitants, 440 of them female, 99 under the age of five, and 49 over the age of sixty-five.[19]

One hundred-fifty nine of the 349 occupied housing units located on the Bad River Reservation, out of 465 total, were owned by the occupants. The average value of the owner-occupied houses was $32,300. The average rent of the 126 rental units was $96 per month.[20]

Another reservation delineated in 1854 is located directly across from the Apostle Islands along the south shore of Lake Superior in present-day Bayfield County. Presently called the Red Cliff Reservation, it was delineated for another portion of the band of Chippewa who also trace their ancestry back to the Loon Clan of the Chippewa. The original settlements were in two bays, now called Raspberry Bay and Frog Bay. At one time, Red Cliff was called Buffalo Bay, in honor of its leader named Buffalo. Later it was renamed Red Cliff because of the red soil there.[21]

In 1981 the Chippewa of Red Cliff, called the *Red Cliff Band of Lake Superior Chippewa*, were operating a successful commercial fishing business, two campgrounds, and an art center on the reservation. In 1990 the reservation consisted of approximately 14,528 acres and had approximately 857 Chippewa inhabitants, 362 of them female, 85 under the age five, and 42 over the age of sixty-five. One hundred eighteen of the 259 occupied housing units, out of 343 total, were owned by the occupants. The average value of the owner-occupied houses was $38,100. The average rent of the 98 rental units was $104 per month.[22]

A third reservation delineated in 1854 is located partially in present-day Vilas County and partially in present-day Iron County, north of Rhinelander in north-central Wisconsin. Presently called the Lac du Flambeau Reservation, initially the settlement was called "Wa-swah-gun-ing," meaning "The Place of the Torch People," a reference to their practice of fishing at night with fire baskets. These baskets contained burning white pine pitch and were suspended from the front of the canoes to light the way and to attract fish. Lac du Flambeau was initially settled in 1745 by members of the Crane Clan of the Chippewa led by a man named Keesh-ke-mun (Sharpened Stone).[23]

In 1981 the Chippewa of Lac du Flambeau, called the *Lac du Flambeau Band of Lake Superior Chippewa*, were operating a successful electrical products manufacturing company, a fish hatchery, and several other commercial businesses on the reservation. In 1990 the reservation consisted of approximately 68,992 acres and had approximately 2,434 Chippewa inhabitants, 712 of them female, 201 under the age of five, and 69 over the age of sixty-five. One hundred forty-six of the 869 occupied housing units, out of 2,593 total were occupied by the owners. The average value of the owner occupied houses was $43,600. The average rent of the 282 rental units was $104 per month.[24]

A fourth reservation was also delineated in 1854. It is located in the area of present-day Sawyer County of northwestern Wisconsin where members of the Bear Clan of the Chippewa had settled along the river near a large lake in 1745. Presently called the Lac Courte Oreilles Reservation, the settlement was initially called "Ottawa-sa-wa-sii'-i-gii-i-go-ning," meaning "The Place Where They Found the Ottawa." This referred to the fact that when the first Chippewas arrived there, some refugee **Ottawas** from Michigan were camping in the area, which was a part of the homeland of the **Santee**.[25]

During the late 1700's itinerant French traders began calling Ottawa-sa-wa-sii'-i-gii-i-go-ning "Courte Oreilles," (which describes their "short ears") because they noticed that the Bear Clan Chippewas living there did not wear the heavy earrings that stretched their ear lobes like the other Chippewas and Ottawas they had previously met. In 1819 Jean Baptiste Corbin, a medical doctor who had fled France during the French Revolution and who was employed by John Jacob Astor's American Fur Company, arrived at Courte Oreilles where he established a trading post. There he married a Chippewa woman, and they had a large family.[26]

Although the Lac Courte Oreilles Reservation had been delineated at the Treaty of 1854, along with the Bad River, Red Cliff, and Lac du Flambeau reservations, six years later in 1860 the United States government took all of the Lac Courte Oreilles reservation land. For thirteen years thereafter, the Lac Courte Oreilles Chippewa had no reservation. Then in 1873, the United States government allocated a reservation for them in the same area as the 1854 reservation, minus much of the prime river and lake frontage property.[27]

In 1981 the Chippewa of Lac Courte Oreilles, called the *Lac Courte Oreilles Band of Lake Superior Chippewa*, were operating a successful construction company, shopping center, and a cranberry growing and harvesting industry on the reservation. In 1990 the reservation consisted of approximately 68,480 acres and had approximately 2,408 Chippewa inhabitants, 888 of them female, 240 under the age of five, and 104 over the age of sixty-five. One hundred ninety-nine of the 796 occupied housing units, out of 1,791 total, were occupied by the owners. The average value of the owner-occupied houses was $46,700. The average rent of the 324 rental units was $90 per month.[28]

A fifth Chippewa band, presently called the *St. Croix Band of Lake Superior Chippewa*, did not have a reservation delineated for them in 1854 because their principal leader, believing that they could stay on their lands as long as they caused no trouble, did not attend the treaty session. Landless according to United States law, they became known as the "Lost Tribe" of Chippewa. Members of the Marten Clan of the Chippewa from Madeline Island had initially settled in the St. Croix River area where smaller rivers such as the Brule, Clam, Namekagon, and Yellow Rivers join the St. Croix in present-day Burnett, Douglas, and Washburn Counties. One of the main settlements in the early 1800's was just east of Shell Lake in present-day Washburn County. Another was the village called Dogtown (so-named because of the large population of dogs in the village) located where the Namekagon River flows into the St. Croix (where the original village of Danbury was located; the present-day village of Danbury is located where the Yellow River joins the St. Croix in Burnett County). The Chippewa villages at Bashaw Lake, Clam Lake, and Sand Lake (also in present-day Burnett County) also developed at that time. By 1804 trading posts operated by both Frenchmen and Englishmen were located in the area. By 1850 many loggers had moved onto the St. Croix Chippewa lands and the members of the St. Croix band, with no reservation of their own, scattered over the area. Finally in 1938, the United States government, under the administration of President Franklin Roosevelt, purchased 1,750 acres of land in scattered parcels for the St. Croix band of Chippewa.[29]

By 1981 the St. Croix Chippewa had land in five different places. They were in the Big Round Lake area of Polk County and in the St. Croix River/Danbury area, in addition to the Bashaw Lake, Clam Lake, and Sand Lake areas of Burnett County. At that time, the St. Croix Band of Lake Superior Chippewa were operating a canoe and boat manufacturing company located in Siren, as well as a store in Danbury (both in Burnett County). In 1990 they had approximately 128 acres located in Barron County, approximately 960 acres located in Burnett County, and approximately 832 acres located in Polk County. Their lands, although they are trust lands, held in trust for them by the United States government, are not a contiguous reservation such as those of the Bad River, Red Cliff, Lac du Flambeau, and Lac Courte Oreilles bands. The St. Croix Chippewa population as of 1990 totaled approximately 505 people; 229 of them female, 61 under the age of five, and 24 over the age of sixty-five. Forty-three of the 147 occupied housing units, out of a total of 163 units, were occupied by the owners. The average value of the owner-occupied houses was $40,100. The average rent of the 95 rental units was $133 per month.[30]

The sixth and final band of Wisconsin Chippewa, the present-day *Mole Lake Band of Lake Superior Chippewa*, did not receive any reservation land until 1937. This band had followed their principal leader, Gih'-tchee-wah-bah-shay'-she (Great Marten) from Madeline Island to the areas of present-day Metonga Lake (located directly south of present-day Crandon in Forest County), Mole Lake (southwest of Crandon in Forest County), Pelican Lake (southern Oneida County), Pickerel Lake (in far southwestern Forest County near the Forest-Langlade County lines), Post Lake (southeast Oneida County and northern Langlade County border area), and White Eye Lake (in present-day Forest County north of U.S. Highway 8, west of Crandon, near the Forest-Oneida County border). Their name for themselves, "Sah-ko'-ah-gun," means "Post In the Lake People," and refers to a post-like stump that was in the middle of the lake called Post Lake. This band of Chippewa, for a long time, thought of that stump as being a Spirit-World-related object with special religious and ceremonial significance.[31]

As early as August of 1826 at a treaty session held at present-day

Fond du Lac, Minnesota, the principal leader of the Sah-ko'-ah-gun Band agreed to keep peaceful relations with the United States. Then in 1847, the United States verbally promised the Sah-ko'-ah-gun Band that the United States would recognize the Sah-ko'-ah-gun Band's right to a twelve square-mile reservation around Mole Lake. This band of Chippewa, however, did not receive any legal confirmation of this from the United States. In 1854, again, the United States verbally promised to recognize that reservation land, but the Sah-ko'-ah-gun were again ignored when it came time to offer written confirmation. For eighty-three more years, the Sah-ko'-ah-gun went without an official reservation. Finally in 1937, the United States government under the Franklin Roosevelt administration purchased 1,680 acres for the Sah-ko'-ah-gun Band located approximately eight miles south of Crandon in Forest County. As is the case with the St. Croix band, these lands, although held in trust for this Chippewa band by the United States government, are not a contiguous reservation as are those of the Bad River, Red Cliff, Lac du Flambeau, and Lac Courte Oreilles bands. Now called the *Mole Lake Band of Lake Superior Chippewa*, as of 1981 they were operating a successful drive-in restaurant and sponsoring a very successful annual summer Bluegrass Festival on their land.[32]

'In 1990 the reservation consisted of approximately 1,856 acres and had approximately 357 Chippewa inhabitants, 155 of them female, 68 under the age of five, and 9 over the age of sixty-five. Fifteen of the 108 occupied housing units, out of a total of 123 units, were occupied by the owners. The average value of the owner-occupied houses was $33,800. The average rent of the 78 rental units was $89 per month.[33]

In August of 1988, a United States federal court judge dismissed a 1986 suit brought by the Sah-ko'-ah-gun Band of Chippewa against the United States in which the Sah-ko'-ah-gun maintained that the band was entitled to the acreage promised to them by the United States in the 1854 treaty. The court dismissed the suit because according to the court, the Sah-ko'-ah-gun had not filed the claim by the 1951 deadline that had been set by the U.S. Congress for such claims.[34]

Much of the present-day Chippewa land is checker-boarded. This means that non-Indian land holdings are intermixed with individually owned and non-allotted Chippewa trust lands within the reservations and other trust-land areas. This largely resulted from the fact that the

United States government failed to prevent non-Indian squatters from entering and settling Chippewa reservation and trust lands between 1854 and the early 1930's.

Some of the Chippewa lands are also checker-boarded because non-Indians acquired allotted lands from the Chippewa, either as a result of outright purchase from Chippewa individuals or through the purchase of land at tax sales held by counties. Those tax sales were of questionable legality, particularly since they often involved sale of land that the counties could not legally tax because they were within the borders of federally reserved trust lands.

Meanwhile, between 1854, when the last treaty was signed, and the end of the nineteenth century, the Chippewas continued to hunt, fish, and gather as they had previously done. They hunted, fished, and gathered off their reservations as well as on them. As the nineteenth century came to a close and as the twentieth century began, officials of the state of Wisconsin increasingly began to harass Chippewas whom they discovered hunting, fishing, and gathering off their reservations. In addition, state authorities began an effort to enforce state game and fish laws on American Indian reservation land. This effort led to the arrest in April of 1901 of John Blackbird, a Chippewa, on the Bad River reservation. An Ashland municipal judge found Blackbird guilty of violating state law and fined him twenty-five dollars plus court costs. Because Blackbird did not pay the fine, he was sentenced to serve thirty days at hard labor in the Ashland County jail. United States attorneys, wishing to challenge the state's authority on federal reservation trust land, appealed the municipal court decision in a case brought before the Federal District Court. They argued that Wisconsin had no jurisdiction to enforce Wisconsin's fish and game laws on American Indian reservations. Federal Judge Romanzo Bunn ruled that the U.S. Major Crimes Act of 1885 had extended exclusive U.S. jurisdiction over American Indian reservations for specific criminal offenses, and that the Congress would provide for the punishment of lesser crimes committed by American Indians, if necessary. Judge Bunn also ruled that state jurisdiction over fish and game matters on reservations was not justifiable in law and ordered the release of Blackbird.[35]

Judge Bunn's ruling did not stop further efforts on the part of Wisconsin officials to extend their authority over the Chippewa. In 1907 a

Chippewa named Morrin, who had become a United States citizen under the provisions of the Dawes Act of 1887, and who had been living in the village of Bayfield (Bayfield County) for more than five years, was arrested by state authorities for fishing with a gill net on Lake Superior. After his conviction, Morrin appealed on the basis of his right guaranteed by treaty to fish in the ceded territory. The Wisconsin Supreme Court, using his appeal as an opportunity to reassert state authority over tribal lands, ruled in 1908 that to exempt American Indians from state laws regulating hunting and fishing within the borders of a state, after that state had been admitted to the Union of the United States, would deprive the state of its sovereign power to regulate hunting and fishing. The court added that to deny the state that right was in conflict with the act of admitting the state into the Union. The court concluded that when the Congress admitted Wisconsin into the Union, the act abrogated the treaty rights to hunt and fish within the borders of the state. The court, ignoring federal Judge Bunn's 1901 ruling, in addition to upholding Morrin's conviction in this specific case, set the basis for Wisconsin's ignoring the treaties' usufructuary clauses for the next seventy-five years, until the federal appeals court ruling in the *Voigt Decision* of 1983.[36]

Meanwhile, some of the Chippewas continued to remember that their ancestors' understanding of the 1837 and 1842 treaties included usufructuary rights on the lands ceded to the United States. The political and social climate of the country, focused on a world war and prohibition, and later preoccupied by a depression and another world war, was such that no segment of the dominant society intervened in behalf of the Chippewas' treaty rights.

Then on January 26, 1970, the Great Lakes Inter-Tribal Council, Inc., an intertribal organization composed of representatives of all the Wisconsin tribal groups except the **Menominee** (who at that time were still a terminated tribe) filed a suit against Lester P. Voigt, then secretary of the Wisconsin Department of Natural Resources. The tribes sought to prevent the state of Wisconsin from enforcing fishing and game laws against their people and their lands. They contended that under sovereign immunity, such action violated the treaties that the tribes and the United States government had agreed to years before. The state asked that the suit be dismissed, but U.S. District Judge James E. Doyle denied the request. At the same time, however, he also ruled that the immunity afforded by limited tribal sovereignty could not prevent state officials from enforcing state statutes, such as conservation laws.[37]

In 1972 a case involving two Chippewas who had been arrested and charged with violations relating to gill net fishing and fishing without a license on Lake Superior reached the supreme court of the state of Wisconsin. A lower court had ruled that although the Chippewas had the right to fish on their reservation, such rights did not extend to fishing on Lake Superior. When the case reached the Wisconsin Supreme Court on appeal, the court ruled that the Chippewas could fish Lake Superior based on the treaties, although their right did not prohibit the state from controlling fishing on that lake.[38]

Two years later in 1974, in the landmark decision *United States v. Washington*, U.S. District Court Judge George H. Boldt ruled that treaties protected Indian off-reservation fishing rights. On June 4, 1975, the U.S. Ninth Circuit Court of Appeals in San Francisco affirmed the *Boldt Decision*. The U.S. Supreme Court declined to review the case, which set an important precedent for the cases involving the fishing rights of other American Indians, including the Wisconsin Chippewas.[39]

Later, a Wisconsin court convicted two members of the St. Croix Band of Lake Superior Chippewa who had been charged with possession of game fish during the closed season and for having a spear on Big Round Lake in Polk County. The defendants appealed and on November 16, 1982 the state Court of Appeals ruled that the defendants had fishing rights on Big Round Lake. Lower courts, however, did not always follow the *Boldt Decision* precedent.[40]

Another important treaty rights case had its beginnings in 1974 as well. On March 8th of that year, two members of the Lac Courte Oreilles Band of Lake Superior Chippewa decided to test Chippewa rights under the provisions of the treaties of 1837 and 1842. Wisconsin game wardens arrested the two at Chief Lake located just off of the east boundary of their reservation. They were charged with illegally attempting to fish with spears while off their reservation. A circuit judge in that area found them guilty. The Chippewa appealed the decision.[41]

In 1979 U.S. District Judge Doyle ruled that the Chippewas' hunting and fishing rights that had been stipulated in the 1837 and 1842 treaties had been dissolved when in the 1854 treaty the Chippewas had relinquished their right to occupy the land. The court further ruled that the Chippewas did not have the right to hunt, fish, or gather wild rice without state regulation or control in off-reservation areas. The Chippewa filed an appeal of the ruling.[42]

Finally in January of 1983, in *Lac Courte Oreilles Band of Lake Superior Chippewa Indians, et al. v. Voigt* and in *U.S. v. State of Wisconsin*, the Federal Appeals Court in Chicago handed down a decision that reversed Judge Doyle's earlier decision and reaffirmed the Chippewas' usufructuary treaty rights. The Appellate Court held that the treaties of 1837 and 1842 did not confer unlimited discretion on the United States to terminate the tribe's usufructuary rights, but rather required that the tribes be denied such privileges only if they were instrumental in causing disturbances with white settlers. The court further held that the Chippewas' usufructuary rights established by the 1837 and 1842 treaties were neither terminated nor released by the 1854 treaty.[43]

In response to the court decision, signs berating and degrading American Indians began appearing in northern Wisconsin. Racial slurs fueled hostilities, creating a time bomb of intense emotions that threatened to explode because of misunderstanding and misinformation.[44]

On May 16, 1986, a special meeting focusing on treaty-based hunting and fishing rights claimed by the Lake Superior Bands of Chippewa was held in Wausau (Marathon County in central Wisconsin). An angry outburst of opinions was heard. One person who attended the forum later wrote that the courts have "handed the American Indian rights far superior to those of all other American citizens." Furthermore, he wrote that American Indians, "laying false claims under the treaty. . . are declaring themselves above the laws of this state in a very arrogant and obnoxious fashion."[45]

An editorial appeared in the *Milwaukee Sentinel* which, while it did not deny that the Chippewa held hunting and fishing rights based on treaties signed in the 1800's, it did raise the question relating to why the Chippewa did not use 1800's traditional hunting and fishing methods. The editorial stated in part, "Now the Indian wants his special season with modern, high powered rifles and an outboard motor-powered aluminum boat, a blazing spotlight and a carbon steel spear." The editorial went on to point out that since the Chippewa were not being traditional in their hunting and fishing methods, their rights should also be modified.[46]

On March 20, 1987, federal Judge Doyle announced that ill health compelled his removal from the case. The case was reassigned to Federal Judge Barbara Crabb, chief judge for Wisconsin's Western District of the Federal Court. On March 28th, an organization called PARR (Protect Americans' Rights and Resources) held a meeting in Wausau to publicize the civil rights of non-Indians in northern Wisconsin in light of the court-guaranteed Chippewa rights.[47]

The controversy between state authority and Chippewa off-reservation rights, as well as that between majority and minority perceived rights, continues to be a major issue.

The violence at the boat landings, which was quite prevalent from 1987 through 1990, seems to have abated quite a bit, largely because of the massive police presence and the very heavy fines imposed on protest leaders. The underlying resentment, however, on the part of the non-Chippewa, may or may not be abating. It is very difficult to legislate or adjudicate people's feelings. Conservation-related issues, civil rights concerns, racial discrimination, and other serious misunderstandings appear to remain and, perhaps, continue to fester.

NOTES

1. The principal sources of information for this chapter include John Boatman, "Historical Overview of the Wisconsin Area: From Early Years to the French, British, and American Intrusions," *An Anthology of Western Great Lakes Indian History*, ed. Donald L. Fixico, rev. ed. (Milwaukee: American Indian Studies, University of Wisconsin-Milwaukee, 1989); E.S. Rogers, "Southeastern Ojibwa," (760-764, 768-769) and Robert E. Ritzenthaler, "Southwestern Chippewa," (743-745), both in *Handbook of North American Indians, vol. 15, Northeast*, ed. Bruce Trigger (Washington, D.C.: Smithsonian Institution, 1978); William W. Warren, *History of the Ojibway People* (St. Paul: Minnesota Historical Society Press, 1885, 1984); Edmund J. Danziger, *The Chippewas of Lake Superior* (Norman: University of Oklahoma Press, 1978). These are also supplemented by information from my notes taken during the time I was a student of Nancy O. Lurie at the University of Wisconsin-Milwaukee in the 1960's.

2. Some of the information about the migration and the name of the island is from Shelley Oxley and Ernie St. Germaine, "The Anishinabe: An Overview Unit of the History and Background of the Wisconsin Ojibway Tribe," *Wisconsin Woodland Indian Project Curriculum* (Rhinelander: Rhinelander School District, Wisconsin Department of Public Instruction and the Great Lakes Inter-Tribal Council, 1982), 9, 12, and 22.

3. Danziger, 27.

4. *The Jesuit Relations and Allied Documents: Travels and Explorations of the Jesuit Missionaries in New France, 1610-1791*, vol. 18, ed. Reuben Gold Thwaites (Cleveland: The Burrow Brothers, 1896-1901), 230.

5. Danziger, 55.

6. "Treaty With The Sioux, etc., 1825," *Treaties and Agreements of the Indian Tribes of The Great Lakes Region* (Washington, D.C.: Institute for the Development of Indian Law, 1974), 13, 16.

7. "Treaty With The Chippewa, etc., 1827," *Treaties and Agreements of the Indian Tribes of The Great Lakes Region* (Washington, D.C.: Institute for the Development of Indian Law, 1974), 18. The location of the "Burnt-wood" River named in the treaty is not identifiable on available *Wisconsin Atlas & Gazetteer* or *Wisconsin Official State Highway Map*. It probably is located in present-day Marinette County and has since been renamed.

8. Donald L. Fixico, "Chippewa Fishing and Hunting Rights and the Voigt Decision," *An Anthology of Western Great Lakes Indian History*, ed. Donald L. Fixico, rev. ed. (Milwaukee: American Indian Studies, University of Wisconsin-Milwaukee, 1989), 194.

9. Ronald N. Satz, *Chippewa Treaty Rights: The Reserved Rights of Wisconsin's Chippewa Indians in Historical Perspective*, Transactions, volume 79, Number One (Eau Claire: Wisconsin Academy of Sciences, Arts & Letters, 1991), 13-17, 155-156. The reader who wishes to know much more about this subject is urged to consult Satz's 251 page book.

10. Satz, 18-19.

11. Ibid., 25.

12. Ibid.

13. Ibid., 156.

14. Danziger, 80-81.

15. Satz, 171.

16. Ibid., 55.

17. Ibid., 53-59.

18. Shelley Oxley, "A Unit on the History of the Bad River Band of Lake Superior Ojibway Indians," *Wisconsin Woodland Indian Project Curriculum* (Rhinelander: Rhinelander School District, Wisconsin Department of Public Instruction and the Great Lakes Inter-Tribal Council, 1982), 4, 6-8.

· 19. Ibid. Statistics are from "Summary Population and Housing Characteristics: Wisconsin," Table 17, *Selected Population Characteristics for*

American Indian and Alaska Native Areas: 1990 (Washington, D.C.: U.S. Department of Commerce, Economics and Statistics Administration, Bureau of the Census, U.S. Government Printing Office), 369; and "Summary Population and Housing Characteristics: Wisconsin," Table 18, *Selected Housing and Household Characteristics and Land Area for American Indian and Alaska Native Areas: 1990* (Washington, D.C.: U.S. Department of Commerce, Economics and Statistics Administration, Bureau of the Census, U.S. Government Printing Office), 370.

20. *Selected Population Characteristics for American Indian and Alaska Native Areas: 1990*, 369; *Selected Housing and Household Characteristics and Land Area for American Indian and Alaska Native Areas: 1990*, 370.

21. Shelley Oxley, "A Unit on the History of the Red Cliff Band of Lake Superior Ojibway Indians," *Wisconsin Woodland Indian Project Curriculum* (Rhinelander: Rhinelander School District, Wisconsin Department of Public Instruction and the Great Lakes Inter-Tribal Council, 1982), 4, 11.

22. Ibid.; *Selected Population Characteristics for American Indian and Alaska Native Areas: 1990*, 369; *Selected Housing and Household Characteristics and Land Area for American Indian and Alaska Native Areas: 1990*, 370.

23. Ernie St. Germaine, "A Unit on the History of the Lac du Flambeau Band of Lake Superior Ojibway Indians," *Wisconsin Woodland Indian Project Curriculum* (Rhinelander: Rhinelander School District, Wisconsin Department of Public Instruction and the Great Lakes Inter-Tribal Council, 1982), 3-7, 17.

24. Ibid.; *Selected Population Characteristics for American Indian and Alaska Native Areas: 1990*, 369; *Selected Housing and Household Characteristics and Land Area for American Indian and Alaska Native Areas: 1990*, 370.

25. Saxon Gouge', Ernie St. Germaine, and Shelley Oxley, "A Unit on the History of the Lac Courte Oreilles Band of Lake Superior Ojibway Indians," *Wisconsin Woodland Indian Project Curriculum* (Rhinelander: Rhinelander School District, Wisconsin Department of Public Instruction and the Great Lakes Inter-Tribal Council, 1982), 4,6,8.

26. Ibid.

27. Ibid.

28. *Selected Population Characteristics for American Indian and Alaska Native Areas: 1990*, 369; *Selected Housing and Household Characteristics and Land Area for American Indian and Alaska Native Areas: 1990*, 370.

29. Shelley Oxley, "A Unit on the History of the St. Croix Band of Lake Superior Ojibway Indians," *Wisconsin Woodland Indian Project Curriculum* (Rhinelander: Rhinelander School District, Wisconsin Department of Public Instruction and the Great Lakes Inter-Tribal Council, 1982), 4, 5, 7, 9.

30. Ibid.; *Selected Population Characteristics for American Indian and Alaska Native Areas: 1990*, 369; *Selected Housing and Household Characteristics and Land Area for American Indian and Alaska Native Areas: 1990*, 370.

31. Shelley Oxley, "A Unit on the History of the Mole Lake Band of Lake Superior Ojibway Indians," *Wisconsin Woodland Indian Project Curriculum*

(Rhinelander: Rhinelander School District, Wisconsin Department of Public Instruction and the Great Lakes Inter-Tribal Council, 1982), 4.

32. Shelley Oxley, 8-10.

33. *Selected Population Characteristics for American Indian and Alaska Native Areas: 1990*, 369; *Selected Housing and Household Characteristics and Land Area for American Indian and Alaska Native Areas: 1990*, 370.

34. *The Milwaukee Journal*, 11 August 1988.

35. Satz, 83-85.

36. Ibid., 85.

37. *Great Lakes Inter-Tribal Council, Incorporated v. Voigt*, No. 68-C-95, U.S. District Court, W.D. Wisconsin, 26 January 1970, *Federal Supplement*, vol. 309, "Cases Argued and Determined in the United States District Courts, United States Customs Court and Rulings of the Judicial Panel on Multidistrict Litigation," (St. Paul: West Publishing Co., 1970), 60-64.

38. *State of Wisconsin v. Richard Gurnnoe, Thomas Connors, et al.*, 2 March 1972, Supreme Court of Wisconsin, 192 N.W. 2d 892.

39. Fixico, 192.

40. *State of Wisconsin v. Richard Lowe and Kenneth J. Mosay*, 16 November 1982, Wis. App., 327 N.W. 2d 166.

41. Fixico, 201, 222.

42. *U.S. v. Bouchard, U.S. v. Ben Ruby and Sons*, and *Lac Courte Oreilles Band of Lake Superior Chippewa Indians v. Voigt*, Nos. 76-CR-70, 72-C-366, 74-C-313, U.S. District Court, W.D. Wisconsin, Federal Supplement, vol. 464, "Cases Argued and Determined in the United States District Courts, United States Customs Court, Special Court, Regional Rail Reorganization Act and Rulings of the Judicial Panel on Multidistrict Litigation," (St. Paul: West Publishing Co., 1979), 1316-43.

43. *Lac Courte Oreilles Band of Lake Superior Chippewa Indians, et al. v. Voigt* and *U.S. v. State of Wisconsin*, Nos. 78-2398, 78-2443 and 79-1014, U.S. Court of Appeals, Seventh Circuit, 25 January 1983, *Federal Reporter*, vol. 700 F.2d, "Cases Argued and Determined in the United States Courts of Appeals in the United States Courts of Appeals and Temporary Emergency Court of Appeals," (St. Paul: West Publishing Co., 1983), 341-65.

44. Fixico, 193.

45. Ibid., 206; and "Old tribal treaties threaten state's future," *Milwaukee Sentinel*, 10 June 1986.

46. Fixico, 208-208; and "Indians should return to primitive fishing," *Milwaukee Sentinel*, 12 May 1986.

47. Fixico, 210-211.

CHAPTER EIGHT
THE ONEIDA

The Oneida, along with the Cayuga, Mohawk, Onondaga, Seneca, and Tuscorora, formed the once very powerful **Eastern Iroquois League**.

The Oneidas' name for themselves, "O-ne-yo-te-a-ka," means "People of the Standing Stone," referring to a large red stone that, according to legend, always appeared near the main Oneida settlement, wherever it might be located. The Oneida people referred to the Eastern Iroquois League as "Ho-ni-no-sho-ni," meaning "The People of the Longhouse."[1]

The first Europeans to make contact with the Oneida were the Dutch, who came into the Oneidas' home region in present-day New York state in 1634, the same year that Jean Nicolet came ashore in Wisconsin. In 1667 a French missionary priest visited the main Oneida village located approximately fifteen miles from present-day Oneida Lake, northeast of present-day Syracuse, New York. This places the village within twenty-five miles of the Lake Ontario shoreline. By 1757 the main Oneida village had been relocated to within six miles of Oneida Lake.[2]

At that time, the entire Oneida homeland consisted of approximately six million acres of land in what is now central New York State.[3]

During the French and English war, the Oneida, who had tried to remain neutral, were drawn in as English allies. The period following the end of that war saw the Oneida become victims of famine, an increase in alcoholism, as well as factional disputes.

In 1767 a fundamentalist Presbyterian minister named Samuel Kirkland established a church among the Oneida, seriously challenging the Oneida traditionalists' beliefs. By so doing, he weakened the position of the hereditary leaders in the ongoing factional disputes. It apparently was Kirkland who influenced the Oneida to support the colonial effort rather than the English Crown effort during the colonial revolution that broke out in 1775.[4]

During the war against England, the Oneidas were strong colonial allies and have been credited with aiding George Washington's starving, freezing troops during the winter of 1777-78 by providing them with food and animal-skin clothing while they were camped at Valley Forge, in the Pennsylvania Colony. The Oneida continued to substantially assist the colonial cause thereafter until the war ended.[5]

When the war ended, the Oneida people were scattered from Niagara to Schenectady in present-day New York State. Most of their villages had been destroyed, their farm fields trampled upon and their traditional societal system seriously disrupted due to their alliance with the colonial forces. Most of the other tribes in the once powerful Eastern Iroquois League, most of whom had supported the English Crown forces, had since become alienated from the Oneida.[6]

In 1784 the Continental Congress, the precursor to the United States Congress, recognizing the contributions and sacrifices that the Oneida had made to the colonial cause during the war, guaranteed that the united colonies would respect the territorial integrity of the Oneida's six million acres in the Treaty of Fort Stanwix. The guarantee was repeated by the newly formed U.S. government in the Treaty of Fort Harmar in 1789 and in the treaties of Canandaigua and Oneida in 1794.[7]

In 1794 at Oneida Village in present-day New York state, the newly created United States government also acknowledged that the Oneida, along with the Tuscorora and the **Stockbridge**, had "adhered faithfully to the United States, and assisted them [the United States] with their warriors." The United States agreed to pay $5,000 to be divided between the Oneida and Tuscorora and agreed to construct a grist mill and sawmill for them, as well as to provide $1,000 for the purpose of constructing a church building for the Oneida (to replace one that had been burned down during the American Revolution).[8]

Although the Oneida had sided with the colonies during the war and the United States had officially acknowledged their valuable assistance and had furthermore guaranteed on three separate occasions to respect their homelands territorial integrity, it did not prevent the state of New York from taking huge tracts of land from them. After the end of the

Revolution, the Oneida also experienced increasing internal problems, including further societal disintegration.[9]

One Oneida faction, led by Shenandoah, was Christian and pro-"American." The other faction, led by Cornelius, who wished to retain the old traditional societal system and religion, was referred to as the "Pagan" faction. By 1805 the division was so great that their territory around Oneida Lake was divided into two separate reservations. The Christian influence among the people of the Oneida tribe, the total population of which was probably not much more than six hundred at that time, temporarily declined after the death of Kirkland in 1808.[10]

In the years after the Revolution, Quaker missionaries also arrived on the reservation and taught agriculture, which Oneida men had been reluctant to take up since it was traditionally considered to be a woman's responsibility. Pressed by famine, however, their interest appeared to increase.[11]

Meanwhile, the Caucasian population of the state of New York was increasing dramatically. It grew from an estimated 589,051 in 1800 to an estimated 1,372,812 in 1820. As the Caucasian population increased, the desire to take the American Indian lands intensified. New York had granted the right of preemption to private land companies. Particularly active in the years after 1815 was the Ogden Land Company, which had gained preemptive rights to American Indian lands in western New York. The company began to pressure the federal government to remove the American Indians, including the Oneida, from New York State.[12]

Immediately after the end of the War of 1812, the governor of New York urged the national government to remove the American Indians from his state. As the pressures for removal of the American Indians from New York increased, the Oneida experienced still another change when in 1816 Christianity among the Oneidas was given a major boost by the arrival of Eleazer Williams on their reservation.[13]

Eleazer Williams was an extremely controversial figure during his lifetime and appears to remain so today. Some sources state that there is evidence that he was the "Lost Dauphin," the surviving son of King Louis XVI of France (assassinated during the French Revolution in 1792). Williams claimed this to be true, stating that he had been spirited out of France and raised as a foster child in England before becoming an Anglican missionary priest.[14]

Other sources state emphatically that Williams was of mixed-English and St. Regis American Indian tribal ancestry. Those sources point out that there is strong evidence that among his ancestors was Eunice Williams, a daughter of the Reverend John Williams. Eunice is believed to have been captured by some American Indians in 1704. Those sources go on to state that as a boy Eleazer Williams had been taken to New England and had received a colonial European education. According to these sources, he subsequently became an Episcopalian and in 1816 he was appointed as a lay reader, catechist, and schoolmaster among the Oneidas. Williams' teaching and preaching in the Mohawk language could be readily understood by the Oneida. It is said that he was dramatically successful in rekindling an enthusiasm for Christianity among many of the Oneidas.[15]

It also appears that Williams' education and his excellent command of the English language enabled him to deal skillfully with both other missionaries and government officials. His knowledge of Iroquoian dialects also enabled him to gain considerable influence as an interpreter.[16]

Working among those Oneida who had remained Christian subsequent to missionary efforts on the part of others, Williams, after forming a strong Christian Party, began to preach to the old Pagan group. He soon began to experience success with them as well. Early in the year 1817, many of the leaders of the old Pagan group publicly professed their Christianity and formed the Second Christian Party. Soon most of the Oneida became professing Christians.[17]

While Williams was achieving success among the Oneidas, a more determined drive was developing to remove the American Indians from New York. David A. Ogden of the Ogden Land Company family whose members were leaders in the removal effort, was elected to the U.S. House of Representatives from New York. At first the objective was to remove New York's American Indians to a region west of the Arkansas River. Staunch resistance to that plan on the part of the tribal leaders, however, led to serious consideration of Wisconsin as an alternate relocation site.[18]

Eleazer Williams became an enthusiastic advocate of relocation and he soon had success in convincing many members of the Oneida First Christian Party about the desirability of emigration. Other Oneidas were far more reluctant and expressed hostility toward any move westward.

It appears that by that time, "Williams imagined himself playing a vital role within a great Indian state west of Lake Michigan."[19]

Albert Ellis, who in 1821 accompanied Eleazer Williams to New York City to meet with Thomas L. Ogden of the Ogden Land Company, stated that from that time on Williams received money from the Ogden Land Company.[20]

After having made several prior trips to Wisconsin, Williams and a group of his Oneida supporters arrived at Green Bay at the beginning of September 1822 to meet with United States government officials, as well as with representatives of the **Menominee** and the **Winnebago** tribes. At the meetings, the U.S. government compelled the Menominee and the Winnebago to cede a great deal of land for use by "the New York Indians," including the Oneida. The amount of land ceded for that alleged purpose eventually totaled approximately six million acres. In actuality, "the New York Indians" never obtained anywhere near that amount of land from the government. The Menominees, however, lost any claim they had to the land, and for many years afterward they bitterly disputed the validity of the decisions made during those meetings.[21]

By the winter of 1822-1823 Williams and some of his Oneida supporters were settled on a portion of the former **Menominee** land in Wisconsin. In March of 1823, Williams married the young Metis daughter of a French Canadian and a Menominee woman. In the summer of 1823, additional Oneidas who were members of the First Christian Party faction settled in the Fox River area of Wisconsin. By 1825 there were approximately 150 Oneidas settled in the area. That summer a large number of additional Oneidas arrived from New York, and they, along with those who had arrived previously, moved to and established a permanent settlement at Duck Creek. This was to become the Oneida reservation in Wisconsin.[22]

In the 1820's and 1830's, a bitter dispute arose as the **Menominee** challenged the validity of the previous land cessions. As the Menominee-related dispute dragged on, non-Indian Yankee and European immigrant land-seekers began to enter portions of the six million acres that "the New York Indians," including the Oneida, were supposedly to have been allocated by the United States government. By 1832 the Oneida lands in Wisconsin had been reduced to 7,680 acres located along Duck Creek in present-day Brown County.

By the fall of 1838 there were approximately 654 Oneidas living on the Duck Creek reservation, and over the next fifty years Oneidas continued to arrive from New York, as well as from Canada.[23]

By the time the 1930's arrived, the Oneidas had lost most of their Wisconsin land to non-Indians, much in the same way that some of the **Chippewa** had lost theirs. As a result, much of the present-day Wisconsin Oneida Reservation is checker-boarded. This means that non-Indian land holdings are intermixed with individually owned and non-allotted Oneida trust lands within the reservation. This is largely a result of the fact that the United States government did not prevent non-Indian squatters from entering upon and settling on the Oneida reservation between 1838 and the early 1930's. Some of the Oneida reservation land is checker-boarded because non-Indians acquired allotted lands from the Oneida, either as a result of outright purchase from Oneida individuals or as a result of purchasing the land at tax sales held by counties. Those tax sales were, however, of questionable legality, particularly since they often involved the sale of lands that the counties could not legally tax because they were within the borders of federally reserved trust lands.

In 1934 the U.S. government, under the Franklin Roosevelt administration, purchased 1,574 more acres for the Oneida. Since that time, the Oneida Tribe has been purchasing acreage, which is subsequently added to the reservation.

In 1990 the Oneida Reservation in Wisconsin consisted of approximately 65,472 acres; 26,560 acres located in Brown County and 38, 912 acres in Outagamie County. There were, according to the United States census figures, 18,033 Oneida inhabitants, with 1,240 of those being female. A total of 319 people were under the age of five and 201 people were over the age of sixty-five. At that time, 449 of the 5,761 occupied housing units, out of 5,910 available, were owner-occupied. The owner-occupied dwellings had an average value of $52,200. The average monthly rent of the renter-occupied dwellings was $177.[24]

The Oneida presently own and operate several commercial enterprises, including a successful hotel and convention center complex near the Green Bay airport, as well as a major gambling casino on their reservation. They also, in addition to operating their own school system, lease commercial land to non-Indian business enterprises.

NOTES

1. Jack Campisi, "Oneida," *Handbook of North American Indians, vol. 15, Northeast,* ed. Bruce Trigger (Washington, D.C.: Smithsonian Institution, 1978), 489; William M. Fenton, "Northern Iroquoian Culture Patterns," *Handbook of North American Indians, vol. 15, Northeast,* 320. The reader who wishes to learn a great deal more about the Oneida is advised to read Fenton's chapter (pages 296 through 321), as well as Campisi's chapter (pages 481 through 490).

2. Campisi, 481.

3. William A. Starna, "The Oneida Homeland in the Seventeenth Century," *The Oneida Indian Experience: Two Perspectives,* ed. Jack Campisi and Laurence M. Hauptman (Syracuse, N.Y.: Syracuse University Press, 1988), 9. The reader who wishes to learn a great deal more about the Oneida is also advised to read this entire 207 page book.

4. Campisi, 482-483.

5. Barbara Graymont, "The Oneidas and the American Revolution," *The Oneida Indian Experience: Two Perspectives,* 37-38, 40; and Introduction, 7.

6. Campisi, 483.

7. Ibid., 484.

8. "Treaty With The Oneida, etc.,1794," *Treaties and Agreements of the Indian Tribes of The Great Lakes Region* (Washington, D.C.: Institute for the Development of Indian Law, 1974), 1.

9. This, as well as much of the other information contained within this chapter, is based on information contained in Reginald Horsman, "The Origins of Oneida Removal to Wisconsin, 1815-1822," *An Anthology of Western Great Lakes Indian History,* ed. Donald L. Fixico, rev. ed. (Milwaukee: American Indian Studies, University of Wisconsin-Milwaukee, 1989). The reader who wishes to learn a great deal more about this phase of Oneida history is advised to read Horsman's chapter. Other information, unless otherwise cited, is from my notes taken during the time I was a student of Nancy O. Lurie at the University of Wisconsin-Milwaukee in the 1960's.

10. Campisi, 484; Horsman, 89.

11. Horsman, 89-90.

12. Ibid., 90-91.

13. Ibid., 92-93.

14. *Wisconsin Historical Collections,* vol. 2 (Madison, Wisconsin: Wisconsin State Historical Society, 1856), 418-420; *Wisconsin Historical Collections,* vol. 6 (Madison, Wisconsin: Wisconsin State Historical Society, 1872), 308-342; *Wisconsin Historical Collections,* vol. 8 (Madison, Wisconsin: Wisconsin State Historical Society, 1872), 322-369.

15. *Wisconsin Historical Collections,* vol. 2, 418-420; *Wisconsin Historical Collections,* vol. 6, 308-342; *Wisconsin Historical Collections,* vol. 8, 322-369; Horsman, 93-94.

16. Horsman, 94.

17. Ibid.

18. Ibid., 94-97.

19. Ibid., 98, 101.

20. Ibid., 102.

21. Ibid., 107.

22. Ibid., 107-108.

23. Ibid., 108-109.

24. "Summary Population and Housing Characteristics: Wisconsin," Table 17, *Selected Population Characteristics for American Indian and Alaska Native Areas: 1990* (Washington, D.C.: U.S. Department of Commerce, Economics and Statistics Administration, Bureau of the Census, U.S. Government Printing Office), 369; "Summary Population and Housing Characteristics: Wisconsin," Table 18, *Selected Housing and Household Characteristics and Land Area for American Indian and Alaska Native Areas: 1990* (Washington, D.C.: U.S. Department of Commerce, Economics and Statistics Administration, Bureau of the Census, U.S. Government Printing Office), 370.

CHAPTER NINE
THE STOCKBRIDGE, THE MUNSEE, AND THE BROTHERTON

The present-day tribe called the **Stockbridge** developed from remnants of eastern coastal area tribal groups, particularly those of **Mahican** ancestry, whom the English either persuaded or compelled to settle at an English, Protestant (probably Presbyterian) mission located in the Massachusetts Colony after 1735.[1] The mission was named after a town in England called Stockbridge, and eventually the American Indians living at and near the mission were called Stockbridge Indians. The present-day **Munsee** developed from remnants of eastern coastal area **Delaware** tribal groups from the Delaware River valley and adjacent areas, particularly from those groups living in the Hudson River highlands located between the Hudson River and the Delaware River west of Long Island Sound.[2] The group called the **Brotherton** is another mixed group of Atlantic coastal remnants, including **Narragansetts** from Rhode Island, who between 1759 and the mid-1800's moved to and settled at a Protestant mission community called Brothertown in New York. **Mohegans** from coastal Connecticut joined the Narragansetts at Brothertown after 1775. At that time also, **Montauks, Poosepatucks,** and **Shinnecocks** from Long Island joined the growing intertribal group at Brothertown.[3]

The word *Mahican* may derive from the Dutch pronunciation of their **Munsee** interpreters' own pronunciation of *Muh-hea-kun-neuw*, the name by which the "Mahicans" called themselves. The word may also derive from some other Algonquian-speaking tribal groups equating the name to *Meegun*, an Algonquian word for "wolf." The word *Muh-hea-kun-neuw* apparently comes from *Muh-hea-kun-nuk*, referring to the region where the tidal water of the Hudson River ebbs and flows as far upriver as present-day Albany, New York. Some tribal sources state that the name "Mahican," deriving from "Muh-hea-kun-nuk," means, "The People From the Area Where the Waters are Never Still," or, literally, "Like Our Waters, Never Still."[4]

The word *Munsee* is apparently derived from the general Delaware designation for those Delaware peoples whose home base was Minisink Island located in the upper Delaware River.[5]

The first European contact with the Mahicans was when a Dutch group led by Henry Hudson met with them in 1609. By 1613 the Mahicans were fighting against the Mohawk of the **Eastern Iroquois League** over the growing competition in the European fur trade. That year, the *first treaty between North American tribal peoples and Europeans* was made when the Mahicans agreed to let the Dutch construct a trading post, Fort Nassau, on what became known as Castle Island in the Hudson River. In 1624 when Dutch colonists built Fort Orange upriver along the west bank of the Hudson River (present-day Albany, N.Y.), the Mahicans relocated one of their major villages to the shore opposite the fort. From there the Mahicans controlled the tribal trade with the Dutch at the fort.[6]

By 1628, however, Mohawk and other tribal groups had forced the Mahicans to leave the area. By 1630 the continued intrusion of more Dutch colonists resulted in the Mahicans moving further from the Dutch and developing intertribal alliances with other smaller eastern seaboard tribal groups. Hostilities between the Mahican alliance and the Mohawks continued. In September of 1664, when the English defeated the Dutch and took Fort Orange, the Mahicans resisted any alliance with England.[7]

During the early period of the French and English hostilities, which culminated in the French-English war (1754-1763), the Mahicans actually considered moving to the St. Lawrence River region and joining the French alliance. Finally in 1675, peace between the Mahicans and the Mohawks was achieved; although, having been ravaged by epidemic diseases on three separate occasions, the Mahican population had been reduced to such a state that they had ceased to be a major tribal power. By 1681 the Mahicans and the **Munsees** were together cooperating with the **Eastern Iroquois League** tribes in the trade. It appears that the Mahicans by that time had obtained permission from the **Ottawa** and the **Miami** to seek furs in their homeland areas. Apparently some of the Mahicans also merged with the Miami, with whom they had been living in the southern Michigan-Ohio border area. Mahicans and **Munsees** were also actively competing with the **Cherokee** in the southern Allegheny mountain area, as well as in the Ohio valley. Also at that time, the Mahican and the Munsee became involved in an alliance with the **Shawnee** and by 1692 had developed a Mahican-led "River Indian Confederacy," which included those Shawnee who had moved to Munsee territory.[8]

In 1721 a number of Mahicans moved to the Kankakee River region of present-day Indiana, where they settled among the **Miami**. In January of 1735, their population severely depleted by epidemic diseases from Europe, and suffering from the negative effects of alcoholic beverages introduced by both the Dutch and the English, the Mahican-led River Confederacy leaders met with a Presbyterian missionary named John Sergeant, at his request. Sergeant told them that he wished to establish a mission village for them. They consented and he established the village that he called Stockbridge, named after a town in England. By 1738 nearly all of the American Indians in that region, Mahican as well as others, had moved to the village at Stockbridge, where a church and school had been established. At the village, Reverend John Sergeant was assisted by a Mahican named John Quinney. The tribal children were placed in a boarding school located in the village, so that they might become Christian and adopt the values of Anglo-European society.[9]

During the 1754-1763 war between France and England, commonly called the French and Indian War, most of the Mahicans and their tribal allies, by that time called the **Stockbridge** Indians, assisted the English. With that war over and England victorious, many of the Stockbridge again assisted the English in the English war against Pontiac's intertribal confederacy in 1763. Many Stockbridge lost their lives fighting on the side of the English during those wars. Nearly one-half of their male population was lost during that time. Not all of the Stockbridge supported the English, however. Most of those Mahicans and their affiliated tribal peoples living in the western Pennsylvania frontier region relatively far from New England, supported both the French and Pontiac.[10]

During the North American colonial revolutionary war against

England, approximately sixty western-region Mahicans supported the English. Most of the eastern region **Stockbridge** supported the colonies; some of them provided quite significant support to George Washington's army. In 1794 at the Oneida village in present-day New York State, the newly created United States government acknowledged that the **Stockbridge**, along with the Oneida and Tuscorora, had "adhered faithfully to the United States, and assisted them [the United States] with their warriors." Four Stockbridge leaders "signed" the treaty. Their "signing" was witnessed by Reverend John Sergeant.[11]

At the end of the war and with the founding of the new United States, the **Stockbridge** discovered that they were no longer wanted at the village in Stockbridge, Massachusetts, where Caucasians had taken over the local government and wanted the tribal peoples removed. The dispirited and disillusioned **Stockbridge** then accepted an invitation from the **Oneida** to come and live amongst them. In 1783, 420 **Stockbridge** Indians, remnants of once-powerful tribal nations, relocated from Massachusetts to lands located along Oneida Creek in New York. By 1786 most of the **Stockbridge** and other Mahican-related tribal remnants had resettled there, and the place became known as New Stockbridge. There the Stockbridge, many of whom could both read and write English, began to work at establishing farms. By 1800 they had established a relatively stable community at New Stockbridge, modeled after English-American rural communities. Factionalism arose, however, as a traditionalist element persisted in wearing "Indian" clothes and speaking their native language. As non-Indian "profiteers" exploited the factionalism, excessive use of alcoholic beverages increased, especially among the non-Christian "traditionals."[12]

It was at that time that some of the **Stockbridge** leaders, wishing to remove their people from the influence of the exploitative non-Indians and remembering the old agreement with the **Miami** in northern Ohio and Indiana, began to investigate the possibility of relocating the **Stockbridge** to the White River region of Indiana, where a group of **Munsee** had previously settled, and where the **Stockbridge** had been promised land by the government (some sources state that it was Thomas Jefferson himself who had promised them the land).[13] Their move was delayed during the Tecumseh War and the War of 1812, but with those wars ended, a group of approximately 75 **Stockbridge**, led by John

Metoxen, departed for Indiana in 1818. After their long journey, they arrived there only to find that the United States had compelled the **Miami** and the **Munsees** to cede the land to the United States. They were told that they could not stay there.[14]

Then, as noted in previous chapters, beginning with the treaty session held in August of 1825 at Prairie du Chien, the **Menominee** tribe was compelled to cede approximately six million acres of their Wisconsin homeland to the United States for use as a new homeland for the "New York Indians." One-half million acres of that total, located on the east side of the Fox River in the Green Bay area, was specifically designated for a new home for the **Stockbridge** and the **Munsee**. As early as 1828 a mixed-tribal group from New Stockbridge, New York led by John W. Quinney migrated to and began to settle on their new homeland They were soon joined by the group that Metoxen had previously led to Indiana. According to oral traditions preserved among some of the Wisconsin tribal peoples, it was a group of **Stockbridge** at Kaukauna in present-day Outagamie County who built the first Protestant church in Wisconsin. Other **Stockbridge** tribal peoples from New York also migrated westward to Wisconsin, the last group leaving New Stockbridge in 1829. The Stockbridge in Wisconsin were joined by approximately 100 **Munsees**, bringing the total number living in the settlement on the east side of the Fox River to approximately 325 by 1831.[15]

Then, to their astonishment and dismay, at the end of October of 1832, the **Stockbridge** and the **Munsee,** who had settled on their new homelands, were informed that the U.S. government had decided to change the location of their new homeland. The new location was to be 46,080 acres on the east side of Lake Winnebago, land that the U.S. government had also taken from the **Menominee** tribe. An additional 23,040 acres in the same region was specified "for the use of the Brothertown Indians [the **Brotherton**]."[16]

The **Stockbridge** and the **Munsee** had no alternative but to move, again, this time to the region east of Lake Winnebago in present-day Calumet County. Five years later in 1837, that community's population increased as the result of the arrival of a group of **Munsee** who had been living in Canada subsequent to leaving New York.[17]

In 1839 the United States government, as part of its effort to remove all native tribal people living east of the Mississippi River to lands further west, convinced approximately 70 conservative **Stockbridge** and approximately 100 **Munsees** to move to the Missouri River region. Most did not survive the hardship and disease they encountered there. This effort was followed in 1843 by another social experiment, in which the U.S. government offered citizenship and individual land-holdings to the **Stockbridge**. The issue proved to be quite controversial, splitting the Stockbridge into a new "Indian Party" and a "Citizen Party." Many of those who opted for U.S. citizenship eventually lost the land to non-Indians.[18]

Many **Brothertons** also opted for citizenship at that time.

In February of 1856, the United States government compelled the **Menominee** to give two townships (46,080 acres) located on the southwest corner of the Menominee Reservation, to the **Stockbridge** and the **Munsee**. That land later became part of Shawano County. The land east of Lake Winnebago where the Stockbridge and Munsee had been living was desired by newly arriving immigrants from Europe. Between 1856 and 1859, with the exception of some of the Stockbridge and Munsees who had become citizens, the Stockbridge and Munsee tribal peoples were compelled to move, again, this time to the land which the U.S. government had taken from the **Menominee** Reservation. On the new land, they were joined by some **Brothertons** who had previously migrated to and settled in Wisconsin, as well as by some new arrivals from New York. Following the U.S. General Allotment Act of 1887, individual Stockbridge and Munsees who were now settled on the newly acquired lands, chose allotment. This eventually also resulted in an additional substantial loss of land to non-Indians.

Initially, with the lumber industry very active in their area, the Stockbridge and Munsee maintained a reasonable standard of living. They marketed seventeen million feet of timber in 1895 alone. When logging ended, however, their community became very economically depressed.[19]

The **Brotherton**, who were not absorbed by the **Stockbridge** or the **Munsee**, are not federally recognized as being American Indians, have no reservation or trust land, and are essentially scattered throughout the United States, most of them living in Wisconsin.

As of 1981 there were an estimated 750 Stockbridge and Munsee combined living on the reservation, and an estimated 450 more living elsewhere, including on a reservation in New York and on one in Canada. At that time, most employment opportunities were located off the reservation, resulting in the necessity to commute to work. Unemployment was running as high as fifty percent.[20]

In 1990 the **Stockbridge-Munsee** Reservation in Wisconsin consisted of approximately 22,272 acres in Shawano County of central Wisconsin. There were, according to the United States census figures, 581 people living there (this figure was not broken down by separate tribal identity). Two hundred nineteen of the 581 inhabitants were female. Thirty-two individuals were under the age of five and 62 people were over the age of sixty-five. At that time, 112 of the 197 occupied housing units, out of the 228 available, were owner-occupied. The owner-occupied dwellings had an average value of $33,700. The average monthly rent of the renter-occupied dwellings was $150.[21]

NOTES

1. This, and much more detailed information about the tribe known as the Stockbridge may be found in T.J. Brasser, "Mahican," *Handbook of North American Indians, vol. 15, Northeast*, ed. Bruce Trigger (Washington, D.C.: Smithsonian Institution, 1978), 198-212. The reference to the Presbyterian church is supported by several references to the tie between the missionaries who worked among the Stockbridge and the group known as the Society in Scotland for Propagating Christian Knowledge (a Presbyterian group); see, for example, "Documents Relating to the Stockbridge Mission," *Wisconsin Historical Collections*, vol. 15 (Madison, Wisconsin: Wisconsin State Historical Society, 1900), 39.

2. This, and much more detailed information about the tribe known as the Munsee, may be found in Ives Goddard, "Delaware," *Handbook of North American Indians, vol. 15, Northeast*, ed. Bruce Trigger (Washington, D.C.: Smithsonian Institution, 1978), 213-239.

3. This and more information about the group known as the Brotherton, may be found in Laura E. Conkey, Ethel Boissevain, and Ives Goddard, "Indians of Southern New England and Long Island: Late Period," (181, 184); Jack Campisi, "Oneida," (481), both in *Handbook of North American Indians, vol. 15, Northeast*, ed. Bruce Trigger (Washington, D.C.: Smithsonian Institution, 1978).

4. Brasser, 211; Shelley Oxley, "A History of the Mahican and the Munsee Indians," *Wisconsin Woodland Indian Project Curriculum* (Rhinelander:

Rhinelander School District, Wisconsin Department of Public Instruction and the Great Lakes Inter-Tribal Council, 1982), 5.

5. Goddard, "Delaware," 215, 236.

6. Brasser, 202-204.

7. Ibid.

8. Ibid., 204-205.

9. Ibid., 205-208.

10. Ibid., 208-209.

11. "Treaty With The Oneida, etc.,1794," *Treaties and Agreements of the Indian Tribes of The Great Lakes Region* (Washington, D.C.: Institute for the Development of Indian Law, 1974), 1-2; Brasser, 209.

12. Brasser, 209.

13. Nancy O. Lurie, *Wisconsin Indians* (Madison: State Historical Society of Wisconsin, 1980), 12.

14. Brasser, 209.

15. "Treaty With The Sioux, etc., 1825," 13-18; "Treaty With The Chippewa, etc., 1827," 18-20; "Treaty With The Menominee, 1831," 24-29; "Treaty With The Menominee, 1832," 39-43, all in *Treaties and Agreements of the Indian Tribes of The Great Lakes Region* (Washington, D.C.: Institute for the Development of Indian Law, 1974).

16. Ibid.; Brasser, 209.

17. Brasser, 210.

18. Ibid.

19. Ibid.

20. Oxley, "A History of the Mahican and the Munsee Indians," 28.

21. "Summary Population and Housing Characteristics: Wisconsin," Table 17, *Selected Population Characteristics for American Indian and Alaska Native Areas: 1990*, 369; "Summary Population and Housing Characteristics: Wisconsin," Table 18, *Selected Housing and Household Characteristics and Land Area for American Indian and Alaska Native Areas: 1990*, (Washington, D.C.: U.S. Department of Commerce, Economics and Statistics Administration, Bureau of the Census, U.S. Government Printing Office), 370.

PART TWO

SELECTED ASPECTS
OF
THE CULTURE
OF
WISCONSIN INDIANS

CHAPTER TEN
THE ORGANIZATION OF THE
TRIBAL SOCIETAL SYSTEM

As is the case with most human groups, the traditional societal systems of tribes in the Wisconsin area were developed and organized in response to the **real need** for the effective and efficient fulfillment of at least five **basic human needs**. These needs included the need for sustenance, protection, leadership, learning (education), and the need to maintain both physical and psychical (including spiritual) well-being. Note that these basic needs are not listed in the order of importance because all of these needs, and their reasonable satisfaction, are of equal importance.

Generally speaking, the reasonable satisfaction of these important needs was accomplished through the arrangement of individuals into what some scholars call the *nuclear family*. The nuclear family consists of the mother, the father, and any children resulting from the union of the female and the male. Nuclear families were gathered together into a number of **extended families**, usually headed by a grandmother or grandfather.

Each extended family was an integral part of one or more **clans**. In some areas, several clans were combined into one or more **bands**.

Clans, and where relevant, bands, were combined into **tribes**. Tribes were sometimes combined into **nations**.

Tribes, and where relevant, nations, were combined into **language/ culture groups**.

LANGUAGE/CULTURE GROUPS AND TRIBES

At different periods in history, tribes from the Algonquian, the Siouan, and the Iroquoian language/culture groups made their homes in the Wisconsin area.

The indigenous Menominee and most of the tribal groups that came into the area between 1610 and 1820, including the Potawatomi, the Sauk, and the Ojibwe (Chippewa), were of the Algonquian language/culture type. The Stockbridge and the Munsee, who came into Wisconsin from the Atlantic coastal area after 1820, were also of the Algonquian type; however, major differences distinguished them from the original Western Great Lakes area Algonquians.

The Winnebago, descendants of the ancient Oneota peoples who came into the Wisconsin area in approximately A.D. 800, were not Algonquian. Some scholars say they are Siouan; however, the Winnebago language is quite closely related to languages spoken by the Iowa and the Missouri tribes and is only remotely related to the language of the Dakota, one of the "Sioux" groups. In the mid-1600's, the Winnebagos' territory in Wisconsin was overrun by intrusive Algonquian tribal peoples fleeing Eastern Iroquois League attacks in their Lower Michigan homelands. A recurrent theme in Winnebago references to this period is that there are few "pure" Winnebagos left today as a result of extensive mixing with Algonquian tribal peoples during that time. Consequently, much was borrowed from Algonquian culture as well.

The Oneida, who came into the Wisconsin area of the Western Great Lakes after 1820, are of the eastern Iroquoian group.

WHO WERE ONE'S RELATIVES?

There were a number of criteria for determining to whom one was related. An individual was, of course, related to those to whom he or she had biological ties (one's "blood-relatives"). One was also related to those with whom one had ties established through marriage. In addition, an individual was also related to all those individuals who were members of the **same clan**.

WHAT IS A CLAN AND WHY WAS IT IMPORTANT?

A **clan** is defined as an organized group of human **extended families** that identifies with and recognizes common ancestry from an ancient ancestor. Most often, this ancient ancestor was non-human, usually a Spirit-Being or an extra-terrestrial. This ancient ancestor was said to manifest in the form of an animal or as some phenomenon in nature, such as one of the winds, thunder, or clouds. Each clan had a special symbol that represented its ancient ancestor.

Clan-groupings were either matrilineal or patrilineal. (Note that these words, and many of the following technical words, are those used by scholars and not by the tribal peoples themselves.) If one traced one's line of descent back in time from one's mother, one's clan affiliation was matrilineal. On the other hand, if one traced one's line of descent back in time from one's father, one's clan affiliation was patrilineal.

If one usually lived in the general vicinity of one's mother's family, one was said to be from a matrilocal societal unit. If one usually lived in the vicinity of one's father's family, one was said to be from a patrilocal societal unit.

If the major decisions in one's community were usually made by a council of female Elders, one was said to live in a matriarchal society. On the other hand, if the major decisions in one's community were usually made by a council of male Elders, one was said to live in a patriarchal society.

One cooperated with and largely depended upon one's clan for the fulfillment of specific needs in the larger human group.

The tribal clan system gradually began to break down after the escalation of the French fur trade in the late 1600's. A band system organized for hunting and trapping emerged in response to the increased demand for furs. Some clan elements, however, remained intact for quite some time after the emergence of the band system.

THE NEED FOR SUSTENANCE

Generally, the need for sustenance was met by clan and/or tribal hunters, fishers, and other food providers such as gatherers and farmers. Those who participated in these occupations were highly respected members of the community.

The most respected occupation in the community was that of the initial provider of human sustenance: the Mother. Through Mother come both initial life and initial sustenance.

THE NEED FOR LEADERSHIP

Many important points about leadership are contained within the following story, which was told by many Elders from the Western Great Lakes area.

Of all the echo-makers in the natural world, the Crane and the Loon are among the most eminent.

Very long ago, Crane, whose calls are both infrequent and unique, was the leader of all of the birds. Because Crane's calls were such, when Crane did call, most other life forms stop their own activity and listen.

One day Loon decided to challenge Crane to become leader of the birds.

Crane was not willing to fight to retain *the burden of leadership* so, as a result, Crane turned over the leadership position to Loon. Loon then assumed the position with much pomp and ceremony.

Most of the other birds were quite relieved that someone other than themselves had assumed *the burden of leadership.* They looked to Loon, as they had previously looked to Crane, for leadership and guidance.

Then in late August, some of the birds went to Loon and told Loon that they were ready to leave for their southern wintering territories. Loon replied that it was too early; that they should wait because all the birds were going to migrate at the same time under the new leadership system.

By the time that Loon was ready to lead the massive migration, many of the bird species had suffered considerable hardships. Some had even died as a result of exposure to temperatures much colder than those to which they were accustomed. Finally, Loon led the great migration toward the south.

Soon, however, problems developed. Some of the birds said the speed of the flight was too fast for them to keep up. Others said that they were flying far too high, while others complained that they were flying too low. Many said that they were flying too far each day without resting. Loon generally ignored the complaints.

Upon arrival at a certain point in southern Tennessee, Loon announced the end of the migration. Many quickly said that they always went much farther south, some into the Caribbean islands. Loon emphatically stated that all were going to stay in the same place that year.

The birds quickly called an all-bird council, after which they called for Loon to resign the leadership position. They told Loon that too little concern had been shown for their differences and their individual species' needs.

Loon responded by stating that the well-being of all, the "general good," had to be considered first. Many of the birds shouted that the "general good" had already resulted in the illness and death of many members of various bird species. Loon, again, responded by emphasizing the need to consider the "all," not just a few. The birds then shouted, "You think to big; you forget the small!"

With that, all the birds left Loon and pleaded with Crane to assume the leadership again, when the need arose for a leader to make decisions.

That is why now Loon is often still alone.

From this story, one should learn that just as Crane calls infrequently, and yet commands attention, so also should *human leaders exercise their prerogative rarely,* and only when there is a real *need.*

In addition, *human leaders should speak infrequently,* just as Crane does, lest they be considered to be shallow-minded.

Human leaders should also be first in action, and not be merely commanders. *They should not speak their own sentiments, but rather those of the group,* emphasizing the importance of consensus, whenever possible.

Leadership was to rely on persuasion in times of real "need," and was not to be constant or permanent. *When the real "need" ended, so should the leadership.* Just as a flock of birds disbands when the flock arrives at its proper destination, human leadership should terminate until a real "need" arises and a new leader is chosen.

Because these principles of leadership are best exemplified by birds, *birds are chosen as the tribal totem symbols for leadership* in many of the tribes.

An important part of the traditional training for leadership was training to "listen" to the thoughts and expressions of others.

Leadership positions were not sought after. Elders observed the behavior of a possible candidate for a leadership position over a lengthy period of time and would, after discussing the relative merits of the individual being considered, approach the individual in a time of real "need" and offer that person a symbol of leadership, such as a ceremonial Pipe of Peace.

Acceptance of the Pipe by the individual who was approached by the Elders was an outward sign of acceptance of the responsibilities and burdens of leadership. In accepting, the chosen one would say, "You have this day made me a poor woman/man!" This was because the individual was aware that it was a burden to lead and that, in addition, *the property of the leader was henceforth at the disposal of the group in times of real "need."*

If the individual believed that she or he was not ready, the individual was expected to respectfully decline the offer of the leadership position.

Chosen leaders who accepted the burden of leadership, were expected to consult regularly with the Council of Elders. This insured that the "needs" of the people were always considered in the adjudication of wrongs, in the settlements of disputes, the allocation of hunting/fishing/gathering territories, in the guidance of migrations, and in decisions that related to either war or peace.

Generally, there were three main types of leaders: civil government leaders, including individual clan leaders; war leaders; and ceremonial/ religious leaders. The leaders were often called a variant of the Algonquian title "Ogima," and *not* by the European term "Chief."

Civil governmental concerns were discussed in the lodge of the most prominent civil leader, who served as chairperson of the Council. The Council was attended by most males over the age of thirty, including the leaders of each clan.

NEED FOR PHYSICAL AND PSYCHICAL WELL-BEING

Medicine People worked at helping to fulfill the need for physical, mental, and spiritual well-being.

They were usually *chosen by the Elders* from among those who were observed to evidence some signs of having parapsychological abilities, as well as having a compassionate nature. Those chosen, and who subsequently accepted the choice, were expected to participate in a long and difficult training and apprenticeship period.

Training usually began under the guidance of the herbalists, during which time the individual became familiar with the medicinal properties of plants.

Normally, an individual did not function as a medicine person until she or he had reached the age of at least 40 to 45, when hair begins to turn the color of the snow. The reason for this delay in becoming involved as an actual practitioner was rooted in the general belief that an individual's ability as a "conductor" for Spirit-World "power" became optimum during the last stage of one's life.

The healers (medicine men and medicine women) generally practiced holistic medicine (medical treatment which dealt with the entire person, both physical and spiritual, mind and body). Being a healer meant being a combination of herbalist, physician, psychiatrist, philosopher, and clergy-person. Healers believed that the well-being of the body was directly related to the well-being of the inner-self, the mind—the Spirit.

Because these individuals dealt with "power" from the Spirit-World, which is inherently amoral and is both positive and negative by nature, medicine people were among the most respected, but at the same time feared, members of the tribal communities.

These individuals, often called "Shamans" by members of the dominant society, played a definite *de facto*, behind-the-scenes role in tribal affairs, including tribal government.

NEED FOR PROTECTION

The need for protection was fulfilled by warriors. They were considered necessary to the community, although both indirectly and directly their very presence in the community was a potential source of conflict.

Warriors were generally not included in the community council; however, they often had a great deal of *de facto* influence, and they served as the tribal police.

NEED FOR EDUCATION

The Elders, who were considered to have lived long enough to have found and developed a positive and balanced "Sun Trail," were the main teachers. They usually employed stories as a medium to teach about life and tribal ways.

The stories were usually such that children enjoyed them, while at the same time they were complex in the depth of the important themes that they contained.

Humor, which reflected the natural element of comedy present in most aspects of life, was an important element in many of the stories. The use of humor in the stories pointed out that one should not take one's self too seriously, lest one fall along the path of one's "Sun Trail."

"Students" were encouraged to draw their own inferences from the stories they heard. Later, after serious contemplation, they were advised to discuss the stories, and the inferences that they had drawn from them, with the Elders.

"Tests" in this type of educational system were quite severe, as they were found in the day to day functioning of every day life. If one had not learned properly, one might find one's self in real danger.

Fish were chosen as the tribal totem symbols for education. This was because knowledge, like the fish which lies hidden in the depths of the swirling water, must be sought out and retained until needed. Once attained, it was not to be flaunted and bragged about; rather, it was to be kept in humble reserve until the need arose.

SYSTEM OF "JUSTICE"

The system of justice that was prevalent among Great Lakes tribal peoples was based on the principle of "an eye for an eye."

Those accused of a capital crime, such as murder or an act of negative sorcery (such as love sorcery, which was thought of as being similar to rape), were brought to the attention of the community at large, and particularly the Council of Elders.

The accused was shielded by the Civil Leader until such time as the

Council of Elders made a determination as to his or her guilt or inno-cence. This determination was made after an extensive investigation of the available facts. If the accused was determined to be guilty, the family of the victim was given the option of dealing with the individual. This could result in community-sanctioned execution or else exile from the protection of the tribal group.

THE CALENDAR SYSTEM

Time was kept by keeping track of sun and moon phases during a year divided into four equal parts of three months each--very much like the ancient European calendar and the ancient calendars of other civili-zations.

The Winter and Summer Solstices and the Spring and Autumn Equinoxes were celebrated with special ritual.

There is some evidence that the mound systems and stone monoliths found in the Great Lakes region were at least partially oriented to this time-keeping system in conjunction with the position of the planets and other astronomical bodies at certain times of the year.

The length of a lunar phase corresponded to the length of a "month" or "Moon." These included the Autumn Moons, the Winter Moons, the Spring Moons, and the Summer Moons.

The first of the Autumn Moons was the "Rice-Making-Moon" (Wild Rice Moon), which generally was from the full moon in August to the full moon in September. This was following by the "Leaves Turning Color Moon" (Moon of the Falling Leaves), which generally was from the full moon in September to the full moon in October. The Autumn Equinox usually occurred during this mid-phase of the Autumn Moons. The last of the Autumn Moons was the "Beginning-Ice-Forming-Moon" (Moon of the Flowing Ice), which generally was from the full-moon in October to the full moon in November.

The Winter Moons began with the "Great Spirit Moon," which generally was from the full moon in November to the full moon in December. This was followed by the "Little Spirit Moon," which generally was from the full moon in December to the full-moon in January. The Winter Solstice usually occurred during this mid-phase of the Winter Moons. The last of the Winter Moons was the "Moon of the

Crust on the Snow" (Moon of the Broken Snow Shoes), which generally was from the full moon in January to the full moon in February.

The first of the Spring Moons was the "Sucker-Spawning Moon" (Moon of the Sucker-Mouth Fish moving upstream), which generally was from the full moon in February to the full moon in March. This was followed by the "Sap Running Moon" (Moon of Our Good Tree Maple), which generally was from the full moon in March to the full moon in April. The Spring Equinox usually occurred during this mid-phase of the Spring Moons. The last of the Spring Moons was the "Budding Moon" (Moon of the Flowers Blooming), which generally was from the full moon in April to the full moon in May.

The Summer Moons began with the "Strawberry Moon" (Heart-Berry Moon), which generally was from the full moon in May to the full moon in June. This was followed by the "Mid-Summer Moon" (Red Raspberry Moon), which generally was from full moon in June to the full moon in July. The Summer Solstice usually occurred during this mid-phase of the Summer Moons. The last of the Summer Moons was the "Blue Berry Moon" (Moon of the Good Blue Berry), which generally was from the full moon in July to the full moon in August.

DUTIES AND RESPONSIBILITIES IN LIFE

What responsibilities did an individual have to one's family, one's neighbor, and one's community? What, if anything, did an individual owe to one's self? Are there any responsibilities from which there is no release—responsibilities that one is obligated or required to fulfill? Do promises made bind the maker to those promises forever?

Many Elders said that, to all of these questions, the answers were to be found individually, according to unique circumstances. The Elders told special stories, from which the listener might derive guidelines to be used in searching for an answer to each particular circumstance. The stories were repeated, from tribe to tribe and from storyteller to storyteller.

The stories stressed that one has the responsibility to take appropriate action to provide for one's own real "needs," because otherwise one will have difficulty meeting the needs and responsibilities of others.[1]

AGGRESSIONS AND ALTERNATIVES TO AGGRESSION

WAR

There is sketchy, and sometimes conflicting, evidence relating to the amount and type of intertribal warfare that occurred in the Western Great Lakes area, including Wisconsin, prior to the intrusion of the Europeans. Oral traditions generally declare that it was somewhat rare. Following the intrusion of the disruptive Europeans, intertribal warfare occurred more frequently, escalating with the increasing intensity and competition of the fur trade.

The personal charismatic qualities and reputation of an individual leader was particularly important in the determination as to who should be the leader of a military effort. Individuals would sometimes report that they felt compelled to lead a war party, as a result of a dream or a vision that they had experienced. Such war leadership was usually temporary, lasting only for the duration of the particular military encounter. In some tribes, the "war power" was vested in "owners" of Spirit-World-related "War Bundles," which contained, among other things, dream and vision-related and inspired items. An example of this is the snake skin, which was believed to potentially provide the "owner" with unique stealth. Participation in war parties allowed young men the opportunity to demonstrate courage and bravery.

The pre-European "wars" usually consisted of quick actions by relatively small raiding parties. Generally the purpose of such action was to avenge perceived "wrongs" committed by "outsiders" against one's group.

An individual organized a war party by sending messengers to others, explaining the purpose of the proposed military activity. The messenger would present a War Pipe to the individuals. If the individual wished to join the war party, he took the pipe and puffed on it briefly as a sign that he accepted the responsibility. He then handed the pipe back to the messenger, who went on to contact other individuals. Individuals were free to accept or reject the pipe thereby signaling acceptance or refusal of the request to join the war party.

At a scheduled time, those who had agreed to join the effort met at the particular war leader's lodge to plan and discuss strategy further and also to partake in a pre-battle feast and ceremony. The ceremony was designed to appeal to the Spirit-World for assistance with the task involved in the military effort, and also served to emotionally prepare the participants for the encounters ahead. A war dance was often an integral part of the ceremony.

During the actual military action, especially in pre-European times (according to oral traditions), the principal objective was to demonstrate bravery and courage by physically striking the enemy, to embarrass him in front of witnesses. This has been termed "counting coup."

Many of the tribal groups also expected warriors with established reputations to perform "police duty" for the tribe. An example of one of the objectives of this activity was to insure that the wild rice areas were not entered by anyone prior to the harvest time chosen by the Council of Elders.

The practice of "scalping," which is a common stereotype applied to American Indians in general, was, according to the oral tradition of the Elders, quite rare in the pre-European Wisconsin area. It is also a subject of controversy since there is evidence that the practice east of the Wisconsin area escalated only after European intrusion, especially after the English began paying tribal peoples for the scalps of American Indians whom the English defined as the enemy.

After the intrusion of the Europeans into Wisconsin, especially during the periods of warfare between France and England and between the united colonies and England, warfare was enthusiastically practiced by some of the tribal groups, and the activity was idealized in "sacred" tradition. Warfare even began to permeate some of the religions and some Spirit-World beings were associated with war activity. Young adult males were expected to seek war honors.

ALTERNATIVES TO WAR

A number of games were often played as alternative outlets for human aggressive impulses that could otherwise lead to war.

The most popular and geographically widespread of these games is known to some tribal peoples by the name *baa-ga'adowe*. The game is commonly known by the French name for it, *lacrosse*. The racket used in this game reminded the French of a *crosier*, the staff resembling a shepherd's staff that Catholic bishops and abbots carry as a symbol of their position.

Many of the tribal groups believed that powerful Thunderer Spirits, who own the game, taught it to humans in ancient times. Humans continue to be allowed to play the game, but it is still owned by those spirits.

When lacrosse was played, it was played to honor its owners, the powerful Thunderer Spirits, and to request assistance from the Spirit-World in curative-related tasks. It was also played for recreation and fun.

The game was usually played after an individual reported having dreamed that he should arrange for and sponsor a match. He would send messengers to other individuals reporting that he had experienced the dream, in which he had been directed by the spirits to sponsor a game. The messengers would offer a pinch of an herbal offering mixture (such as tobacco) to prospective players. If an individual agreed to play, he took the offering and found out the designated place and time. Accepting the offering obligated the player, barring injury or illness, to play in the upcoming match. An individual could refuse the offering, thereby excusing himself from play.

On the day the game was to be played, each individual who had agreed to play brought his own racket (with a design on the handle unique to the player). The player carefully tossed his racket onto a growing pile of rackets at the playing area. The sponsor then selected two team leaders from among the assembled players.

One of them would be blindfolded and led to the pile of rackets. He would then divide the rackets into two separate piles; these became the two teams. The sponsor did not play. He stayed on the sidelines, observing, praying, and awarding prizes to those who scored.

Ordinarily two teams of five players-each played. However, as many as nine could play on a team. On some extremely rare occasions, between fifty and one hundred players were on each team.

The playing field was a level area containing two goal-posts set in the ground some distance apart, one at each end. Sometimes they were as much as a quarter mile apart. During the winter the game was some-times played on a frozen lake, if the snow was not too deep.

The racket was made of wood. It was about four feet long and bent at the non-grip end to form a circular loop, which was filled with leather strips latticed in such a manner that a ball could be caught in the loop. The ball was about the size of a baseball. Often it had a deerskin cover and was stuffed with hair. Sometimes it was made from a knot of wood, charred and scraped to the proper size.

The sponsor started the game by standing mid-field and tossing the ball into the air. The opposing team players then scrambled to get the ball. Players were not allowed to touch the ball with their hands. The ball was moved across the field in the netted-loop of one's racket, having been either scooped off of the ground or caught in mid-air while it was being passed or knocked from another player's racket. A player, after getting the ball, either ran with it or passed it to a team-mate, attempting to avoid interceptions. The object was to score a goal by hitting the ball against the goal post behind the opposing team. Opposing team members attempted to intercept passed balls or to knock the ball out of opponent's racket loop nets. One player on each side acted as a kind of goalie, trying to prevent the opposing team from scoring. This was often an exceedingly rough game, with bruises and even broken limbs not uncommon.

When players scored, they claimed a prize from the sponsor. Normally players were required to give the prize away, usually to one of the females in the game audience.

One of the most significant lacrosse games ever played after Europeans entered the Great Lakes region was one played in front of the English fort at the Straits of Mackinac in 1763. At that time, Chippewa, Sauk, and other tribal peoples used the soldiers' interest in observing the game as a device to capture the fort. The soldiers were convinced to open the fort gate so they did not have to keep climbing down from the walls where they watched the game in order to toss the ball back to the tribal people who were playing. Once the gates were opened the Chippewa and Sauk stormed the fort.

There was a women's version of lacrosse, which was called *Shinny* or *Double-Ball*. It was generally played for the same reasons as lacrosse. The shinny ball consisted of two small oblong deerskin bags joined together by a strip of deer skin, making a "double-ball." The rackets were more stick-like, with curved "hook" at end, intended to allow the strip between the "double-ball" to be caught on the "hook." The rest of the game was quite similar to the males' game, except that the playing field was not usually as large.

Another men's game that was sometimes played as an outlet for aggression was *Atowi*. This game had no religious significance. It was played solely as an acceptable outlet for human aggressive impulses. Rarely planned, it usually started on those occasions when a group of young men had gathered for no particular reason. Suddenly one of the young men would take the notion to shout "Atowi!," upon which he would kick an adjacent man in the buttocks as hard as he could. This man, in turn, would kick another and so on. The object was to see who could best keep an even temper for the longest period of time. Sometimes Elders, who would sit and observe with some amusement, awarded prizes to those who they judged to the obviously deserving winners.

NOTES

1. Some excellent stories that relate to the duties and responsibilities that an individual faces in life may be found in Basil Johnston, *Ojibway Heritage* (Lincoln: University of Nebraska Press, 1990), 73-78.

CHAPTER ELEVEN
THE FAMILY STRUCTURE
AND CUSTOMS

COURTSHIP AND MARRIAGE

Generally, for all of the tribal groups in the Wisconsin area, the clans had *exogamous* rather than *endogamous* marriage rules. That meant that one was prohibited from marrying a member of one's same clan. Exogamous marriages (marriages outside of one's clan) were sometimes arranged by families. Parents tried to encourage their children to marry into prominent families. A young woman's parents paid particular attention to evidence that the prospective husband would be an effective provider, and warrior if necessary. It was very rare for either a young man or a young woman to be coerced into an unwanted marriage.

Most marriages were also monogamous; however *polygamy*, a marital system wherein under special circumstances a spouse of either sex could have more than one mate, was allowed. In this regard, *polygyny*, wherein a male had more than one wife, was more common that *polyandry*, the practice of a female having more than one husband. Polygyny was sometimes practiced among affluent and "powerful" males. The custom of the *sororate*, wherein a male married the sister of his deceased wife, was also practiced. The reader should note that the terms *exogamous, endogamous, monogamous, polygamy, polygyny, polyandry,* and *sororate* are all anthropological terms and not American Indian terms.

From the time of puberty on, young girls were closely watched by their family, especially by their grandmothers, lest males be tempted to take unfair advantage of them.

One of the generally applicable courtship procedures was as follows: A male who was especially interested in a particular female would be expected to first approach the family living in the wigwam (the traditional house) next to the family of the female. He would tell them about his special interest in getting to know the female and her family. He would often be provided with "neighborly-type" information about the female. The neighbors would then inform the female's family about the prospective suitor's special interest.

If the grandmother of the female approved, a trial courtship began after the male was informed of the approval. He would begin by calling on the female, always speaking with her in the presence of her adult relatives, especially her grandmother. If the female told her grandmother that she was definitely *not* interested in the male, the courtship was likely to be terminated by the grandmother, unless some very important political matter that impacted significantly on the welfare of family, clan, or tribe was at stake.

Sometimes *courting flutes* would be used by the male. However, in cases of young, virgin females, this practice was discouraged because it was believed that far too often the sweet, seductive sound of the courting flute was too much for young, virgin females to resist.

If the female being courted indicated to her grandmother that she really liked the sound of that particular male's courting flute, or that she liked him in general, it was an indication that she wanted to continue to pursue the courtship within the constraints of clan and tribal rules.

When the male was told that the female and her family approved the courtship, the next step was for him to go hunting for a deer or other large animal which, according to clan rules, was acceptable for food. When he had obtained the animal, he would leave it at the door of the wigwam of the female's family, thus providing evidence to the family that he could provide for the female and, when necessary, her extended family, especially the Elders and children.

If the family subsequently invited the male to participate in a feast, at which some of the meat he had provided was consumed, his "engagement" to the female was official, and the wedding date was set.

On the day of the wedding, the couple actively participated in religious ceremonies honoring Great Spirit and other spirits, including their individual Guardian Spirits. These ceremonies were followed by a special wedding ritual, the form of which varied from group to group. One or more of the following rituals could take place. A single blanket might be placed over the shoulders of both the bride and the groom (European terms). One sleeve from each of their wedding garments would be sewn together by an Elder. The couple might exchange a pair of moccasins (the traditional footwear), stating that each would support the other on their individual life path. An Elder might hand each some seeds or, together, a small tree, instructing the couple to plant them together.

Where the newly-married couple resided depended on whether the clan was matrilocal (wherein one lived near the female's family) or patrilocal (wherein one lived near the male's family).

Divorce was allowed for reasons acceptable to the Council of Elders, provided there was a definite, good, acceptable plan for the care of any children resulting from their union. The divorce consisted of the placing of the spouse's personal belongings outside the door of the wigwam (which spouse's belongings were to be removed depended on whether the group was matrilocal or patrilocal).

THE BIRTH OF CHILDREN AND THE CARE OF INFANTS

It was believed that before a child could be conceived in the uterus of a female, a Soul had to be sent by Great Spirit from the Atisokanak World (the Spirit-World) into the prospective mother's uterus prior to the conception. It was the presence of this Soul that made conception and the new life possible.

When the time for the birth came, the birth took place in a special birthing lodge. The birthing lodge was normally located away from the clan residential area, but near enough to make the pre-birth journey of the pregnant woman to the lodge safe and practical. The reason the birth took place away from the main residential area was that it was believed that blood from a mother at the time of birth had the potential to become supernaturally dangerous (as did menstrual blood). This was because of the very special Spirit-World-related "power" of female beings. All females were believed to have been created with the ability to be automatic conductors for "power" from the Spirit-World into the Now-World.

A woman about to give birth was attended to in the birthing lodge by other females who were supervised by female Elders.

Some of the tribal groups utilized a special "birthing rack," which consisted of a smoothed pole, two or three feet long, set about two feet above the ground on crotched posts. In her final labor, the woman knelt on a softly padded mat, her chest against the cross-bar. The birth of the baby then occurred naturally, utilizing the force of gravity.

Immediately after the birth, a female Elder would rub her hands with cedar oil (from Grandmother Cedar) and then hold her hands to the baby's face for the baby's first breath. The baby usually took its first breath in response to the pungent odor of the cedar oil, making it unnecessary to spank the baby on the buttocks in order to get it to breathe.

After the birth, the umbilical cord was tied and cut. A portion of it was saved and dried, and later sewn into a small diamond-shaped deerskin pouch. This was then hung on the hoop of the baby's cradle board. It was believed that this would help attract wisdom to the child from the Spirit-World.

A bit of cedar oil was also rubbed on the baby's forehead and on the "life spot," located at the front of the neck. The baby's feet were then briefly touched to the Earth while the Elder told the baby to "behold Earth-Mother." It was believed that this helped start the baby on a positive, Earth-Mother-guided life path.

The newborn baby was bathed in a warm solution containing herbs, including bits of cedar, as well as charred pieces of wood from a tree that had been struck by lightning. It was believed that the latter would help attain for the baby the protection of the Thunderer Spirits against negative Spirit-World forces.

The baby, after being held close by the mother for a time, would then be put on the cradle board. Usually made from cedar wood (from Grandmother Cedar), the cradle board was approximately two feet long, ten to twelve inches wide, and a half inch to an inch thick. It had a foot brace on the bottom, as well as a hoop, often made of hickory, at the head end. This hoop, of shock resilient wood, served to protect the baby's head if the cradle board fell over.

Sphagnum Moss, contained in a shallow birch bark tray (from Grandfather Birch) held in the cradle board, served double-duty as a cushion for the baby's body and as disposable diaper material, which could regularly and easily be changed. A finely ground powder made from rotted oak was dusted on the baby to guard against chafing and diaper rash.

The baby would be given baby-sized moccasins with a hole in each sole. It was believed that if a Spirit of Death came to the baby and tried to coax the baby away from the land of living, the baby's Spirit could then respond that the baby could not travel because its moccasins had holes in them. In cold weather, the baby's feet would be wrapped in rabbit skin, with the fur side in.

The baby was held secure in the cradle board by special wrappings, which were often decorated with floral and/or spiritually significant designs. The designs were initially made from porcupine quills, utilizing a unique quill-art. Later, after glass beads were introduced from Europe, they were often used instead. Initially, the baby was held secure in the cradle board, completely bound by the wrappings, except for around the head. Later, as the baby grew, the arms would be left out of the wrappings.

The cradle board provided a sense of security, kept baby warm, kept baby's back straight, and served as both a baby bed and baby carriage (carried on an adult's back). The baby would be taken from the cradle board periodically during the day for cleaning and for exercise. When the mother was working around the dwelling, she could lean the cradle board against the side of the dwelling or against a tree, or place it in a hammock, where it could rock in the wind. Should the cradle board accidentally fall over, the hickory hoop protected baby's head and helped to absorb the shock.

The baby might be kept on the cradle board from nine months to a year. The child could watch its mother at work, as well as look at, and later when the arms were free, play with the things hanging from the hoop. Some of the things hanging from the hoop were intended solely for amusement, such as little shells and pine cones. Other things, however, like the diamond-shaped pouch containing the piece of umbilical cord, had great significance. Usually these pouches were decorated with a butterfly design because the butterfly was often thought to carry the "Spirit of Child Play." A spider web design (often called a "dream-catcher") was also often hung from the hoop. This was to help catch any negative spirit forces that tried to attack the baby, as well as attract positive spirit forces. Grandmother Spider was considered, by most tribal groups, to be a very powerful, positive spirit.

When ceremonial or social drums were played, the cradle board (with the baby secured in it) was gently tapped to the Earth in time to the drum beat. It was therefore said that baby learned to dance before baby could stand or walk.

The baby was breast-fed, when possible, for as long as two to four years, or until the baby "started to bite too hard." This prolonged period of nursing was, normally, physiologically and psychologically healthful for both the baby and the mother. In addition, it was considered somewhat effective in preventing unwanted conception. The baby was weaned on fish or meat broth mixed with soft wild rice, food staples of the tribal community.

THE INITIAL NAMING OF THE CHILD

Parents or other significant adults often gave the child a nickname by which they were commonly known; however, the child was also expected to receive an initial official name. The initial official name was very special because it was believed to carry an identity given as a gift from the Spirit-World (the Atisokanak World). This gift was given by the Spirit-World through an Elder, who was called the "Namer," and who acted as an agent for the Spirit-World.

This Spirit-World gift name was usually given to the child before the first year of life had passed, and often within the first three months of life. The name involved a special relationship between the Elder "Namer" and the Spirit-World, as well as between the Elder "Namer," the Spirit-World, and the child.

The parents would request an Elder to do the naming. If the Elder accepted the responsibility of being the "Namer," he or she would then seek the name from the Spirit-World through a process involving dreaming and out-of-body travel to the Spirit-World by a part of the Elder's Spirit.

Elders did not casually accept a request to become a "Namer," since the process also involved the acceptance of a very special, partial responsibility for the spiritual well-being of the "named" forever. This responsibility, upon acceptance, was recorded and remained established in the Spirit-World. In addition, the "Namer" gave to the "named" a part of the "Namer's" Spirit-Essence.

The actual naming ceremony took place before three months had passed from the time when the "Namer" had accepted the responsibility to do the naming. The ceremony involved honoring Great Spirit, as well as lesser but significant spirits.

During the ceremony, the "Namer" first would turn to the Direction-Spirits of the Seven Sacred Directions (starting with East), announcing the child's new name to each. Each time the "Namer" announced the name to the particular spirit of a given direction, those in attendance repeated the name in affirmation.

The "Namer" would then hold the child close, stating to the child, "You shall be called [the name]; this is your gift, your name from the Spirit-World. By this name you shall be known and called; you must uphold the honor of this name." At that time, a portion of the "Namer's" Spirit-Essence was passed from the "Namer" to the child being named.

The ''Namer'' then presented the child to each person attending the ceremony. Each individual who wished to then briefly held the child and, in so doing, also accepted a partial responsibility bound in the Spirit-World to help properly educate the child.

At puberty the individual could seek an additional name from the Spirit-World through the puberty Vision Quest. More will be said about this later.

After intensive contact with Europeans and Euro-Americans, many tribal people obtained an additional name for identification and use in Euro-American communities for such things as payroll records. As an example, an individual might simply be called "Jim." His sons would then be called "Pete-Jim," "Charley-Jim," and the like. Often Euro-American last names, such as "Brown," "Smith," or "Johnson," were arbitrarily ascribed to American Indians.

THE DISCIPLINE AND TRAINING OF CHILDREN

Physical beatings and even raising the voice in anger were not commonly used in the traditional discipline and training of children. Instead, discipline was instilled through the systematic relating of unacceptable behaviors that would lead to potential Spirit-World reprisal. Fitting into the proper clan and tribal cultural pattern, while maintaining a positive relationship with the Spirit-World, was the goal of successful child rearing.

Orchestrated and controlled fright was sometimes used to dissuade antisocial and other improper behavior. Individuals called "Frighteners," often wearing ugly masks and dressed oddly, would sometimes walk through the village area. Children would be told that such a person might take them away if they failed to exhibit socially proper behavior. Frightening effigy figures were also placed in areas where there was real potential danger, such as near quicksand.

Many events involving a child that are often treated as emotional and perhaps even catastrophic events by some present-day parents in the dominant society would normally be treated with calmness by traditional tribal parents. An example of this involves an incident in which a young child tripped and fell outside of the wigwam, receiving a rather nasty cut on a leg. The child came running into the wigwam crying very hard, pointing to the cut, which was bleeding profusely. The father, who was in the wigwam with the mother at the time, said in a soft voice to the child, "Why didn't you look where you were going?" He then proceeded to treat the cut without externally showing any anxiety or emotion (other than an evidenced "caring"). The mother made no comment at all as she proceeded to continue what she had been doing before the child came into the wigwam.

This lack of evidenced tension, anxiety, and emotion on the part of the parents was, usually, later reflected in the personality pattern of the child as she or he grew into adulthood.

Generally, young boys were taught to hunt, fish, trap, and otherwise provide food as soon as they were able to follow directions. Sometimes young girls were taught these skills; however, it was considered more important for them to be taught to become effective mothers and home-makers, because it was through them that initial life and sustenance would manifest in cooperation with the Spirit-World.

Children were taught that one must never kill that which one does not really need, or that which one will not eat or use in a positive manner.

They were also taught from an early age not to disturb the nests of birds or any young animals, as well as how to identify and know the proper uses of plants.

In addition, they were taught not to gaze at food others were eating, not to disturb others in the wigwam at night, to respect other people's privacy, and to learn to be quiet when so-directed (this was especially important in times of danger during wars).

They were also taught to practice fasting while very young, so that they would later be able to deal with times when food might be scarce. This was also good conditioning for young males, who were expected to participate in Vision Quest fasting at puberty.

The act of dreaming and the content of some dreams were considered to be very important because dreaming was considered an important means for making contact, establishing a relationship with, and learning from the Spirit-World. It was sometimes said that children went to school in dreams, which were thought of as real social situations in which one interacted with Spirit-World beings. Many dream experiences were considered to be as real as waking experiences. Consequently, children were generally encouraged to dream and to remember and discuss their dreams with Elders, whom the children were taught to listen to and respect.

Some tribal groups had a "village crier" who went through the village at dusk, reminding those youths who had misbehaved (without specifying the misbehaver's identity) that their behavior had not gone unobserved, telling them also that they had better mend their errant ways. The "village criers" also made important announcements of general interest and concern to the community. After dark, they announced that young men who were "courting" should go to their own homes at the proper time.

PUBERTY AND THE VISION QUEST

At puberty an Elder would approach a young male one morning at breakfast time and present to him a choice of a dish of his favorite breakfast or a piece of charcoal. From a very young age, young males were taught to be prepared for this time. If the young male chose to pursue his Vision Quest experience, he took the charcoal and rubbed some on each of his cheeks. If, on the other hand, the youth determined that he was not yet ready, he took the food, knowing that he would be given another opportunity to pursue the Vision Quest.

If he chose the charcoal, the next morning his father or another significant adult male would accompany him to a secluded area of the forest where he would choose the location of his Vision Quest lodge.

There he would remain alone for three nights (four days). He would abstain completely from food, ingesting only water or tea. An adult would periodically check on the youth during this time to be sure that he was all right while he sought contact with the Spirit-World. The adult, however, would not communicate with the young man.

During the four day period, if the Spirit-World approved, the young man would be approached by a Guardian Spirit from the Spirit-World. The Guardian Spirit would offer to teach him about his (the young man's) purposes in life and would give him a special Vision Quest Spirit-Name. With this name came a certain amount of ability to conduct Spirit-World "power" which, because it is inherently amoral, could be utilized for either positive or negative purposes. Sometimes the youth also received special parapsychological abilities from the Spirit-World.

On the fourth day, the youth would return to his village where he would discuss his experience with a respected Elder. The Elder would often be witness to undeniable "signs" that something unusual had happened during the youth's Vision Quest experience. These "signs" were clues to the identity of the youth's Guardian Spirit. An example of this would be an Elder reporting witnessing flashes of lightning and/or crashes of thunder on an otherwise clear day--evidence that the Thunderer Spirits were looking favorably on the youth. The Elder would explain to the youth that, apparently, a Thunderer Spirit had chosen to be the youth's Guardian Spirit. The youth would, as a result of accepting the guardian, acquire a Thunderer-related Vision Quest name.

The spiritually-related "gifts" acquired at the time of the Vision Quest experience involved reciprocal obligations on the part of the youth. These reciprocal obligations remained with the youth for the remainder of his life, and he was to be ever mindful of the need to honor his Guardian Spirit.

In some tribal groups, the youth would later paint the symbol of his Vision Quest-acquired Guardian Spirit on his personal drum and other important belongings.

Females did not have to undertake the Vision Quest since by the very nature of being female, they were created by Great Spirit with an automatic relationship with the Spirit-World, which included the ability to conduct Spirit-World "power." Great Spirit's designated "Female Primacy" entailed the female's special role as a conductor for Great Spirit's Life-Giving-Force, as well as her special role in Great Spirit's Sacred Cycle of continual creation, destruction, and re-creation in the Space-Time Continuum. Females did, however, have to learn to fine tune and appropriately use the automatic ability.

Some tribal groups discouraged young women from taking on a Vision Quest, for fear that they might become too spiritually powerful.

When a girl evidenced signs of her first menstrual period, she went to a secluded, special menstrual lodge (sometimes called "the Moon Hut") for a period of from four to ten days. If a young woman did have a Vision Quest-type experience while in the menstrual lodge, she was considered to be extraordinarily "special."

Some tribal groups observed taboos associated with menstruating women such as the prohibition against drinking from the same cup from which a menstruating woman had previously drank. It appears that these taboos were based in males' fear of potential harmful Spirit-World intrusion through such a woman. In some groups, smears of menstrual blood were sometimes put on cradle boards or over wigwam entrances to ward off negative Spirit-World forces, as it was believed that many powerful negative Spirit-World entities would not dare to confront the Spirit-World "power" conductivity of a menstruating female.

CHAPTER TWELVE
PHILOSOPHY, RELIGION, AND CEREMONY

The pre-European tribal philosophy and its value system were based in an understanding and acceptance of one's special relationship to the multidimensional space-time continuum, as well as to a specific geographical place on Earth Mother. As a result, these humans shared a sense of "belonging" to "a place" rather than to "a time." The religion that flowed from this understanding was thought of as being like a golden thread woven through the fabric of life. Consequently, most human acts were thought to have some religious significance, and religion was not something that was set aside or reserved for one day of the week or for a certain time of the month or year. In addition, an individual's religious beliefs, although often manifested in group ritual and ceremony, were also thought of as quite personal. Consequently, in this chapter, I shall not go into great detail. The reader who wishes for more detail about certain ceremonies and rituals may find helpful information in two of Basil Johnston's books, *Ojibway Heritage* and *Ojibway Ceremonies*, as well as Edward Benton-Banai's book, *The Mishomis Book*. The reader may also find it useful to consult my first book, *My Elders Taught Me: Aspects of Western Great Lakes American Indian Philosophy*.

Tribal peoples generally believed that there are two types of worlds. One type is a readily observable and experienced "Now-World," such as Earth. The other type is the not nearly so perceptible multidimensional "Spirit-World" composed of pure energy, often called the *Atisokanak World*.

From the perspective of this traditional belief system, every created thing in and on the Earth Now-World is alive and is a person—or was alive at one time, but has since died. As a result, many things that the dominant Euro-American society considers to be inanimate are considered animate and are included in the category of person in the traditional belief system. Humans are thought to be only one type of person among many, many types.

All created Now-World forms are believed to have (or to have had) a "Spirit" consisting of two aspects. The primary and life sustaining aspect is the immortal *Soul*. The other aspect is the *Ghost*, which is capable of traveling outside of the body in both space and in time.

The traditional tribal peoples also believe that there are a variety of special persons in the Spirit-World, and that these persons are ranked according to the degree of power they hold in a Spirit-World hierarchy. In addition, tribal peoples believe that there are special two-way places of passage between the Spirit-World and the Now-Worlds, including the Earth. Spirit-World persons may readily travel between these worlds. The Ghost aspect of a Now-World person's Spirit (including that of humans) may also travel between these worlds with the assistance of a Spirit-World person or persons. Humans were taught to try to live their lives in such a manner that they will be aware of the possible interactions between these worlds and their persons.

The tribal peoples were also monotheistic, believing in only one supreme being or god, who was often called "Gitchi Manitou" or "Maec-awaetok," both words meaning Great Spirit.

Great Spirit was thought to be both creator and prime sustainer, female and male, containing the potential for both positive and negative interactions, which are held in universal balance by Great Spirit. This understanding of the concept of god is quite different from that held by much of the dominant society, which normally refers to God as "He." The tribal peoples did not believe in the existence of a supreme evil spirit similar to the Christian concept of the devil prior to the intrusion of the Europeans. Such a belief was introduced into the tribal belief system from the European belief system after contact.

The tribal peoples believed in the existence of many, many lesser spirits who were created by Great Spirit. These lesser spirits were thought of as inherently amoral, but with the potentiality for behavioral manifestations, which may be perceived as being either "evil" or "good." Beings such as a great water "monster;" a cannibalistic, vampiristic, ice and snow "monster;" and many others, were thought to be associated with the manifestation of "evil." Beings such as the "Thunderer Spirits" and the "Guardian Spirits" were thought to be associated with manifestation of "good."

The tribal peoples also believed in the existence of a being who was part "Spirit-Being" and part human, often labeled as a "trickster." This being often was involved in making mischief, doing both good and not so good things as a means of both teaching and testing humans. This being was called by several names, including Waynaboozhoo and Manabus.

SHAMANISM AND SORCERY

It was believed that some humans had a special relationship with the Spirit-World that resulted in their becoming technicians of the connections through which Spirit-World "power" flows from the Spirit-World into the Earth Now-World. These individuals, females as well as males, had the ability to fine-tune these power connections. In the English language, they are called shamans and shamanesses (or sorcerers and sorceresses), and their activity is called shamanism or sorcery. In some of the tribal languages, they were referred to as being either Mide, Wabano, or Jesako practitioners.

OFFERINGS TO THE SPIRIT-WORLD

A mixture of various plant leaves, sometimes including various scrapings from tree and shrub barks, was used as an offering to the Spirit-World and its beings. The mixture was often called *kinnikinnick*, which means "much-mixed." Tobacco was also used and, especially later in history, became an acceptable substitute for other kinnikinnick substances.

Whenever tribal peoples went on a journey, whenever a storm was approaching, or before hunting, fishing, or gathering and harvesting plant products, or when coming upon a place in the natural world that was considered particularly special (such as a waterfall, an unusually shaped tree, a unique-appearing rock), the tribal people would "put down" some kinnikinnick for the spirits that may be present at that time or place. The spirits would be requested to be kind to the humans present who were engaging in the particular activity and to forgive the human intrusion, if it was considered intrusion. If individuals did not have kinnikinnick or tobacco, they "put down" a piece of their hair as an offering.

RELIGIOUS SOCIETIES

Among the ancient religious societies was the Waubanowiwin (also variously spelled Wabenowiwin and Waubunowin, etc.), which in the English language was called the Society of the Dawn, the Morning Star Society, and the Society of the Heavens. Some individuals have also called it the Society of Witches. Others have said that it was associated with and drew its powers from evil forces in the universe.

Another ancient religious society is the Midewiwin (also spelled Midewewin, and alternatively spelled and called Mitiwin by the Menominee), which in the English language was called the Grand Medicine Society, partly because of the society's knowledge and use of plant medicines and because of its emphasis on rituals intended to assist those who were ill. Some of the tribal Elders, upon hearing about and/or observing individuals who appeared to be emotionally troubled, often advised the troubled person "to go sit among the trees. . . because the power of the trees would clear the mind."[1] For a more detailed description of both the Waubanowiwin and the Midewiwin, which also appears to be objective and fair, see Basil Johnston's *Ojibway Ceremonies, Ojibway Heritage*, and/or Edward Benton-Banai's *The Mishomis Book*.

Still another ancient religious society was the Jesakowiwin, whose practitioners made use of a shaking-tent from which advice from the Spirit-World intended for those gathered around the tent was heard.

In approximately 1870, a religious society that originated in the plains area west of the Great Lakes arrived in the Wisconsin region. It is called the Big Drum or Drum Dance Religion, and after a time, elements of it began to mix with elements of the Midewiwin.

In the early 1900's another religion, the Native American Church, which originated in Mexico and in the southwestern United States, was introduced in some tribal areas of the Great Lakes region. Also called the "Peyote Religion" because of its use of the bud of the mescal cactus in its ritual, it never did attract a large number of tribal adherents in the Wisconsin area.

MUSIC AND DANCE

Like religion, and intimately related to it, music and dance were important, integral, and essential elements of everyday life. The tribal peoples believed music and dance to be so important because they readily observed that both are integral components of the natural world. Consequently, music accompanied most tribal activity, and both its rhythm and melody were inspired by the natural world. American Indian music "has endured through the passing of time," despite all the changes that occurred in the American Indian societies as a result of the contact with, intrusion of, and dominance by the European-American peoples, "because it is an extension of [American] Indian people [and is]. . . the means by which [almost] all aspects of history, religion, and culture have been remembered and recorded."[2]

The rhythm is provided primarily by the drums. The drumbeat is thought to represent the combining of four heartbeats: the heartbeat of the drummers, the heartbeats of the drum-Spirit, Earth Mother, and all other life forms in the universe.

The source of the melody is found everywhere in the natural world. At the time of the creation of the Earth, Great Spirit, after creating the winged-ones (the birds), gave them the gift of music to give to and share with all the other created beings on the Earth. That is why we can hear the music in the whisper and the wail of the winds and in so much of the natural world.

When we walk along the lake, river, or stream shore, we can hear the songs of the waters, whose melodies may be smoothly flowing, laughing, or crashing amongst the rocks. When we go among the trees we can hear their songs, too. Each of the created ones has its own unique song. Great Spirit then asked these other created beings to share the gift of music with the humans, who were last to be created. As the humans traveled about the Earth, they learned songs from all the other previously-created beings.[3]

Tribal peoples began to learn and often imitated these natural sounds through various throat and voice sounds called vocables. These vocables were often without specific meaning, except for their imitation of various sounds found in nature. The music often involved a great deal of repetition because this repetition was thought to be effective in attracting and holding the attention of Spirit-World entities.

Many other songs were said to have been inspired by individual dreams or visions. These songs could be obtained from another individual, either as a gift or by purchasing them.

Dances were often imitative of the movements of birds and animals. For example, there is a Deer Dance, a Fish Dance, and an Eagle Dance.

Some dances, such as the Snake Dance, had a great deal of special symbolism. In the performance of the Snake Dance, a number of dancers imitate the actions of a snake crawling along the ground and then shedding its outer-skin as it crawls over a log or other object. The performance of this special dance symbolizes the shedding of one's negative habits and the renewal of one's self in a positive manner. Thus, the Snake Dance symbolized positively-intended rebirth and renewal, which is important for positive growth, just as Medicine Snakes themselves symbolize healing and renewal.

There were other dances that were primarily for competition and were tests of individual dexterity. One of these involves the dancer attempting to pick up a feather from the ground, using only the dancer's teeth, while at the same time the legs are to keep time continually to the beat of the drum. No hands could be used in the process.

In more recent times, dances such as the 49-dance, a dance which honors veterans of military service, and social dances such as a Two-Step, have become popular. Nearly every tribal group has composed a "Flag Song," which has become an American Indian anthem, similar to the national anthem of the dominant society. All present are expected to stand quietly when the Flag Song is played and sung.

TYPES OF DRUMS

Most of the early traditional drums were made from a hollow log or a log that had been hollowed out utilizing a technique called "reduction by fire" involving repetitive burning and scraping.

These drums were normally between fourteen and twenty inches high, but they could be smaller. One or both ends were covered with animal hide drawn tight over the end and secured there, forming the drumhead. Sometimes the drumhead had spiritually-related symbols painted on it.

A special drum of this type was the Water Drum. Water was added to this drum, to varying depths, through a hole in the side. When played, the result was a unique, peculiar sound, which could be heard over a considerable distance.

Another of the early traditional drums was a drum that was made from a circular wooden frame, normally about eighteen inches in diameter and about two and a half inches wide, that was completely covered with thin hide. Often both drumheads were painted with spiritually-related symbols. This drum is commonly called the "tambourine drum" because strung across the interior near each drum head were two parallel cords, to which short sticks were attached, producing a tambourine-like sound when the sticks inside vibrated against the drum heads. Sometimes pebbles were also placed inside, producing a rattling effect. The drummer rested the drum vertically on his or her knee or held it in the crook of his or her arm, striking the drum with the wrapped end of a short drumstick.

The third major drum is the drum called the "Four Winds Drum," the "Dream Drum," or the "Big Drum." Probably derived from the plains tribes in the 1800's, this drum is the largest and most dramatically decorated of the drums. Both top and bottom are covered with stretched drumheads made of hide. The top drumhead was usually painted in a unique manner. One half, colored blue, was always oriented to the north when the drum was used. This blue half symbolized the "cool" and related aspects of the natural duality found in the world. The other half, colored red, symbolized the "warm" and related aspects of natural duality, and was oriented to the south when the drum was used. Across the center, between the blue and the red halves, was a yellow stripe. When the drum was used, this yellow stripe was oriented east-west, symbolizing the sun's path, as well as the positive "Sun Trail" that one must aspire to in life. This drum was usually suspended in crotched stakes when played and normally did not touch the ground during ceremonies. The drum was also often "dressed" with Spirit-World-related designs.

Rattles made of gourds or deer dew claws were also used as musical instruments, as were flutes, which were usually made of cedar. There were, however, special restrictions imposed on the use of flutes.

Individuals were cautioned, lest it be inferred that they were practicing forbidden "love sorcery," as it was believed that often the seductive sounds of the flute might be too irresistible for humans present.

THE POWWOW

Originally, the Powwow was a small, local, clan or village gathering to celebrate special events. It involved music and dance, as well as feasting. In the late nineteenth century, after American Indians were forced to stay on reservations, the Powwow grew in size and gradually became intertribal in scope and participation. It became a social occasion "for renewing old acquaintances," for making new ones, and often, in the mid-twentieth century, for "reaffirming one's Indianness."[4]

DEATH, BURIAL, AND MOURNING

Death, often referred to by tribal peoples as "westing," was *not* thought of as "the end." It was, instead, thought of as a step, phase, or transition in Great Spirit's non-linear space-time continuum.

Death was believed to occur when the life-sustaining Soul left the body and journeyed to the Spirit-World. The Ghost aspect of the Spirit might, or might not, accompany the Soul at that time. It was believed that the Soul journeyed for four days to reach the Spirit-World.

Burial customs varied from tribe to tribe. What is herein described may be generally applicable to many of the tribal groups in the Western Great Lakes area, including Wisconsin.

Upon death, the body would be washed and the hair would be combed and, depending upon custom, sometimes braided. The body would then be dressed in the individual's finest garments.

Sometimes a spot of brown with a horizontal red line running through it would be painted on each side of the face. This symbolized both Earth Mother and the positive Sun Trail. Sometimes grey streaks would be painted on each side of the face as well. These symbolized the fact that the Soul might stop on its journey to the Spirit-World in order to participate, briefly, in the dance of the Spirits at the Northern Lights.

A small amount of kinnikinnick or tobacco would be placed in each fist of the deceased. Sometimes the tobacco would be enclosed in small pouches of hide.

The body would be laid out in the ceremonial lodge on a sheet of birch bark or other mat material if birch bark was not available. The feet of the body would be oriented to the west. If the individual was a member of the Midewiwin, the individual's Medicine Bag would be tucked under the left arm of the body.

The funeral ceremony would be held before four days had passed since the death. At the funeral ceremony, the religious leader conducting the ceremony would offer kinnikinnick or tobacco to Great Spirit and other spirits, following which he or she would speak to the Spirit of the deceased, describing the four day journey to the Spirit-World. The Spirit of the deceased was told that in the Spirit-World he or she would be reunited with previously deceased family and friends. The Spirit would also be told to be sure and stay on the correct Spirit-Trail to the Spirit-World and would be cautioned that he or she would come to a Spirit-River. There he or she would see a log, apparently over which one was expected to cross. The log, however, would begin to quake, not actually being a log, but rather a Water-Spirit. The deceased was instructed to respectfully greet the Water-Spirit and offer some of the spirit of the kinnikinnick or tobacco that had been placed in the fists of the deceased. When that was done, the "log" would cease quaking and the Spirit could cross safely to the Spirit-World.

The religious leader would then conduct a Fly Away ceremony, in which he or she would do a special Eagle Dance while waving some Eagle feathers from the dead body to a western opening in the ceremonial lodge four times. This was done to remind both the Soul and the Ghost aspect of the Spirit that it was time to journey west to the Spirit-World, if they had not already done so.

At the end of the funeral ceremony, the body would be carried by several men through the western opening of the ceremonial lodge. In later times, when ceremonies were held in buildings with windows, the body would be taken through the west window. The body was never taken through the entrance door, as that could result in the Ghost aspect of the Spirit staying around and causing problems.

The body was carried to the "Giving Back Place," the burial grounds or cemetery, where it was given back to Earth Mother from whom it had come. The body, wrapped in birch bark, would be placed into the grave along with some of the individual's favorite possessions, which were first deliberately broken in order to symbolically release their spirit essence. In the grave, the feet of the body would be oriented to the west.

Logs and large stones would be placed over the grave to protect the remains from scavenger animals. Later, when saws and sawed boards became available from the Europeans, little houses of board were constructed over each of the graves. These little houses had a small opening at the west end. Under the opening there was a small ledge upon which bits of food and kinnikinnick (or tobacco) would be placed periodically for potential use by the possibly remaining Ghost portion of the Spirit. The Ghost portion of the Spirit could linger for an indefinite period and could cause many types of mischief or be an annoyance in some other manner.

If it was winter and the ground was frozen, the body would be additionally wrapped in hides and placed on a high scaffold or in a tree.

A grave marker, with the individual's totem symbol carved or painted on it, would be placed next to the grave. Sometimes the symbol was carved in an adjacent tree. The symbol was carved or painted upside down, denoting that the Soul had left and the body was dead.

In some of the tribal groups, members of the Rabbit Clan were not buried in the ground. It was believed that long and severe winters might result if a member of the Rabbit Clan was buried in the ground. Consequently, they were cremated instead.

Periodically, usually in time intervals of four, Ghost Suppers were held in an effort to placate the Ghost portion of the Spirit, which might still be present on the Earth-plane. The ceremony hopefully would convince the Ghost to journey to the Spirit-World and join its previous companion-Soul there. The Ghost Supper ceremony consisted of invited individuals bringing various favorite foods of the deceased to a designated place. There, a small portion of each type of food was placed on a sheet of birch bark, along with a small amount of kinnikinnick (or tobacco). This was placed in the ceremonial fire, where the essence of it would be consumed by the Ghost. Words, spoken politely, would be said to encourage the Ghost to journey to the Spirit-World, if it had not already done so.

A period of mourning was usually observed for one year. Often the mourner's hair would be cut short as a sign of mourning. Individuals in mourning also sometimes painted black circles around each eye with charcoal-based paint. Sometimes pine resin was added to the charcoal, making it much more difficult to ignore the requirements of mourning publicly. Those in mourning were not to touch children, for fear that misfortune would fall upon the children. As this was often very impractical, especially for parents with small children, the custom of utilizing substitute mourners, who were often Elders, was practiced. This use of substitute mourners, however, had to be approved by the Council of Elders first.

At the end of the designated period of mourning, the Council of Elders would meet to determine whether the mourning period had been properly observed by the appropriate people. If the Elders determined that the mourning period had been observed properly, a special ceremony was held officially releasing close relatives, especially a spouse, from required mourning. If the Council of Elders decided that the mourners, especially the spouse, had not been sincere with the mourning, they would direct the mourners to mourn for another year, after which time they would be judged again.

In some of the tribal groups, a special ceremony called the Feast of the Dead was held, usually at four year intervals. This ceremony consisted of disinterring all the remains of the dead who had not been placed in the proper community "Giving Back Place" since the time when the last Feast of the Dead had been held. The remains of those who might have been placed on a scaffold, in a tree, or buried far from the community because death had occurred while traveling far from the home area, were taken to a designated location where a ceremony honoring their Spirits was held. A Ghost Supper was often held as part of the Feast of the Dead ceremony. At the end of the ceremony, the remains were buried together in one large grave.

NOTES

1. Shelley Oxley and Ernie St. Germaine, "Religions of the Ojibway: The Midewiwin," *Wisconsin Woodland Indian Project Curriculum* (Rhinelander, Wisconsin: Wisconsin Department of Public Instruction and the Great Lakes Inter-Tribal Council in the Rhinelander Wisconsin School District, 1982), 29.

2. Shelley Oxley and Ernie St. Germaine, "Music of the Woodland Indians," *Wisconsin Woodland Indian Project Curriculum* (Rhinelander, Wisconsin: Wisconsin Department of Public Instruction and the Great Lakes Inter-Tribal Council in the Rhinelander, Wisconsin School District, 1982), 3.

3. Ibid., 4.

4. Thomas Vennum, Jr., *Ojibway Music from Minnesota: Continuity and Change* (Minnesota Historical Society Press, 1989), 4.

CHAPTER THIRTEEN
FOOD ACQUISITION
AND PREPARATION

The tribal peoples had many rules that governed food acquisition; however, one rule overrode all the others. This overriding rule stated that humans were allowed to take plant and animal people only when they really needed to take them, keeping in mind that to want and to need where not the same thing!

With this rule in mind, food acquisition activities primarily consisted of fishing, hunting, and some trapping, supplemented by the periodic gathering of plant products such as Wild Rice, maple sap, and various plant parts, including roots. Some tribal groups also engaged in some sustained agriculture, the extent of which was limited by geography and climate.

Generally, prior to the intrusion and settlement of the Europeans, tribal peoples did not domesticate and raise animals. Some tribal peoples never did engage in this practice, even after such practices were introduced from Europe.

Regarding the "domestication" of the dog, traditional legend relates that it was the dog that chose to stay with the humans, rather than the humans who domesticated the dog. Accounts written by Europeans and European-Americans relating to sacrifice and eating of dogs are, according to my Elders, exaggerated and overgeneralized. On those rare occasions that it did occur, it was an act of sacrifice quite similar to some of the acts reported in the Old Testament of the Bible wherein sacrifices to the deity were made from among those things that were most cherished.

It should be noted that all created forms were thought of as being "persons" having Spirits composed of a life-sustaining Soul and a Ghost. All created forms, consequently, were thought to have inherent rights similar to those of human persons. Humans were *not* thought of as superior, but rather only as different. As a result, there were very special rules with regard to humans taking and using all other created forms.

SPECIAL RULES REGARDING HUMANS TAKING AND USING OTHER CREATED FORMS

An overriding rule stated that humans could only take other created forms only when there was a *real need*. It was important to know and remember that to need is not the same thing as to want.

When a human believes that there is a real need to take another created form, the human is obligated to make a brief ceremonial offering of kinnikinnick or tobacco to Great Spirit and to the Spirit-Master of that particular life form prior to taking. In addition, the human is obligated to be sure that all that is taken is used; no waste is allowed. Furthermore, humans must never take all of the members of a particular created form in an area. Regarding those created forms from whom only a particular part is needed, humans may take only those parts.

In the case of plants, if the plant reproduces by seed, the human must leave a sufficient quantity of the seed-producing part of the plant. If the seed is ripe, the human is obligated to scatter or plant some of the seeds. If the plant reproduces by root, the human must leave enough root to ensure future growth. If the human is not sure how the plant reproduces, the human is obligated to leave enough of the seed (or seed-producing part) and root.

In the case of animals, including birds and fish, the human may not take the female of the species in times of presumed pregnancy. Humans also may not take females who are still caring for their young. The very young, such as fawns and cubs, are also not to be taken or killed. In addition, females in general are to be spared if there are males available; one male can impregnate many females.

As a general rule, one did not hunt and take one's clan totem-symbol animal.

Meat, taken under proper and acceptable conditions, was either used at the time the animal was killed, or was smoked or dried and kept for future use. Illustrative of the practice of processing food for future use is the making and use of pemmican, a type of food prepared from dried strips of meat, which are pounded into a paste and then mixed with fat. Sometimes bone marrow is added as well. Often the mixture contains crushed berries or cherries. The mixture is then either pressed into small cakes or stuffed into sections of intestine much like present-day sausage. In the case of the latter, the ends are made airtight with melted tallow, resulting in a sausage-like pemmican that was known to keep for years and was a favorite traveling food.

Parts of animals, taken under proper and acceptable conditions, were also used as follows: Hides, either with or without the hair, were used for clothing and robes. Hair was used for stuffing cushions and mattresses, as well as game balls. Large bones were used for farming tools. Ribs were used for making arrow-straighteners. Very large ribs were used to make snow sled runners. Ends of small bones were chewed on, after which they were used for paint brushes. Hooves were used for rattles or made into glue. Horns were used for making some arrow-heads, as well as being used in making some aphrodisiacs. Sinew was used to make thread and to make bow strings. Sinew was also wrapped tightly around mid-sections of bows to increase their springiness. Teeth were used in necklaces. Gallstones were used to make a yellow paint. Tallow, rendered from fat, was mixed with wood ashes to make a soap. Porcupine quills were used for special artwork that was common prior to the introduction of glass beads from Europe.

Fish, when proper and acceptable conditions were met, were either hooked with bone hooks using sinew or plant-fiber lines, netted, or caught through the ice in winter. Some were speared when there was a real need. Night fishing, utilizing torches whose light attracted the fish, was also common.

Fish were used immediately, or either dried or smoked and stored for future use. Fish bones were used for needles. Non-edible parts of the fish were used for plant fertilizer.

Some animals were taboo; they were not to be taken or killed under any circumstances. The taboos were quite consistently observed prior to the escalation of the European-introduced fur trade.

Taboo animals included the eagle, who is symbolic of the Thunderer Spirit. In addition, the eagle travels each day over the land, from east to west, and reports to Great Spirit as to whether or not there are any human groups worthy of being spared from total divine destruction.

The Hawk was also generally taboo because of its relationship to the eagle.

The beaver, which during the European fur trade period was highly coveted, was traditionally taboo because it was thought to be far too intelligent and beneficial, as it made houses and dams.

The otter was taboo because it played a very important role in the initial development of the Midewiwin.

The owl was taboo because it was considered to be a special Guardian of Souls that had become lost on their way to the Spirit-World. In addition, owl was said to be both a bringer of medicine and a messenger of the Death-Spirit. It was owl who is believed to have brought special "Hunting Medicine" to the Menominee and some other tribal groups.

Feathers from taboo birds were used for ceremonial purposes, including on ceremonial headdresses; however, they were not to be killed for their feathers. Rather, selected individuals would watch these taboo birds almost constantly, and after a bird died of natural causes, some feathers would then be taken.

LIMITED AGRICULTURE

The limited agriculture that took place in areas where geography and climate permitted involved a technique called "companion planting." This technique took into account the natural growing patterns of plant species which were thought to act as "companions" to other species. It involved planting various types of plants together in the same area rather than separating each species in different fields, as is the case in contemporary agriculture. Companion planting helped plants resist disease and repel insects, since some plants are immune to the diseases of others while still others issue odors that repel some insects and pests. Companion planting also promoted a natural form of soil conservation because some plants return certain nutrients to the soil that other plants deplete.

The plants that were cultivated prior to the intrusion of the Europeans were corn, beans, squash, and pumpkins.

Corn, which is indigenous to Central America, was brought north and passed from tribal nation to tribal nation. It was cultivated in gardens by Wisconsin American Indians wherever geography and climate allowed. Fresh ears of corn were roasted in husks and eaten. Sometimes the husks were pulled back, exposing the corn kernels, after which the ears of corn were dried by hanging the husks from a drying rack or from the ceiling of a lodge. In addition, corn was cut before it was fully ripe. It was then shelled and the corn kernels were spread on mats or sheets of birch bark to dry. Later, these dried kernels were boiled and seasoned with maple syrup. Corn was also parched in hot kettles, causing some of the kernels to pop open, after which they were eaten like popcorn. Those kernels that did not pop open, but rather simply dried, were later put into a hide bag and laid on a flat stone. The bag containing the dried kernels was then pounded with another stone until the corn kernels inside became corn meal.

The corn meal was later used to make corn bread or was used to make a corn soup containing deer meat or fat. Kernels of corn that were not fully ripe were also removed from the corn cob and ground to a paste between two stones. The resulting substance was then divided into small cakes, which were individually tightly wrapped in green corn leaves. These were then covered with moist earth and baked in hot coals for about an hour. The charred leaf coverings were then removed, the baked cakes taken out, and the cakes were either eaten with bear fat or sunflower oil, or they were dried and stored for winter use when they were either boiled with meat or steamed and eaten. Corn was also made into hominy by boiling the corn kernels in a lye solution made from hardwood ashes. After boiling in the lye solution, the corn was rinsed in clear water and then boiled a second time in clean, clear water. Meat or animal fat was added for seasoning and sometimes beans were also boiled with the corn.[1]

Succotash was made by putting the kernels from several ears of corn that were not fully ripe into a kettle with partially cooked beans and meat. This was covered with water and cooked together until all the contents was tender. The succotash was then thickened with corn meal or sunflower meal and seasoned to taste.[2]

Corn cobs were dried and used as an alternate fuel. Dried corn cobs, with the husks still on, were sometimes used to make dolls.

SUGARBUSHING

An area where maple trees were abundant was referred to as a "sugarbush," and in regions where maples were plentiful, maple sap was an important staple food.

As in the case with all major tribal activities, including food acquisition, a ceremonial offering must be made prior to beginning the "sugarbushing" process. Kinnikinnick or tobacco is offered to Great Spirit and the maple's Spirit-Master at that time.

Just before the sap begins to run, usually sometime in March, some members of all of the extended families would go into their designated area of the maple forest to prepare the area for the "sugarbushing" activities, including making necessary repairs on the "sugarbushing" lodges or possibly constructing new ones. Some of the lodges were for members of the extended family to live in during the "sugarbushing" process. Other lodges were for storing necessary equipment, while some of the larger ones were for doing certain "sugarbushing" activities during inclement weather.

After the sugarbush area preparation was completed, more members of each extended family would go to their designated areas to begin the process of "tapping" the maple trees. The trees would be "tapped" by making a small horizontal gash in the tree, approximately three to four feet from the ground. A spout, often made of cedar, would then be inserted in the gash at an angle so that one end pointed down toward the base of the tree. A container, often made of birch bark and called a "makuk," would be placed under each "tapped" tree and positioned in such a way that the sap would drip into the container as it oozed from the tree and through the spout.

Family members kept a close watch on the containers. Before they reached the point where they would overflow or spill when lifted, they were emptied into carrying-buckets. Two of these buckets would be carried at a time, sometimes utilizing a neck-shoulder yoke, to a central working area. There the sap was poured into cookers, which were often made of pottery prior to the European introduction of metal containers. The sap would then be boiled until it began to thicken to the point where it extended in strings from a stirring paddle.

The thickened, hot sap was then strained. Prior to the European introduction of cloth, the straining was done through basswood fiber mats. After the sap was strained it was poured into rectangularly shaped wooden troughs. Once in the troughs, the thickened, strained sap was "worked" with wooden paddles as it cooled. As it cooled while being "worked," the sap began to granulate. The granules were then pulverized and the sugar stored in makuks until needed.

Sometimes the still warm, thick, almost-granulated sap was packed into small molds forming little maple sugar cakes, which could be eaten like candy. The author recalls an older American Indian woman who usually had several maple sugar cake "candies" in her apron or dress pockets.

Maple sugar was used as seasoning on fruits, vegetables, cereals, meat, and even fish. It was also added to herbal medicines to make them taste better, especially when those medicines were given to children and the elderly. Maple sugar was sometimes added to water, in small quantities, making a pleasant-tasting, refreshing beverage.

While at the "sugarbush" camp, it was a time for renewing old acquaintances, cementing alliances, and engaging in generally pleasant social activities. Almost everyone engaged in drumming, singing, and dancing, especially in the evenings around the camp fire and when the actual "sugarbushing" activities did not require everyone's time.

WILD RICING

Wild Rice, a type of cereal grass that grows in shallow lakes and streams, was also an important food staple. The rice plants need calm, slow-moving water and a lake or stream bed with sufficient nutrients for the plant to grow and sustain itself.

Since the rice ripens in late summer, selected women would go into the ricing areas in early August to do whatever light maintenance was necessary on the lodges and on the ricing mats. If unusually heavy work was required, young men would accompany the women to assist with the tasks.

Great care was taken to make sure that the Wild Rice crop was not harvested until the clan or tribal council officially authorized the harvest. Tribal guards were posted near the rice areas of the lakes and streams. Often an elderly woman was the individual who kept track of the crop growth and maturation, and it was she who advised the council as to when the rice was ready. Sometimes several elderly women had this responsibility, and they also determined which specific lake or stream areas individual families could harvest. The clan or tribal council usually supported the decisions of these Elders.

As was the case with "sugarbushing," each extended family had its own designated ricing area. Also, as is the case with "sugarbushing" and other food acquisition activities, a ceremonial offering of kinni-kinnick or tobacco is made to Great Spirit and the Spirit-Master of the Wild Rice prior to beginning the "wild ricing" process. An offering was also made to the Spirits of the waters in which the rice grew.

As was also the case with the "sugarbush" camp, the Wild Rice camp was a place for renewing old acquaintances, cementing alliances, and engaging in pleasant social activities, including drumming, singing, and dancing.

Before the rice ripened, representatives of the extended families went to their designated areas and tied special markers on a number of rice stalks, indicating that those areas were theirs. The stalks of rice were sometimes also tied into sheaves which looked like curved "pig tails" or "shepherds crooks."

To tie rice stalks into sheaves, two individuals would get into a canoe and move in rows through the rice. One poled the canoe through the shallow water where the rice grew while the other tied the sheaves. The purpose for tying the rice was to keep large quantities from falling into the water as it ripened, especially as a result of birds landing on it—although each family group was also responsible for making sure that sufficient rice fell into the water so that the rice might reproduce, insuring that there would be rice for other years and other generations. Families also made sure that the ducks and birds got their fair share. Ducks and birds, through eating and excreting some of the ripe rice kernels, "planted" the rice as well. Poling the canoe was usually done with a crotched sapling between ten and sixteen feet long. The bottom stalk of the rice near the root was grabbed with the crotched end. By twisting the pole, the canoe would be propelled slowly through the water amongst the stalks of rice. Sometimes elders sat in front doing the tying while a younger person poled the canoe through the rice.

When the rice grains were no longer milky when broken open and had begun to harden, the rice was ripe. After ceremonially requesting that Great Spirit and the other relevant spirits grant assistance with the harvesting process, particularly by allowing at least four consecutive days without rain, the harvest began. At that same time, almost the entire area was alive with ducks and birds who were beginning their own harvest.

The harvesting process required teamwork. One person slowly poled the canoe through the rice beds. The other person did the actual harvesting. If the rice had been previously tied, it was first untied and the rice knocked into the canoe with a short "knocking stick." If it had not been tied, the canoe was poled by one person while the other alternated knocking the rice into the canoe, first from the left, then from the right, and then back again. At this time, family groups were again responsible for being sure that enough rice landed in the water so that the rice might reproduce, as well as to ensure that the ducks and birds had their fair share. It was important that the poling was neither too fast nor too slow so that the maximum amount of rice could be harvested by the person doing the knocking.

After the canoe was reasonably filled, it was returned to shore where the rice was put into containers and carried to the processing area. Sometimes a number of men picked up the full canoe and carried it. At the processing area, a small amount was cooked the first night and ritually offered to the spirits.

The harvested rice, still in its hull or husk, was spread out onto mats, after which extraneous materials such as twigs, pieces of stalk, worms and other insects were removed by hand. Usually all the family members except for the very small children and the very elderly participated in this process. The rice was allowed to sun-dry for a time on the mats and was periodically moved about so that all sides would dry.

Small amounts of rice with the hull intact were then put into medium-sized fire-proof containers. In pre-European times, the containers were made of either pottery or copper. Iron kettles were used after European. The container was tilted over a small, hot fire and stirred constantly so that the rice became parched, not scorched or burned. This process further helped dry the hull still encasing each rice grain, making it brittle. It also removed moisture from the rice grains themselves, thereby curing the rice.

The rice was then ready for the "pounding" process. Not all groups included this step, preferring to go directly to the threshing process instead. The pounding process involved pounding small amounts of rice with a wooden mall to loosen the hull so that it separated from the rice grain. The individual doing the pounding had to be extremely careful that she or he did not smash the rice kernels in the process.

Threshing, often called "dancing the rice," was a more commonly practiced step to separate the rice kernels from the hull. Some tribal groups included both the "pounding" process and "dancing the rice."

The threshing process consisted of first digging a hole in the ground to a depth of approximately one foot. The hole normally was between two and three feet across. A clean animal hide was then put into the hole to function as a liner. A small amount of dried rice was then put into the hole on top of the hide lining. An individual wearing special clean, dry moccasins containing cuffs reaching above the ankles then "danced" upon the rice while leaning on a stout pole for support and balance, often to the accompaniment of a drum and special rice-dancing songs. This music focused on light, "jumpy" melodies in an effort to keep the dancer light on his or her toes so that the rice kernels were not crushed. This process was repeated until all the rice had been threshed.

Later, with the European introduction of wooden tubs, tubs placed on the ground were used, substituting for the holes in the ground.

The next step consisted of the winnowing process. An amount of rice was placed in a large, shallow birch bark tray and then the rice was tossed approximately six to eight inches into the air, the rice kernels falling back into the winnowing tray while the air current created by moving the tray up and down causes the lighter hull material to blow away. Winnowing was especially effective on windy days, the wind accelerating the process. Experienced winnowers were able to process two to four pounds at a time without losing any rice kernels from the tray. The winnowed rice kernels were then stored in makuks (birch bark containers).

Sometimes when a family knew that they would be returning to a rice-processing area later, they buried a canoe filled with processed rice on a sunny slope of a hill (if there was one). Most rain and melted snow would run off, keeping the buried rice relatively dry. Rice cached in this way would keep as long as two years without spoiling.

Wild Rice was boiled and eaten with corn, beans, and squash. Meat was often added, and sometimes maple sugar was added for special flavor. Babies were often weaned on a mixture of soft Wild Rice and other food staples.

NOTES

1. "Corn: The Gift of the American Indian People," *Wisconsin Woodland Indian Project Curriculum* (Rhinelander: Wisconsin Department of Public Instruction and the Great Lakes Inter-Tribal Council, 1982), 25.
2. Ibid., 25, 32.

CHAPTER FOURTEEN
CLOTHING AND
BODY PAINTING

Traditionally, clothing was either functional or ceremonial, and considerations of style were not particularly important. People generally put more articles of clothing on as the temperature became colder and, conversely, took more off as the temperature became warmer.

Where practical, near nudity or complete nudity was allowed, depending on the circumstances. It was not considered to be a crime or a religious offense.

The average clothing for males consisted of a breechcloth (breechclout, loin cloth), the purpose of which was to protect the genital area, especially when one was in brush, thorns, or the like. When one was in brambles and thorny areas, such as when picking raspberries or blackberries, as well as in very cold weather, one wore hide leggings. Animal hide robes were also used. Moccasins were worn on the feet.

The average clothing for females consisted of a sleeveless garment, sewn together at the shoulders and with a opening for the head. Its general purpose was to protect the body, especially when working around fire and cooking. Females also wore leggings, robes, and moccasins, the functions of which were the same as for the males.

In cold weather and when one's head needed protection, an animal fur was wrapped around the head and then sewn, fitting like a fur turban.

CEREMONIAL HEADDRESS FOR MALES

The traditional ceremonial headdress in most of Wisconsin and adjacent areas was the "roach." Usually made of deer and porcupine hair, it was held by a bone or wooden roach-spreader, which produced a "brushed-up" effect across and down the center of the head, from the forehead to the back of the neck. Sometimes parts of the roach were dyed red. Sometimes a single eagle feather swiveled in a bone socket at the center of the roach-spreader.

The feathered war bonnet, seen so often in "Cowboy and Indian" movies, was *not* indigenous to the Western Great Lakes area. It was, instead, introduced into this area from the western plains of the United States during the early 1900's, arriving in this area with Buffalo Bill's Wild West Show and other western shows, which were then popular in European-American communities.

HIDE PREPARATION AND TANNING

Large animals, like deer, generally provided all the necessary ingredients for the preparing and tanning of the hides. Antlers and larger bones made useful flesh and hide scrapers, while small bones could be used to make hide needles. Thread could be made from sinew. The animal brain was used to soften and cure the hide.

Techniques used for tanning varied according to individual and clan custom; however, in most cases, the process was quite similar to the one described below, with variations.

Fresh, "green" animal skins were preferred, although dried or salted skins could be used. Salting a hide in order to preserve it over a period of time was, generally speaking, a post-European intrusion practice.

Summer hides were easier to tan than fall or winter hides, which were thicker. Summer hides, although they were thinner, were considered to be tougher than winter hides. As a result, summer hides were preferred for making clothing. Hides from younger animals were easier to work with than those from older animals.

The first step in the hide preparation process, after removing it from the animal, was to wash the blood and dirt from the skin. Once wet the hide became heavier and more difficult to handle.

Next, the skin was soaked in water for several days, with periodic rinsing recommended. One the skin had been soaked and rinsed for a sufficient period of time, the hide began to expand and the animal hair began to "slip," making it relatively easy to remove. The hair's readiness was tested by pulling sharply on a few hairs. One tested the hide in several places, noting that the hair in the shoulder area was often particularly tenacious. If the hide was ready, the hairs would come out fairly easily when pulled sharply. If the hair fell out, on the other hand, one could assume that the skin was rotten. Some tribal people hurried the "slipping" by spreading wood ash on the hair side of the skin. When water was added to that side, the lye in the ash leached out, accelerating the "slipping" of the hair. One was cautioned, however, that the lye in ashes could discolor the hide.

Individuals had to be keenly aware that no matter which preparation and tanning method was being used, one had to be ready to work the hide when the skin was ready and not necessarily when the individual was ready! Most of the tanning processes were preferably done in the shade or on cool days.

The next step in the process, "fleshing the hide," took up to two or three hours to complete. For this process, the hide was draped over a log while all the flesh and fatty tissue was removed using a "flesher" instrument. The "flesher," usually made of bone with a slanted scraping edge, was held with the scraping edge against the hide. Small bits of flesh and fatty tissue were removed a little at a time, with care being taken not to cut into the skin itself. When all of the flesh and fat had been removed properly, the skin had a non-greasy, whitish surface. It was particularly important to be sure that all the fat had been removed because otherwise it would be absorbed into the hide later as it dried, making it hard and unmanageable. In warm weather especially, this had to be watched for since then the hide absorbed fatty portions rapidly. If the hide started to appear yellowish-tan in color, it was dampened with water.

After "fleshing," the hide was washed again in fresh water in order to be sure that any clinging particles of flesh or fatty tissue had been removed. If not, they were carefully removed and the hide was washed again.

The hair on the hide was then ready to be removed, a process that could take from two to five hours.

The hide was draped, hair side up, over a six to eight foot-long log (sometimes called a "beaming" log), which was set into the ground at one end and angled upward at an approximately forty-five degree, "belly-high" angle. Wooden supports held the higher end of the log in place. The entire apparatus had to be sturdy so that it did not move during the hair removal process. The log had to be carefully inspected prior to selection to be sure that it did not have pits or projections that would catch on the skin or cause the hair removal tool to dig into the hide. The tool used for removing hair was similar to the "fleshing" tool.

The individual removing the hair from the hide leaned over the belly-high projecting end of the beaming log, gripped the hair removal tool in both hands, and with the scraping edge tilted, began making long, downward strokes away from the belly end, thereby removing the hair. The hide, which was repositioned several times on the log as the process continued, also stretched some during this process. Some individuals took care to wear protective clothing during this process, as it could be dirty and odor producing. At one time, the hair from this process was sometimes used to stuff mattresses and other items.

When all the hair was removed, the hide was again washed thoroughly, after which it was wrapped around a small tree with a small, stout stick tied to the overlapping ends. This stick was then turned, causing the water to be wrung from the hide as it tightened against the tree. This wringing process was repeated several times so that the hide was completely wrung of excess water. The hide then appeared to have a bluish-white color.

The next step was called "braining," and involved first simmering the brain material in a container with enough water to cover it. This was simmered until the solution was gray-white in color, usually about fifteen to twenty minutes. The mixture was then mashed and simmered for a while longer, after which the mixture was allowed to cool to the point where it wouldn't burn one's hands when handled. When cool enough, the mixture was gradually worked with one's hands into the entire hide using a kneading motion. After that, a container large enough to hold the entire hide was filled with the brain-mixture and water. The hide was then left to soak in that mixture overnight. Sometimes, depending on the individual hide, two braining procedures were necessary.

After soaking in the brain mixture overnight, the hide was wrung again, after which it was attached to a stretching frame for the next step. This frame consisted of four poles, approximately eight feet long and four inches in diameter, two of which were set quite firmly into the ground about six feet apart. It was important that these two poles were firmly in the ground so that the pressure of working on the hide during the stretching process did not dislodge them. The other two poles were attached horizontally to the vertical ones, one at the top and the other some distance above the ground (often at knee-level); the exact distance was determined by the width of the hide to be held within the frame. The rectangular opening created within the poles was made somewhat larger than the estimated final size of the finished hide.

The hide was then secured all around its outer edge with cords that were then attached to the stretching frame so that the hide hung in the middle. Using a stretching tool, somewhat resembling a blunt end axe handle, and being careful that the tool was not sharp enough to tear the hide, one pushed against the hide over and over again. The object was to attain a hide which, as it stretched, appeared to have a uniform thickness.

Periodically checking both sides of the hide, while also re-tying the cords to keep the hide tight as it stretches from the pressure of being worked with the stretching tool, the process was continued. Long, arc-like, sweeping strokes, utilizing both pressure and some speed, were quite efficient. As this process was quite exerting, it was best to do it under shade, and if possible, on a day that was not too dry and windy, since then the hide would dry too fast. Because one's arms would tire quickly from this process, experienced individuals recommended that two individuals work as a team, taking turns with the stretching movements.

The goal of this entire stretching process was a soft, pliable, whitish, dry hide. This may have taken anywhere from two hours to almost an entire day. If it was one's intention for the final product to remain white in color, the tanning process ended here.

If, on the other hand, a color was desired, the hide was smoked for a period of between ten minutes and four hours. In addition to coloring the hide, smoking helped the hide return to a more flexible state later when it got wet. Smoking the hide also helped to repel many insect species.

For the smoking process, the hide was secured around a cone-shaped frame which was placed over a fire contained within a pit of hot coals. Smoke, not flame, was what one needed. Through an opening at the bottom, various fuels were added, with great attention paid so that the flame didn't become too high and burn the hide. The hide was periodically adjusted so that it smoked evenly on both sides.

The color produced depended upon the type of fuel used and the length of time allowed for the smoking. Some experienced tanners recommended rotted hemlock or sumac.

When the smoking had achieved the desired effect, the hide was taken down, rolled up, and laid aside to give the color time "to set." After that, it was hung outside in the weather for a few days to help rid it of some of the unpleasant odor. Caution had to be taken to hang it high enough so that the dogs wouldn't get at it.

BODY PAINTING AND TATTOOS

Sometimes parts of the face and upper torso would be painted for purposes of camouflage in a manner similar to that now practiced by some bow-hunters. Paint would also be applied to the face to represent the omnipresent duality found in the natural world. This often involved painting one side of the face one color and the other side another color.

Permanent tattoos were sometimes applied by perforating the skin in such a manner as to obtain a desired design. The design was then traced over with a mixture of powdered charcoal and a plant dye.

CHAPTER FIFTEEN
HOUSING, TRANSPORTATION, WEAPONS, AND TOOLS

HOUSING

For traditional tribal people, the "house" and "home" were **not** the same thing.

The house, also often referred to as the "lodge" or "wigwam," was one's everyday dwelling place, which besides providing shelter and a place to rest and sleep, was a place to keep one's personal and family belongings. The house was located in the "home." The "home" was the geographical territory to which one felt one belonged.

The wigwam, made from abundant and renewable resources, was a sensible and environmentally sound structure. Of varying sizes, it was usually round and dome shaped; however, some were rectangular and elongated. The word "wigwam" comes from the Algonquian-derived word *wigwass*, which means "birch bark" in some of the tribal languages.

The average wigwam was made by first gathering approximately one dozen straight, sturdy, small trees approximately sixteen feet in length. Tamarack, ironwood, or maple were preferred, in that order of preference. If none of those were available, other trees would be substituted, provided that they were straight. The gathered trees became the main frame poles for the structure. Six to eight additional trees, more slender but approximately the same length, were also gathered for use as the material for the side frame. The actual number of trees gathered depended on the desired size of the finished wigwam.

Strips of basswood tree bark, with the inner layer intact, were gathered for tying the poles together when building the frame. The basswood strips were soaked in water for some time, preferably overnight, after which the soft and pliable wood was separated into thinner, ribbon-like strips measuring approximately one-half inch in width. The strips of basswood remained immersed in water to keep them pliable until needed.

The main poles were sharpened on one end and then placed securely into the ground, in either a circular or rectangular shape, to a depth of approximately ten inches. The poles were not planted into the ground vertically, but rather were put in on an angle so that they slanted slightly outward at the top.

The top part of the wigwam's main poles were then bent inward two at a time and tied together with the strips of basswood bark that had been soaking in water. These strips would be used while they were still wet. The basswood strips contracted as they dried, forming a tight binding that made the joints very strong and sturdy. Each of the poles was thus tied, two together, forming a dome-shaped or rectangularly-shaped oblong frame.

Next, the slender side frame poles were tied securely to the main poles on the inside of the frame, spacing them so that room was left for the door. One started approximately sixteen to twenty-four inches from the ground and secured these smaller poles horizontally, conforming to the shape of the frame. Each junction of main and side pole also became very strong as the basswood strips dry. The next horizontal row of side poles was secured in the same manner, usually about two feet above the first ring of horizontal poles. This process continued until the last row of the frame was secured toward the top. The number of rows and the amount of space between them depended upon the desired finished height of the wigwam.

The builder was then ready to attach the siding of bark, reed mats, or hides. Usually birch, basswood, black ash, or elm bark were used for siding material. Birch bark was preferred, if available, because it was easier to work with.

Birch bark was removed in sheets from the tree by cutting into the outer bark vertically and horizontally, with great care being taken not to cut too deeply so as to damage the inner layer and risk the life of the tree. A birch tree whose bark had been correctly removed would normally grow another covering, albeit not the same as the whitish paper-like-appearing bark removed. When the proper cuts had been made both vertically and horizontally, a stick the length of the vertical cut was inserted under that cut, and the sheet of bark would be literally rolled off the tree. This bark had to either be used immediately or kept moist until it was used, otherwise it would dry out and curl excessively, or possibly even crack.

Other barks were removed in a similar manner; however, much deeper cuts had to be made with stronger, sharper cutting instruments, and because these barks were bulkier, they were more difficult to remove and handle. Often these heavier barks had to be laid on the ground, outer bark upward, and then covered with large stones or logs to flatten them before use. Since, unlike the birch tree, these trees do not grow a replacement bark, they eventually died, and their wood was used for other purposes, including fire wood.

Bark siding was attached to the wigwam in sheets, starting at the bottom of the structure. With thin barks, such as birch bark, perforations were made through which basswood strips were strung to secure the bark to the frame at each frame pole junction. Thicker barks were similarly secured; however, this again was more difficult.

Regardless of the type of covering one used, one started at the ground and worked upward so that a shingle effect was created, thereby allowing rain and melting snow to run off the outside of the structure while the inside remained dry.

A heavy hide was secured over the door frame area, serving as the door.

Inside the finished wigwam was a central fireplace. Along the sides were sleeping platforms, which utilized rope "springs" for comfort.

Wigwam frames were often left at the sugarbush camps and the ricing camps, as well as at the main summer and winter villages. Sometimes additional frames were constructed and left at places between these main sites. Sometimes spring and summer dwellings near river banks were built on scaffolds to prevent flood waters from entering the dwelling.

Other types of lodges, not necessarily built for long-term habitation, were lodges used for religious and ceremonial purposes, sweat lodges, and the menstrual lodges (sometimes called the "Moon-Hut").

Temporary A-frame shelters, as well as *plains-type* tipis, were also utilized when needed.

TRAVEL AND TRANSPORTATION

Prior to European intrusion, and for many years thereafter, the most common form of travel in the Western Great Lakes area was by foot. The second most common form of travel was by birch bark canoe. A second type of canoe, the "dug-out," made by hollowing out a very large log through a process of repeated burning and scraping, was far less common and considerably more difficult to maneuver. On the other hand, in areas where birch bark was not available, dug-outs were often necessary for water transportation. The burning and scraping technique was referred to as "reduction-by-fire." Horses were rarely used in this area, as they simply were not efficient in the brush and forests.

THE BIRCH BARK CANOE

The birch bark canoe common to the Western Great Lakes tribal area, largely because of its fine design and workmanship, was the stereotype of the "Indian canoe." The French and later intrusive Europeans quickly copied this design, enlarging upon it and adapting it for the famous "Voyageur" canoes of the fur trade.

The average birch bark canoe was twelve to fourteen feet long; however, some were as large as twenty feet in length.

Birch bark canoes had many advantages. Among the foremost of these was the fact that they were relatively fast, capable of covering from fifty to eighty miles a day. This made them particularly valuable during the time of the fur trade. In addition, they could be relatively easily portaged (carried from one river or stream to another) because of their light weight.

Birch bark canoes were also relatively strong and stable because of their design, capable of holding at least three adults and their supplies. They were also relatively safe in rough water because they would not capsize easily since the principle power source, the paddler, also steered. Consequently, they could shoot rapids. In addition, because they displaced only a few inches of water, they were quite buoyant, a distinct advantage in shallow waters.

Because they were made of materials that were relatively accessible in the immediate environment, repairs were not unreasonably difficult.

The frame of the birch bark canoe was made from white cedar, while the canoe covering was birch bark. Spruce or Jack pine roots were used for securing the covering and tying the frame together. Pine pitch, sometimes mixed with charcoal, was used for sealing seams.

There were some disadvantages involving the birch bark canoe, however. These included the fact that the pitch sealing material became brittle, making it necessary to check the seal daily, and if necessary, to replace portions that need replacing.

In addition, the canoe's lightness and buoyancy, which were normally a distinct advantage, became a disadvantage in very high winds and extensive rapids. Consequently, extreme caution was required lest one either capsize or damage the canoe under those conditions.

WINTER TRANSPORTATION

Snow shoes, of which there were two principle types, were extensively used for transportation in winter. One type of shoe, often referred to as having a Catfish design because of its oblong shape and pointed-toe, was best for use in open country where the snow was crusted by the cold and the winds. The other type, known as a Bear Paw shoe because of its oval design, worked best where snow was deep, as well as in heavy bush where the snow was seldom crusted.

The frames of both types were preferably made of ash wood, which is very strong, yet light weight. Birch or willow was sometimes substituted when ash wood was unavailable.

"Green" (freshly cut) wood, which could be bent, but which dried hard and strong, was best. Sometimes the wood was steamed first and then bent and tied to hold its shape until it dried.

Caribou or beaver rawhide was best for the netting because they did not stretch when they got wet. Deer or moose rawhide may have be substituted.

Sinew or plant fiber twine was used for the finer netting and for fastening the entire netting to the frame. These materials could withstand the twisting action that occurred at the joints of the netting when the snow shoes were in use.

The tribal peoples in this area also made and used toboggans, as well as sleds, which were often pulled by humans or dogs.

WOOD CRAFTS, BASKETRY, TOOLS, AND WEAPONS

Bowls, trays, plates and spoons were all made from wood by the process of carving or by utilizing the "reduction-by-fire" technique. Some items were made by using a combination of the two techniques.

Intricately designed baskets were made from strips from the log of the black ash tree. Other containers were made from birch bark.

The typical bow was the flat-bow, which was approximately four feet long and two inches wide at the center and tapering and becoming narrower in width at each end. The bow was made preferably of well-seasoned (for at least a year) hickory wood. Elm, hemlock, or white oak were substituted when hickory wood was unavailable. Sometimes the bows were wrapped with sinew to increase their springiness. Bow-strings were made of sinew or plant fibers. Sometimes they were made from the skin off the neck of snapping turtles.

Arrow shafts were usually made from cedar or pine. They were fletched with hawk or turkey feathers, which were attached with sinew.

Arrow heads were usually made of chipped stone (flint or white quartz were preferred), as well as of bone or antler. Arrows with knobbed, blunted ends were used for small game.

PIPES

As noted previously, short-stemmed pipes with small bowls made of clay or other pottery were indigenous to the Wisconsin region. The long-stemmed "Calumet" pipe, the bowl of which usually comes from south central Minnesota, arrived in the Wisconsin region later.